Advance Praise

Challenging political correctness, *Secular Sectarianism* shows that subalterns are partly responsible for their conditions because of their inner divisions and their sheer ignorance of the very principles they claim to promote, including equality and secularism. This powerful and very original argument is made on the basis of a series of well-chosen case studies ranging from caste groups to tribes and religious minorities.

Christophe Jaffrelot, Senior Research Fellow,
CERI-Sciences Po/CNRS, Paris;
Professor, Indian Politics and Sociology
King's India Institute, London;
Non-resident Scholar,
Carnegie Endowment for International Peace

This is an original and compelling investigation into the fraught question of 'intra-subaltern' conflict. Moving beyond the theoretical and political complacencies of elite domination and subaltern resistance paradigms, the authors in this timely volume offer an impressive range of finely crafted, empirically rich studies of the sociology of conflict and the unpredictable dynamics of minority political agency. The volume engages audience across disciplines and reaches well beyond area studies to engage fundamental questions of political and social theory.

Srirupa Roy, Professor and Chair, State and Democracy
Centre for Modern Indian Studies, University of Göttingen,
Germany;
Director, International Centre of Advanced Studies
'Metamorphoses of the Political' (ICAS:MP)

Around the world, academics use the language of elites and the subaltern. In *Secular Sectarianism: Limits of Subaltern Politics*, Ajay Gudavarthy has assembled a group of scholars to show how this binary fails to capture the messy reality of Indian politics. There is not one solid class on top and one solid class below in India. Rather, Dalits, Muslims, women, OBCs and Left-Brahmins often fight with each other, while right-wing forces have gained the support of elites within subaltern social groups. The book is an essential read for those who wish to understand contemporary Indian politics and how the Right (Hindutva, the Bharatiya Janata Party, Prime Minister Modi) is triumphing over the Left (Congress Party, Communist Party). More than that, the book poses a challenge for Left activists and scholars around the world: How is it possible to form political coalitions that are internally diverse but still work together to fight economic and cultural oppression?

Nicholas Tampio, Professor, Political Science
Fordham University, New York City, USA;
Author of *Kantian Courage* (2012), *Deleuze's Political Vision* (2015),
Common Core (2018) and *Learning versus the Common Core* (2019)

SECULAR SECTARIANISM

SECULAR SECTARIANISM

Limits of Subaltern Politics

Edited by **Ajay Gudavarthy**

Los Angeles | London | New Delhi
Singapore | Washington DC | Melbourne

First published in 2020 by

SAGE Publications India Pvt Ltd
B1/I-1 Mohan Cooperative Industrial Area
Mathura Road, New Delhi 110 044, India
www.sagepub.in

SAGE Publications Inc
2455 Teller Road
Thousand Oaks, California 91320, USA

SAGE Publications Ltd
1 Oliver's Yard, 55 City Road
London EC1Y 1SP, United Kingdom

SAGE Publications Asia-Pacific Pte Ltd
18 Cross Street #10-10/11/12
China Square Central
Singapore 048423

Published by Vivek Mehra for SAGE Publications India Pvt Ltd. Typeset in 10.5/13 pt Bembo by Zaza Eunice, Hosur, Tamil Nadu, India.

Library of Congress Cataloging-in-Publication Data Available

ISBN: 978-93-532-8677-4 (HB)

SAGE Team: Abhijit Baroi, Neena Ganjoo and Anupama Krishnan

To
Professors DNR and V. S. Prasad
for their unflinching support

Thank you for choosing a SAGE product!
If you have any comment, observation or feedback,
I would like to personally hear from you.

Please write to me at **contactceo@sagepub.in**

Vivek Mehra, Managing Director and CEO, SAGE India.

Contents

Part III: Left and Its Fragments

Introduction
Prolegomenon to a Critical Theory of Secular Sectarianism

The world is getting globally connected and locally divided.[1] Unfulfilled aspirations are asking searching questions about seeking, not justice, but reversal of the sense of injury. The question is no longer about equality but about relative mobility expressed as retributive mobility. Anne Phillips argues that, globally, equality is no longer on the political agenda because we do not know how to make people equal, even as economic inequalities have risen exponentially. Forget for a moment lesser developed economies of the global south, within the centre of capitalist economy like the United States, opportunities have fallen drastically, even as expectations have been steadily growing. Michael Sandel notes, in the context of the United States, 'of those born in the bottom fifth of the income scale, 43 percent will remain there, and only 4 percent will make it to the top fifth' (Sandel 2018). Further, the project of 'cultural recognition', by way of politicizing differences, has hit a road block. Hyper-politicization of differences has led to a craving for community, order, unity and reviving ancient cultural forms, as against the invasions of 'Western enlightenment' and liberalism in general. Ironically, while equality has disappeared from the agenda of capitalist nations, culture is moving to the centre stage of a communist country like China. Tiziana Lippiello argues that President and General Secretary of the Chinese Communist Party, Xi Jinping, launching a campaign 'to revive Chinese culture' is trying to avoid the pitfalls of Western-style liberalism.

---

[1] Political philosopher Akeel Bilgrami in a recent article noted that 'Obama radiated hope, Trump channeled rage' (Bilgrami 2018). This is as much relevant to India. While Congress generated aspirations, Modi is converting it into rage.

Lippiello, following Michael Sandel, writes:

> Chinese thinkers, and in particular Confucian thinkers, have foreseen the limits of an abstract notion of universal justice and have otherwise affirmed the importance of a proper behavior, righteousness and a moral disposition to do good, together with cardinal moral values such as humaneness, social rites and wisdom.

She claims that amongst Chinese scholars and philosophers, 'there is a general consensus on the adoption of traditional values and their positive psychological and social impact'. Yet, Lippiello also acknowledges that the Communist Party's insistence on the 'unity of thought' can assume totalitarian forms (Kaul 2018: 348).[2]

However, the sociology of conflict in India is no longer 'merely' between the majority and the minority, between upper and lower castes, between the economically powerful and the weak, between the governors and the governed. In other words, it is no longer between the elite and the subaltern, even as those modes of conflict continue to exist. The theatre of much of street conflicts and mobilization has shifted or percolated to conflicts within the marginalized groups. Today, we cannot understand social dynamics exclusively as conflicts between the dominant and the dominated. While such conflicts are relatively easy to frame as initiating a process of social change, how do we problematize a process of one marginalized group targeting the other? How do we theorize the dynamics of subjugating the weaker

---

[2] In a somewhat similar manner in India too, as Meera Nanda (2011) observes, *how globalization is making India Hindu*. 'Against expectations of growing secularism, India has instead seen a remarkable intertwining of Hinduism and neoliberal ideology, spurred on by a growing capitalist class.' It is this "state–temple–corporate complex"', she claims, that now wields decisive political and economic power and provides ideological cover for the dismantling of the Nehru-era state-dominated economy. According to this new logic, India's rapid economic growth is attributable to a special 'Hindu mind', and it is what separates the nation's Hindu population from Muslims and others deemed to be 'anti-modern'. As a result, Hindu institutions are replacing public ones, and the Hindu 'revival' itself has become big business, a major source of capital accumulation (Nanda 2011).

amongst the weak? What is the political subjectivity of such a subject? How do these conflicts speak to the traditional social conflicts? Why do various social constituencies find it difficult to come together or even express solidarity? Why do subaltern social groups fail to articulate issues beyond their immediate concerns and identities? This book is a preliminary attempt to theorize and problematize this terrain of intra-subaltern conflicts that has been left under-theorized in much of social sciences in India, amongst other reasons, for want of relevant social categories and the tyranny of political correctness. Voices from below and those representing such voices have remained steadfastly selective, if not attempting an erasure. The social reality gets only further complex when the very nature of secular ethos becomes the frame for structuring the social content of intra-subaltern conflicts in India.

Subaltern social groups have claimed to locate themselves within the secular ethos, wanting to move beyond immediate identities and narrow ethnicity. However, the post-independence politics of India has been a witness to repeated failures of such politics forging any meaningful solidarity or political dialogue. Increasingly, social groups have remained narrow, communal, parochial, ghettoized and isolated. These politics are all mostly intervening from singular or exclusivist standpoints that fail to understand the viewpoint and the nature of power dynamics and its implications for other groups that are both below and also laterally located. It is this sustained failure that is here referred to as secular sectarianism.

In the past three decades, we witnessed sub-caste conflicts between various segments of Dalits, conflicts between other backward classes (OBCs) and Dalits, and conflicts between Dalits and tribals; OBCs and Dalits have been at the forefront of riots against Muslims; Muslims have remained steadfast in their gendered attitudes and social conservatism; minority Muslim universities have refused to follow reservations for Dalits and OBCs; Kashmiri Muslims have moved to growing radicalization and younger generations are less accepting about the return of the Pandits to the valley; there is a growing mobilization of 'sons of soil' where migrants and urban poor had to bear the brunt of exclusion and insidious violence; Left politics has faced a sustained decline and has entered into irrevocable conflict with caste-based Dalit and OBC politics, amongst many other such issues. There is a pressing need to take a relook at some of these conflicts beyond contingent and ad hoc theorization. This edited volume is a preliminary attempt to capture some of these dynamics through the prism of secular sectarianism.[3]

UNEVEN AND UNEQUAL

Much of the question of agency of subaltern political mobilization has been framed through the discourse of subalternity.[4] However, there is an impending need to re-frame the question through the lens of social power being, at least partially, internally constituted. In other words, subaltern social groups—including caste/Dalits, religious minorities/ Muslims, and class politics/Left—are also structured by centring power that is accrued by the same social structure that also marginalizes them. Such power is though skewed in comparison to the traditional social elites—upper castes/Brahmins, Hindus/majority, rural–urban divide— and therefore social power is both *uneven and unequal*. It is not only gravely unequal when compared to the traditional social elites but also uneven in the very constitution of subaltern social groups. Political mobilization, strategies and the question of agency are split between questioning the unequal and preserving the uneven. Thus, social conflicts in India, mostly, have questioned the hegemony of those above them, much more than empathizing or extending solidarity with those below them in social hierarchy. Questioning the powerful is also supported by the *search for the weak* (Gudavarthy 2014). I, therefore, propose the fundamental feature of secular sectarianism is this complex matrix marked by the phenomenon of uneven and unequal.

Secular sectarianism is a specific social condition that allows for incremental mobility for itself while actively arresting the same for social groups that are placed well below them. This has mostly been understood through the frame of elite–subaltern framework, where

---

[3] For sub-caste conflicts, refer to Rao (1998); for OBC–Dalit conflicts, refer to Teltumbde (2008); for participation of Dalit–OBCs in communal riots, refer to Teltumbde (2000).

[4] In the Indian context, this has specific relation to the Subaltern Studies project initiated by Ranahit Guha and others.

the subaltern belongs to an 'autonomous domain' and therefore retains the ability to resist. At the same time, I would argue that resistance is a moment within the matrix and is neither exclusive nor the dominant feature of such a social condition. Resistance and suppression or mobility and reification are inextricably intertwined to allow for any easy separation. Revolution and 'counter-revolution' are not, as Ambedkar suggested, two independent moments but constitutive of each other (Ambedkar 2015). The political condition in the post-independent India was 'always already' precariously situated between moving towards a more inclusive secular ethos, and a deeply sectarian marginalization of the 'other'. Secularism, in philosophical terms, is not merely about separation of state and religion but essentially refers to a social ethos of the ability to trust the stranger: trust as a social condition for mobility. In the Indian context, the very groups identified as harbingers of 'secular upsurge'—Dalits, Muslims, women, OBCs and the Left—have initiated a process of sectarian ghettoization. Political alliances did not result in social reform of hierarchies. Reified social hierarchies and expanding political representation are the constitutive conditions of secular sectarianism. Naturalized social hierarchies go along with the contingent historical vagaries of political exigencies. Internally constituted social content is ostensibly detached from externally operating political dynamics. The endemic divide between *the political and social* domains is a sub-feature that actualizes the generic social condition marked by what I refer to as the uneven and unequal.

I would go a step further and argue that the hiatus between the political and the social has allowed for a more 'legitimate' articulation of social hierarchies through the very secular–democratic/constitutional processes that were set in motion. Ironically, expanded political representation meant more reified social subjectivity. Subaltern social groups carried the 'internal' social power into the secular–democratic political process. Constitutionalism or constitutional morality by default became the concern of tiny cosmopolitan-liberals who were signified as the traditional elites, but this was more rhetorical than historical because the 'elite' themselves found constitutional provisions inimical to their own social standing. While constitutionalism, liberal institutional arrangement and democratic process as such were conservative for the subaltern, these were subversive for the traditional elites. Understanding the process through rhetorical political articulation or everyday forms of mobilization can misrepresent the substantive content of the process.[5] Much of the liberal and post-colonial scholarship in India suffered from this epistemic limitation and, therefore, by default belonged to the same 'epistemic community'.[6]

The chapters in the volume are case studies that provide the necessary empirical and theoretical bases for the formulation of secular sectarianism, without necessarily agreeing with the formulation itself. The authors act as interlocutors to further expand the scope of the idea.

CRITICAL THEORY OF SECULAR SECTARIANISM

Contemporary critical theory offers us a reasonable entry point to negotiate some of the complexities, although it does not present any neat alternatives necessary to frame the question in the Indian context. Some of the debates initiated by critical theory can help us in reframing the issues in order to further explore the formulation of secular sectarianism. Though critical theory itself is not framed in the context of social power being uneven and unequal but it provides us an interesting set of questions and debates that are, nevertheless, relevant in theorizing the idea of secular sectarianism.

Nancy Fraser has inaugurated contemporary critical theory with her agenda of formulating the question of justice as the possibility of reconciling recognition, redistribution and representation. Her core argument begins by pointing to the 'recognition–redistribution dilemma', where while recognition requires differentiation, redistribution requires de-differentiation. In other words, culture is about claiming specificities, while class is about undoing the class differences linked to cultural specificities. She, therefore, offers a critique of identitarian model of recognition that instantiates the problems of 'reification' and

---

[5] A good example of this misreading is Partha Chatterjee's formulation of political society. I edited a critical volume on its possible political limits. Refer to Gudavarthy (2012).

[6] I attempted to explore this convergence in my book *Politics of Post-Civil Society* (Gudavarthy 2013).

'displacement'. Identity politics reifies the given identities and displaces class politics. She proposes a shift from the 'identity model' to the 'status model' (Fraser 1995). Iris Marion Young, in contrast, argues that all identity politics is a means to achieve economic mobility, and one cannot draw on a false dichotomy between recognition and redistribution. While Fraser empowers recognition as an end in itself, Young expands the scope of identity politics by suggesting its inextricable continuity with redistributive agenda. While Fraser brings centrality in making recognition an independent dimension of justice, Young perceives it as a mode of disconnecting it from issues of distributive justice (Young 1997).

Fraser further argues that the only way to reconcile recognition with redistributive class politics is to emphasize deconstructive cultural politics that aim to make all identities, historical, fluid, unstable and beyond the limits of binarized signification. Does replacement of differences with deconstruction undermine the very specificity of culture itself? Anne Phillips (1997) refers to this as 'cultural politics without culture'. Is culture being subsumed to the imperatives of class and, therefore, aiding the project of 'cultural imperialism' that robs the marginalized social groups of legitimate modes of mobilization? Therefore, it becomes important to unhitch 'cultural imperialism' from secular sectarianism. Can all claims of specificity be referred to as sectarian? Or is sectarianism a specific condition of cultural recognition? Do we have the tools to separate the two? Here, Frasers' argument that identity not only reifies but becomes a tool of social elites internal to such group differences—Muslims, Dalits, amongst others—is significant. Essentialized identities can displace the modes through which social elites exclude those internal to that identity under one axis but remain external in other. For instance, Kashmiri Muslims of the valley are rightly recognized as internally colonized, but the social elites amongst them exclude Muslims belonging to Ladakh and Rajouri, and those belonging to the Gujjar caste, amongst such other constituents. Essentialization itself needs to be historically analysed. For Young, differences are claimed to puncture naturalized constitution of those groups as raced and inferior. In contrast, for Fraser, essentialization naturalizes historically constituted identities by claiming the identities as those that cannot be breached. This dialectic between naturalization and historicity is significant in understanding how subaltern politics can congeal power to conceal internal exclusions. Keeping such identities open-ended internally needs a bottom-up process as much as a secularized critique of power relations. When the sub-caste question came up for political mobilization in India, while it was perceived a significant move to internally open-up spaces for marginalized sub-castes, the 'dominant' castes within the Dalits perceived it as a ploy of 'Dividing Dalits', and the caste Hindus took the opportunity to rob the Dalit movement of its moral standing and push it further to delegitimize all strategies, such as affirmative action policies, meant to provide mobility (Rao 1998).

Judith Butler provides us a way out. She proposes that in such conditions unity cannot mean synthesis but a mode of sustaining conflict in productive way. She refers to this as 'equivalence without becoming each other', where 'one social movement comes to find its condition of possibility in another'. Difference is both the condition and limit of identities. Identities gain specificity in difference but the same difference also constitutes the limit on its final realization (Butler 1997). She refers to it as 'conflictual encounter'. While for Butler difference is a condition of solidarity, for Slavoj Zizek difference is marked as distance, and as for Fraser difference is marked by displacement. While difference as solidarity refers to the possibility of secular ethos, difference as distance imbricates a sectarian social process. When difference is seen to break naturalized readings of subaltern, exclusion is, in contrast to difference, opening the possibility of naturalizing historically produced identities.

If this process was merely horizontal and lateral, then what Butler is suggesting as difference being a condition of secular solidarity would offer us an opening; however, when power and prejudice are integral to cultural recognition and difference, as Richard Rorty suggests, then difference becomes unmistakably sectarian. Here, Rorty, instead, suggests replacing the emphasis on cultural recognition with a politics for eliminating prejudice. He makes an intriguing argument that the civil rights movement in the United States in the 1960s was concerned with eliminating prejudice; however, it was with the second-wave feminism that the focus shifted to cultural recognition because women as a social identity was despised and inferiorized but not stigmatized and therefore they could lay a claim to distinctness. Cultural recognition only distanced social groups, and, therefore, he argues there is a need to move back to an emphasis on 'common humanity' based on everyday banality of facts, such as anyone who is pierced would bleed. Common pain and suffering is a more powerful way of breaking the sectarian hold over social groups rather than pushing down, forcefully, an agenda of cultural recognition (Rorty 2000).

In current neoliberal times, recognition and accompanying corollary of victimhood have become the new templates of aspirational politics. Hyper-recognition marked by separation, rather than emphasis on shared ethos, holds wider appeal. A turn to common humanity needs an ethical project of self-limiting subjectivity. The question that still remains in uneven and unequal social conditions is whether social groups hold the same kind of social power to declare themselves as sovereign selves. Can moral or human equivalence replace unequal material positioning? Would it not be true to argue that the difficulty of imagining deconstructive politics in real concrete also holds true for actualizing the ideal of 'common humanity'. This also leaves us with the question of the equation between justice and secular sectarianism.

Axel Honneth would argue that what makes issues of inequality question of justice are only when they are framed in terms of interpersonal ethics of what we owe to our fellow beings. Distributive questions are issues of justice only when we demonstrate the issue of valuation involved that robs the subaltern of a good life. Good life is a positive affirmation of a thickly ontological view of human beings having the innate need for self-realization through reciprocity and mutuality. Such self-realization is articulated for Honneth through the processes of self-confidence, self-respect and self-esteem, signifying emotional security, legal rights/citizenship and achievement and solidarity. Justice, then, is deeply moral, not merely political. Redistribution cannot be an end in itself; it is instead a symbolic struggle over the legitimacy of socio-cultural valuation with 'equal moral worth'. In the Indian context, Gandhi took somewhat a similar approach, of posing the *satyagrahi* as a 'moral exemplar' whose experiential and lived conditions alone lent the ideals the moral velocity and not merely political heft. Justice is as much about inner self, as it is about power. In fact, power needs to be contested by self for Honneth, and by 'soul-force' for Gandhi.

Sectarianism is a condition of approaching justice without the idea of inner self and good life. It is more about alienation than equality. Equality made sense in terms of its implication for a self alienated from the collective based on mutuality and reciprocity. Here, the condition of secular sectarianism is marked by divesting the question of justice from issues of inner self that finds its resonance in deeply invested social life (Yar 2001).

It is imperative to ask if class is itself an identity and can produce sectarianism of its own variant rather than expect an easy transition from the sectarianism of identity to secular ethos of class. Class politics, as represented through Left politics, can produce not only vanguard-ism external to identity and difference formation but also a specific kind of secular sectarianism that undermines independent political articulations that foresee unity as the erasure of culture. Andrew Sayers argues that in order to break this conundrum, we need to invoke what he refers to as 'lay normativity' that is played out in everyday life as pride, envy, compassion, shame and resentment. These are not just affect or experiential but 'evaluative judgments of how people are treated'. They constitute 'emotional reason'. Normative character or issues of justice and secular solidarity do not have a necessary rational basis but exist as 'moral sentiments'. They are influenced but not predetermined by social positions within the social field. Everyday morality spills beyond social position—habitus—and sometimes even ignores it (Sayers 2005). While historical materialism taught us the lesson that morality has a material basis, it is equally important to note that materiality itself has a moral basis. The idea of the social or col-lective is based on a certain universal moral reasoning. For instance, abilities to feel shame and pride are universal, so is the need to frame sectarian issues in universal moral registers. For instance, no individual asking for employment or struggling against domination ever asks to be liberated without questioning the very moral justification of being unemployed or remaining under the yoke of external domination in denial of her personhood.

Sayers here is drawing our attention to cross–class agreements about ways of life and its valuation. Class politics as we witnessed over the last century undermined the potency of cross-class agreements and reduced politics to bare materiality, in the process producing a sectarian logic that undermined the very conditions necessary for class-based collectives. It may be relevant to ask, even if class operated like an identity, the nature of secular sectarianism that it produces in terms of indifference to those that lie beyond the pale of material analysis have itself undermined the legitimacy of class politics, which eventually impacted the core constituency that the Left was mobilizing. This is a process that is as true of de-radicalization of Dalit politics as it is for the way religious minorities lost legitimacy in popular politics in claiming equal moral worth.

SECULAR SECTARIANISM AND LIMITS OF SUBALTERN POLITICS

The chapters in the current volume take a close look at some of the theoretical issues referred to in the previous section. The first part, titled 'Casting Sectarianism, Engendering Secularism', looks at caste and gender as the nodal points to interrogate how issues of narrow articulations have been dealt with. P. Thirumal and Dickens Leonard reflect on the recent political mobilization surrounding the suicide of Rohith Vemula. Rohith's death was deeply political, not merely in highlighting the institutionalized modes of discrimination but also the letter he left behind highlighted the impending need to move the 'thing' called identity and how one is reduced to one's immediate identity. The authors, in various ways, argue that Rohith 'invites the Dalit movement to resituate and transform itself from its undue reliance on legal and representational politics'. One mode of challenging the 'Brahmin Modernity', they note, was the demand of 'rewriting of Dalit movement not purely in identitarian terms'. The way forward could possibly be sighted in revisiting the emphasis Ambedkar laid on the idea of fraternity, and what could be its concrete social form remains important. Ambedkar had noted fraternity is not easy to translate into constitutional principle and therefore his later-day experiment of converting into Buddhism. P. Thirumal and Dickens Leonard note that 'perhaps death raises the question of immunity, sociality and fraternity much more intimately for the Dalit community as a social precedes an eventual death'.

Suratha Kumar Malik, based on an ethnographic survey, takes a close look at a long-standing conflict between Dalits (Panas) and tribals (Kandhas) in Odisha. He concludes:

> The reaction of *Kandhas* and upper caste *Hindus* to *Panas'* new-found assertiveness was predictable. The *Kandhas* suffered from a feeling of loss, and the upper castes felt threatened. While *Panas* think that it is their industriousness and adaptability that were responsible for their betterment, but the *Kandhas* frequently refer to the 'treacheries and low cunning of the *Panas*'.

The upper caste Hindus share the same view as that of the Kandhas, albeit in a more articulate and prejudiced way. The upper caste views the Panas as great exploiters; they loot the illiterate Kandhas and disrupt the moral order of the village. That is, the increase in the Panas' political and economic power had been at the expense of the Kandhas'. Why do subaltern social and collective modes often overlap with hegemonic forms relating to social power? The limits of subaltern politics are entrenched in replicating the existing forms even as they take rhetorical recourse to more universal modes of moral posturing. Does the lack of social power sufficiently explain the innate compulsion to replicate existing modes in order to further subaltern groups' interests? Suratha Kumar Malik concludes by arguing that

> The intra-subaltern conflicts between the tribals (Kandhas) and Dalits (Panas and other Dalit castes like Dombo, Rilli in case of Narayanpatna) from the above three case studies has confirmed that 'the large subaltern consciousness' and the 'mega project' have been fragmented with the material reality, resource conflict, religious sentiment and owing to the political game played by the state and the dominant.

The last chapter in the first part, again based on a rich ethnographic study, looks at the interface between caste and gender. Tarushikha Sarvesh makes a similar point to the previous chapters as to how hegemonic articulations find their presence even in what are considered as subversive techniques, in relation to women's issues. She argues, 'The women from the lower castes have been the victims of exploitation by the upper castes. Such exploitations have also been analysed and understood through textual narratives and legends' (Lorenzen 1991: 49). That is why in the subverting claims by portraying the Sati of low castes or ex-untouchables as virgins—the purest and most holy figures—they challenge the upper castes' version of a monolithic reality. Here we get to witness the claims, which do have the potential to undercut the dominant representation of reality. The problem with such claims is that, although they appear to be constructive and favourable to the female members of the community, in reality they keep the women trapped in the same ideals of hegemonic traditions—be it Brahmanical or other religious principles of purity/pollution, honour/dishonour, pride/shame and so on. As pointed out earlier, 'lay normativity' operates at the cutting edge of cross-class/caste agreements. They cannot be made sense of in terms of either hegemony or 'double consciousness', but public morality itself seems to be structured beyond the limits of social positions. In fact, social positions are themselves, at times, made sense of through available moral frames that tend to hold more universal appeal. Morality here is not merely experiential but used as evaluative judgements to make sense of social processes and how power is structured in society. It is imperative to make sense of how the universalizable dimension of moral frames themselves structure social conditions necessary for secular sectarianism.

The second part of the book titled as 'Limits of Minority-ism' focuses on religious practices and the specific forms in which it produces a sectarian logic. Even as religious minorities lay emphasis on secular ethos that demand the majority community to look beyond its immediate interests, and augment a process based on mutuality and reciprocity, one has witnessed a sustained process of minority-ism where the religious minorities give prominence to cultural differences over cultural affinity. Here, it is clear that both state policy of secularism and multiculturalism, and religious mobilization have articulated difference more as distance than as solidarity. Judith Butler's point that difference as both the condition of identity formation and the limit to its fuller or final realization, while understandable, nevertheless, seems to tilt towards creating distance in search of a final articulation. The dialectic is arrested to produce a sectarian hegemonic logic rather than subversive politics. Samir Gandesha, in his theoretical exploration of the difference between homecoming and forced conversion, makes a more philosophical point on the conditions necessary for a more universal self. He argues:

> Here as in the Western philosophical tradition, as suggested above, there's an intimate connection between exile, on the one hand, and the realization of human flourishing, on the other. That in order to pass from consciousness to self-consciousness, from being-in-itself to being-in-and-for-itself, it is necessary for the self to lose itself by externalizing and alienating itself in the world and then, subsequently, finding or re-finding itself. *That in order to truly be at home in the world, one must take one's leave of it through a process of self-estrangement.*

As I argued in invoking Honneth and comparing him to Gandhi, the idea of self remains pivotal in making secular ethos a more lived reality. While Samir Gandesha poses this important question in the context of the majority practices, it is equally important to articulate it in the context of religious minorities as to how do they practice a sense of 'estrangement' or, in Habermasian terms, 'self-limiting' in order to reinforce secular ethos.

Some of this is taken up upfront in three chapters by Afroz Alam, Mursed Alam and Seema Ahmed, and Shadab Arab. All three of them, in various ways, point to the 'internal' limitation of Muslim politics in the post-independence period. Afroz Alam revisits the question of uniform civil code (UCC) and asks, 'do Muslims need the existing personal laws?' He connects the issue of UCC and the way Muslim politics approached it to the question of 'internal' social elites, reminding us of the point Fraser makes in why essentialization of identity allows for reification of identity and disallows for internal distribution of social power and resources. Afroz Alam is unequivocal in his reading and says:

> In my considered opinion, the right-wing forces, present in both the communities and mostly having the background of high castes, are working in consensus to keep the religious wedge issues alive to

preserve their existential relevance. The diverse interests and opinions of various other groups on UCC and Muslims personal laws are tactfully marginalized by creating hype around the threat to religion.

He concludes by arguing,

In fact, the plurality within Muslim community has also been deliberately ignored and sidelined to serve the designs of privileged groups of both Muslims and non-Muslims. The invocation of religious-cum-emotive issues such as Ram Mandir, Uniform Civil Code, Urdu and so on are being looked upon with distaste among the Pasmanda scholars. They are of the view that these issues are often circulated to keep the development concern and aspiration of Pasmanda Muslims at bay. The heterogeneous character of the Muslim community bars them to have unitary interests when it comes to personal laws. In fact, over-emphasis on Islamic personal laws and Islamization is only to reinforce the caste distinctions.

Hegemonic articulation of majority Hindu community finds its roots to reproduce itself in social elites of the minority religious community; without connecting the two, one cannot analyse the nature of minority politics and its regressive character.

Secularism in the Indian context needs be re-theorized to connect issue of internal power structures with those of external power dynamics. This gets reflected in the slogan *Dalit-Pichda Ek Saman, Hindu Ho Ya Musalman* (Dalits and the Backward are the same, whether they are Hindu or Muslim). Mursed Alam and Seema Ahmed refer to Imtiaz Ahmed's formulation to argue,

Imtiaz says that there have been two kinds of Muslim political response in post-colonial India—they either act as a political pressure group using their demographic dividend for political demands, and/or supporting a national political party. Imtiaz suggests a 'third way' which consists of aligning with the other marginalized sections of other communities and work on a common platform.

Similarly, Shadab argues that Dalit–Muslim unity is the way forward, although such experiments have remained in the margins due to the threat they pose to caste Hindu domination. He argues further,

[A]ny attempts to form the same have been thwarted time and again by both communal and secular outfits. Maulana Nasir Maudani from Kerala, who was trying to forge a Muslim–Dalit unity in the 1990s, was put behind bars for years on flimsy charges of terrorism. Similarly, Asaduddin Owaisi, who is known for articulating the constitutional rights of the community and their daily concerns, has been asked time and again why he only talks about Muslims. He is often reduced to a religious fanatic and a fundamentalist by the secular outfits.

All the three chapters by Afroz, Mursed and Seema, and Shadab look at the future of Muslim politics in terms of an alliance with Dalit politics. Does this require a kind of deconstructive politics that Fraser refers to or an idea of common humanity as Richard Rorty does? Does it involve mere overcoming of prejudice or invocation of 'participatory parity' as a condition of justice? In attempting an alliance across the religious divide on the basis of the commonality of social and economic position, does it necessarily signify 'cultural politics without culture'? Or, as Young would say, it smacks of 'cultural imperialism'? While these issues will remain important signposts in guiding our way through, the question of an alliance beyond cultural/religious limits remains pivotal in overcoming the current regressive content of Muslim politics in India.

The last chapter of the second part takes a look at the issue of Kashmiri Pandits, and whether they constitute a minority in a Muslim-majority Kashmir valley. The question of Kashmiri Pandits is important in many ways. It highlights the limits of framing questions within the limits of the secular discourse of majority–minority distinctions. Pandits are a minority in a Muslim-majority province, while Muslims are a minority in a Hindu-majority nation. Further, it was a Hindu-ruled province, where a majority of Muslims remained socially and economically backward, while Pandits who suffered displacement were socially dominant. Culture and economy do neatly fit or reinforce each other as 'bivalent categories', as Nancy Fraser formulates; instead they limit the way they connect to each other. While Pandits, after moving out, have become a symbol of Indian nationalism, Muslims, who continue to bear the brunt of exceptionalism, seem to be moving towards increased radicalization. It is in this context Nathalene Reynolds refers to K. N. Pundita's views on the nature of secularism in Kashmir. He argues:

[T]he conditions in rural Kashmir were different. The Pandit minority was very thinly dispersed in villages and smaller towns. They were not close to the corridors of power nor had they a toehold in the administration of the State. As such they were not in any position to be munificent to the majority of Muslims in their neighbourhood. Conversely, they were dependent on their Muslim neighbours for assistance in their agrarian activities. Thus appeared the class of 'kashtkaran', the actual tillers of land. And they were all from the majority community. Crop sharing became the basis of contract between an owner and the tenant. Both understood the imperative of mutual understanding and support. In this way developed another facet of Kashmir secularism.

Secularism here had a political economy basis, not cultural. How does one approach the question of cultural differences in the context of economic interdependence? While Kashmiriyat and Sufi traditions of Kashmir were considered to be one kind of a basis, political economy and redistribution of land became another, without necessarily reinforcing each other. Here we could also refer to the third dimension of justice, the question of representation and the specificity of the role of state and law in producing and determining the contours of cultural politics. Leonard Feldman refers to this as 'states self-concealing production of status'. The state eliminates its own constituting power and law becomes the handmaiden for producing/manufacturing recognition. Subaltern groups self-represent themselves through the technologies of the state, beyond the operative dynamics of culture and economy. Secular sectarianism, in this context, cannot be captured 'merely' through a cultural lens but through the role nation-state plays. The state produces political status, which in turn impacts cultural self-representation and economic opportunities, both of which determine the social conditions of secular sectarianism (Feldman).

The final part of the book titled 'Left and Its Fragments' turns to looking at whether Left politics in India too produced sectarianism of its own kind. If so, how was it any different from that of caste, gender and religion? How did it interact with other kinds of sectarian logics operative within the same temporal and spatial dimension? Anindya, Manas and Tirthankar pursue Ernesto Laclau and Chantal Mouffe's plea to break from classical Marxism and move towards 'Left populism' with multiple and irreducible 'antagonisms' at the heart of politics. In India, although the Left argued for a universal class politics, it in reality spoke from a certain caste vantage point. It lacked, more so in Bengal, the political alacrity to understand and adapt to newer modes of political articulation. What it resulted in was a new kind of a political divide that I refer to as Left Brahmin and Right Bahujan. Left, by default, came to represent a certain kind of constitutional/institutional elitism moving away from its mobilizational techniques, and this over a period resulted in the mass of subaltern moving rightwards in search of a more authentic experiential politics. It resisted the need to invent new political idiom, connect to the existing cultural idiom, and in the process also lost the understanding of the nature of capitalism in India. Anindya, Manas and Tirthankar make an earnest plea for the revival of the Left and argue:

> 'Strategy of electoral clientelism' resorted to by the left resulted in democratic vacuity and that was usurped by the right wing. It is high time the left reenergized the agonistic political sphere through a con-flictual mode of Left populism which practices a people-centric form of democratic governance.

The next chapter in this part attempts to raise similar concerns, again in the context of Bengal. Dhritiman Chakraborty asks:

> But, what the Left leaderships can do in a scenario like this? Should it just try combine these spaces that are sometimes contradictory in nature and reformulate its class question to accommodate identity issues, or should it play an anchoring role and try to tease out the materialist issues that are nevertheless operative in new domains of coercion and marginalization.

The problem of heterogeneity and solidarity or, as Habermas puts it, between autonomy and solidarity will remain central. There cannot be a generalized framework, but what one could venture to emphasize is the constant need to combine the logic of 'irreducibility of multiplicity' with mediated solidarity. What could be the concrete social form? What kind of a self-limiting self does it demand? What could be the notions of fraternity that are ethicopolitical in form and content so as not to burden the subaltern with moral utopias? These and many such questions will remain significant in times to come.

The last—concluding—chapter of the volume is an essay that lays out the preliminary outlines of what the formulation on secular sectarianism intends to communicate. It is in no way fully fleshed out. The ideas and chapters in the current volume, I hope, have managed to take the idea further in offering a *secularized critique* of subaltern politics in India. We need to more closely contend with the way social power is internally constituted, and even as it jostles with externally imposed hegemonies, the internal aspects seem to enter into an unholy nexus, making it difficult to mark subalternity to a normatively certain zone that was referred to as an 'autonomous domain'.

REFERENCES

Ambedkar, B. R. 2015. *Revolution and Counter-revolution in Ancient India*. Available at: https://www.amazon.com/Revolution-Counter-Ancient-India-ebook/dp/B0127X347S (acessed on 17 September 2019).

Bilgrami, Akeel. 2018. 'Reflections on Three Populisms'. *Philosophy & Social Criticism* 44 (4): 453–462.

Butler, Judith. 1997. 'Merely Cultural'. *Social Text* 15 (3–4): 265–277.

Feldman, Leonard. 2008. 'Status Injustice: The Role of the State'. In *Adding Insult to Injury*, edited by Kevin Olson, 221–245. London: Verso.

Fraser, Nancy. 1995. 'From Redistribution to Recognition? Dilemmas of Justice in a "Postsocialist Age"'. *New Left Review* 1 (212): 68–93.

Gudavarthy, Ajay. 2012. *Reframing Democracy and Agency: Interrogating Political Society*. London: Anthem.

———. 2013. *Politics of Post-Civil Society*. Delhi: SAGE Publications.

———. 2017. 'Sectarianism of the Secular Brigade'. *The Hindu*, 20 November.

Lippiello, Tiziano. 2018. 'The Paradigms of Religious Philosophical Plurality: The Return of "Spirituality"'. *China Today Philosophy and Social Criticism*, 44 (4): 371–381.

Kaul, Volker. 2018. 'Populism and the Crisis of Liberalism'. *Philosophy & Social Criticism*, 44 (4): 346–352.

Nanda, Meera. 2011. *The God Market: How Globalization Is Making India More Hindu*. New York: Monthly Review Press.

Phillips, Anne. 1997. 'From Inequality to Difference: A Severe Case of Displacement?' *New Left Review* 1 (224): 143–153.

Rao, Chinna, ed. 1998. *Dividing Dalits*. Delhi: Rawat Publications.

Rorty, Richard. 2000. 'Is "Cultural Recognition" a Useful Notion for Leftist Politics?' *Critical Horizons* 1 (1): 7–20.

Sandel, Michael J. 2018. 'Populism, Liberalism and Democracy'. Philosophy & Social Criticism 44 (4): 353–359.

Sayers, Andrew. 2005. *The Moral Significance of Class*. Cambridge, New York, NY: Cambridge University Press.

Teltumbde, Anand. 2000. *Hindutva and Dalits*. Delhi: Samya Books.

———. 2008. *Khairlanji. A Strange and Bitter Crop*. New Delhi: Navayana.

Yar, Majid. 2001. 'Beyond Nancy Fraser's "Perspectival Dualism"'. Economy and Society, 30 (3): 288–303.

Young, Iris Marion. 1997. 'Unruly Categories: A Critique of Nancy Fraser's Dual Systems Theory'. *New Left Review* 1 (222): 147–160.

PART I

Casting Sectarianism, Engendering Secularism

Chapter 1

Incommensurable Sacral–Secular Sectarianism?
Rohith Movement and the Emergence
of the Inappropriable

P. Thirumal and Dickens Leonard

Modern institutions, including educational institutions, breathe a
Brahmanic mode of representation—which is a particular mode of
representing things, relations between things and an orientation towards
things. Indian modernity in that sense presents Brahmin modernity.
It would not be wrong to say that colonially mediated modernity co-
appeared with Brahmanic modernity, that is, the capital along with the
Brahmin. This co-appearance, perhaps, conflates both secular sectarianism and communal sectarianism. The Dalit critique of Left or the vice
versa, therefore, suggests a limit, and this reaches its finest articulation
in the Rohith movement.

The indirect question that seemingly emerged during the Rohith
struggle was an implicit awareness of a Brahmanic form of knowing and experiencing the world and how this was dovetailed into a
modern secular and objective form of understanding the human and
non-human worlds. The networked Brahmin being, while connecting

with the logic of capital, disconnects others (Dalit Bahujan) from access to both the sensorial grasp and the disembodied and distant forms of understanding the self and the world. This mode of representation does not just speak of bodily inscription, but also attaches itself to sense generativity, which helps the Brahmanic self to seek flight from capital whenever it is necessary. The struggle clearly pointed fingers at the Brahmanic subject as not merely the self-sufficient subject, but as a richly networked being having a disposition to obscure and disenfranchise the singular plural being of Dalit Bahujans (both rational and embodied).

The movement seriously differed from the Brahmanic mode of representation—in terms of both its affect and its direction/disposition. Unlike the public character of the Rohith episode, the force of the disposition is generally experienced but rarely visible. It practices some kind of 'infra-red' politics which registers its force at the level of skin, flesh and body. An extreme manifestation of this force or an acute Dalit-Bahujan sensitivity to this force may result in death as in the case of Rohith. This intervention is an attempt to examine theoretical/ conceptual possibilities, and it consists of two sections. One of these primarily describes and discusses the Rohith movement and the letter he left us. The second part reflects and suggests a philosophical take on the sense and meaning of the Rohith movement in relation to progressive emancipatory radical politics as well as regressive communitarian politics in contemporary times. We not only argue that the Rohith movement inspires a radical moment to exceed conventional solidarities, but it also invites the Dalit movement to resituate and transform itself from its undue reliance on legal and representational politics.

When Rohith Vemula committed 'suicide' on 17 January 2016, his death sparked off a massive students' agitation and widespread Dalit mobilization across the globe, which expressed an emergent political language against caste, with an insistent difference. Rohith became an anti-caste icon across the subcontinent, and a new meaning to student struggles was added after his 'suicide' note was circulated far and wide. Ever since, the institutes of higher education have increasingly become sites of anti-caste struggles. Particularly Hyderabad—home to an assertive anti-caste student politics since the 1990s—in South India has become a battleground for such an incessant rage, almost all the time. However, one needs to glean away and attempt to describe the amorphous and formless nature of this student politics which made this emergent language possible through the 'deaths' of Dalits, that differed and deferred from the conventional Left and Right language of politics.

Though there have been many anti-caste student movements across the country, ever since the 1960s, they had largely worked within a vernacular or regional space. The Rohith movement, and the events that followed, brought to light the newer political energy of an anti-caste consciousness and an emergent mobilization not only within an English-speaking audience but also across vernacular, regional and global spaces. Dalits across the globe agitated, mobilized themselves and brought out protest statements. Academics, writers, journalists, workers, street hawkers and students together became a part of this uprising. Many public personalities came out openly about their Dalit identity. It became a social movement across the country, starting from a university in southern India. Perhaps for the first time in India, an agitation in a university became a rallying point for a global resistance against caste. And Rohith became an iconic presence in any protest against caste discrimination thereafter. But this moment, however, has a longer history and context in the higher educational campuses in India.

AMBEDKARITES ON CAMPUS

The Ambedkar Students Association (ASA), for which Rohith worked until his death, offers one of the most interesting contexts and contents to reflect on the emergent and insistent nature of this political language as a critique of the neatness that Left and Right politics reaffirms. ASA was formed in the year 1993 as part of a longer resistance movement across the country, and by the efforts of Dalit-Bahujan students at the University of Hyderabad. The student organization states that it does not affiliate with any political parties outside the campus. Its manifesto states that it believes in the ideology of Dr B. R. Ambedkar and engages in propagating his thoughts and ideals along with social revolutionaries such as Jyotibha Phule, Savitribai Phule, Ayyankali, Narayana Guru, Birsa Munda, Komaram Bheem, Periyar E. V. Ramasamy Naicker, Gurram Jashua and other anti-caste leaders across the subcontinent. This list is open and not closed, and this indicates that the organization is not conventionally just bound by one or two ideologues as such—it intends to discover more—desiring to 'promote education, transform experiences and meaningfully increase the social empowerment of the community'.

Bearing multiple attacks from its inception, rage and struggle imbibed by active ideas such as 'educate, agitate and organize' seems to set the tone of this politics. ASA had made its presence felt by bringing to light the untidy nature of academic spaces and conventional politics. What looks tidy is not indeed one—be it the constitutional provisions, administration and management of the university, or educational and social welfare schemes. Its work was indeed to state that this appearance of modern reality is indeed dirty. This is much reflected in the way ASA was targeted and socially boycotted in the recent struggle of which it was a part, where it lost the student leader and writer Rohith Vemula. Thus, it is pertinent to reflect on the anti-caste critique that it offers as philosophical and political.

SENSE AND MEANING OF THE ROHITH STRUGGLE

In our opinion, the Rohith struggle has strived to put together a philosophy that is at once political. In that sense, the Brahmanic mode of representation of a secular or of a sacral kind cannot but be political. This is not to say that there is an unchanging essence to the Brahmanic mode of representation. It is our contention that in the last 200 years, its influence has only strengthened as it allows for contradictory forces to operate. It opens up caste for certain modern operations and allows caste to be amenable to extremely pre-modern traditional functions. From the traditional Sringeri Mutt to the corporate giant Infosys, there is a lineage that modern Indian institutions imbibe in post-colonial India—a mode of representing that is at once continuous and discontinuous. Its styles of opening and closing ensure that electoral democracy is at work, bureaucracy and other modern economic as well as cultural institutions like the universities formally function alongside ritual practices and maintenance of caste–kinship relations.

In the neoliberal world, the opening of caste to modern operations would mean that they would withdraw reservations in public sector institutions (recent move to reduce intake of scheduled caste/scheduled tribe [SC/ST] teachers in universities) and make a token gesture of providing employment to Dalits in Hindu temples of Kerala. With scarce jobs, inaccessible Hindu gods, the Brahmanic mode of representation is showing fissures at one end but the Left rhetoric has not been able to exploit the situation because its representational mode fails to tear the caste and the Hindu patriarchal fabric. The technological character of Brahmanic thought, which produces affection within one's own caste (Brahmin or Sudra), and the distance between graded and hierarchically organized caste communities (Brahmin versus Sudra) are rigid and porous at the same time. A more extreme position would be to suggest a deracinated individual within one's own caste and community. This deracination happens due to the co-appearance of both capitalist modernity and self-fashioning technologies. While we consider philosophy as a dominant Western mode or way of knowing the world, the Brahmanic mode of representation offers other ways of knowing the world through attenuated sensory practices which inscribe ways of looking, touching, tasting, smelling and hearing. This does not attribute a coherent philosophical self, while it cohabits with a secular, rational, modern, capitalist individual self.

The desire for a politics of body that does not treat innumerable castes as organs performing specific functions and without which the body ceases to function informs the massive anti-caste Rohith struggle. The struggle, while emphasizing the violent and exclusionary nature of Brahmanic self-fashioning technologies, did not merely agitate against the deferred and absent social but sought to restrain any social from appropriating the inassimilable fragment. The movement rendered Ambedkar an inappropriable icon for the Brahmanic mode. It is not just a call for a reformed social, but actually for any form of an inappropriable sharing and dividing as a social ideal. In that sense, the nation experienced a certain kind of moment through the Rohith movement, where it could be argued that it set limits to all other movements—be it the Left, Dalit or other progressive emancipatory projects. It provided a more radical rendering of Ambedkar against law, 'God' and market.

The philosophical project to understand caste as social brings two problems: First, philosophy cannot handle the specificity of the social (caste); second, at the same time, no social (reformed or regressive) can provide redemption. The movement did not aim at merely giving importance to a supposedly dispensable organ, in fact it re-evaluated the whole project of secular or sacral emancipation. In that sense, the movement has made the philosophical political because of the recalcitrant nature of the event itself. Therefore, it questions the need to look for an essence of politics. The need to exit the modern Hindu mind in its secular avatar (Left) and the Hindu body in its communal avatar mark the critique originating from the Rohith movement. It calls for distancing from a dysfunctional secular rationality oblivious to caste inequities and a purging of an imperceptible caste sensorium, whose origins are difficult to retrieve and a socio-historical critique is at best inadequate. This would envision a critique of alienating work through diversifying the possible vitalities, and the irreducibility of the Dalit as merely a labouring subject. Who else can provide a critique against alienating work, commodifying relations or the pleasures and poesies of worklessness than the toiling Dalits? This may be considered as an inappropriable critique of labour and of contemporary debates on merit.

The conventional Dalit movement's perspective seems to have an essence, but from the Rohith movement onwards, the Dalit movement questions any essence—Brahminical or otherwise. Caste practices are considered as giving rise to seriously distorted appearance of things; thus, caste obscures beings. Secular rationality, on the one hand, and Hindu religious identity, on the other hand, have only deepened this distortion. For the Left, caste seems to hide economic relations, and for the Right it obscures an authentic Hindu self. It appears, since colonialism, the idea of the social has constantly been deferred both by the Left and the Right political forces. The Left secular rationality makes the being of beings appear in commodity form (economic rationality and the production of a social form); and the Hindu lived reality (sensorial orientation and affection/distance towards things and beings) provides a closure to a non-coercive social mingling and democratic aspirations of lower caste communities. But the Rohith movement announces itself against any determinant form of social.

The critique of secular rationality against the technological character of commodity relations in its concrete, everyday making in the market-place, and its historical development is important. However, it fails to adequately account for the technological making of caste in everyday context and its historical/poetic evolution. Technology or technique refers to making things appear and how in the process the technique itself disappears. Can secular rationality dis-assemble this technique which re-assembles stardust into caste bodies? The co-appearing of the Brahmanic caste arrangement within capitalist determined social form cannot be seen as the former being fully domesticated by the latter. But modern Brahmanic institutions use both techniques of representa-tions and technique of presentation: one is disembodied and the other is embodied and performative. The capitalist logic of production or modern secular forms of representation and the Brahmanic techniques of presentation work in tandem. Much against the grain of post-colonial scholarship's argument that the heterogeneous Brahmanic temporality and mode of presentation offers a critique against capitalist forms of representation and production; the Rohith struggle seems to suggest that they reinforce each other rather than posit towards a heterogeneous temporality and a plural singularity for the Dalit. Signifying polyphony and polymorphy, Rohith wanted to be a writer of science fiction. For Rohith, science emerges as a struggle between matters of fact and mat-ters of concern. In that sense, science is constantly not in monologue with itself for Rohith, but relates itself to an audience realizing its democratic orientation. In other words, the monochromatic nature of the Dalit movement (as science is conventionally understood) had the potential of being radically transformed. Intriguingly, Rohith had qualified a research fellowship each in the life sciences and the social sciences, resonating a figure of a polymath. Perhaps he was interested in unshackling of forms—be it in disciplinary forms of knowledge or affective forms of social mobilization.

Even in the context of the Rohith movement, the generativity of caste sense is more crucial than the inscribing of the hierarchy of caste bodies. The presentation of caste in each instance is not much dependent on caste inscription but on the sense generativity of Brahmanic thought. It was this sense generativity that produced the structure of *Velivada* (Dalit Ghetto) on the University of Hyderabad campus and the movement exteriorized the concealed Brahmanic technique of presentation into a recognizable anti-caste technique of representation. The structure (being) disclosed hidden space and spatial (caste) disposition. The many works of art that were assembled at the site of *Velivada* and in the social media *unconceal* Brahmanic techniques of presentation, to unfold the multiple origins of the caste present and the caste past.

On another note, in present times, Brahmanic temporality and capitalistic temporality cohere to stifle, crush and dismember the lower caste bodies in such modern spaces as cinema houses, libraries, laboratories and universities, on the one hand, and temples, culinary and inter-dining practices including marriage across castes and communities, on the other hand. The violence of Brahmanic temporality co-appearing with market temporality on an everyday basis results in the de-constitution of multiple lower caste sensibilities and techniques of world forming and community imaging/imagining. Lack of funding for public universities means Brahmanic forms of representation will take over and cohabit with forms of relations based on exchange value and once again regain the sacrality of modern *gurukula* systems (master-disciple tradition of Indian schooling). Secular rationalities based on commodity relations fail to adequately account for the varied appearance of this insistent social form. Rohith's last abstract was about questioning the Brahmanic ordering that overlay the scientific institutional ordering of the laboratory (*News Minute* 2016).

It is true that there was considerable support for the movement from progressive civil society and political formations. But it must be noted that the initial thrust of the movement questioned a unificatory project of the Hindu Right as much as it questioned the categorical violence wrought by the language of class struggle and workers' revolution. Interestingly, it also demanded the rewriting of the Dalit movement not purely in identitarian terms. The political possibilities of the emergent Dalit critique, we would like to argue, make an effort to disembody the blinding sensorial luminosity, which accompanies the Hindutva mode of emaciating contemporary anti-caste movements. In its place, it seeks to institute the practice of re-embodied corporeal politics—that of exteriorizing the *Velivada* including the performative power that exudes in the originary suicide note that Rohith had written.

EYE OF THE STORM

Despaired after struggling against social boycott at the University of Hyderabad, five Dalit research scholars—student leaders from the ASA—bore the brunt of the institutional powers of the nation. But Rohith's death sparked off widespread protests across the world, where Dalit politics converged along with students' and social movements against caste discrimination in higher educational spaces across the country. His death was considered as an institutional murder, and a case under prevention of atrocities against the SC/ST Act was filed in the High Court at Hyderabad. However, Rohith's desire to be a writer was fulfilled only in his death. And all he got to write was this 'last letter for the first time' (Vemula 2016). Rohith Vemula—an aspiring writer and academic—son of a single Dalit mother (divorcee) became an iconic catalyst for a movement against caste discrimination in contemporary India. However, Rohith and his family are now denounced as non-Dalits, and even in his death, his birth is clarified through enumerative categories to apprehend his life and others (Henry 2016; Mondal 2016; *News Minute* 2017).

However, in the eye of the storm was Rohith's haunting yet philosophical 'suicide' note:

> I loved Science, Stars, Nature, but then I loved people without knowing that people have long since divorced from nature. Our feelings are second handed. Our love is constructed. Our beliefs colored. Our originality valid through artificial art. It has become truly difficult to love without getting hurt. The value of a man was reduced to his immediate identity and nearest possibility. To a vote. To a number. To a thing. Never was a man treated as a mind. As a glorious thing made up of star dust. In every field, in studies, in streets, in politics, and in dying and living.

> I am writing this kind of letter for the first time. My first time of a final letter. Forgive me if I fail to make sense. My birth is my fatal accident. I can never recover from my childhood loneliness. The unappreciated child from my past …

He went on further to state, in a Christ-like manner:

> No one has instigated me, whether by their acts or by their words to this act. This is my decision and I am the only one responsible for this. Do not trouble my friends and enemies on this after I am gone. (Vemula 2016)

While his death was considered a sacrifice, it was also widely perceived that his aspiration was humiliated, rejected and reduced to death. The Dalit presence is, then, perhaps ontologically never human enough as increasingly cows are holier than a Dalit and a Muslim in contemporary India. The Dalit presence in academic spaces haunts the privileged and the dominant as they are made to belong to a different time, who, however, occupy—non-meritoriously—the present, 'modern', spaces that are largely populated and designed by/for the 'upper' castes. Though rejected over dead meat, they haunt through their presence as socially dead beings. They are subjected as incompatible beings in life but become powerful icons in their deaths. They, perhaps, are ghost presences. However, Rohith rejected this rejection, wilfully, through his death.

ROHITH'S SHADOWS

Rohith Vemula wrote in his *un*-departing note (and we repeat) that, for some, birth is a curse; and his birth is a fatal accident (Vemula 2016). Is there any birth that is not a fatal accident, one wonders? One could also extend whether the birth of nation, the birth of what is to be human, who is an untouchable—are they not accidents? If they are indeed just accidents, why is a person never treated as a glorious being made out of stardust? Why she or he is reduced to an identity, to a number, to a vote, to a thing? Desiring to be a writer of science, Rohith became a ghost writer of sorts in his eventual death.

Rohith's gesture against violence—his sacrifice, his gift of life and death[1]—is perhaps against caste that 'things' human beings to their immediate identity and nearest possibility. A question of values against the notion of 'what it is to be' was raised. Did Rohith's death signify the death of a community? Or did it signify the political valency of the community of deaths? Is death, an offering to the community, a gift? What about the death—a living social death—before the physical death, which is inscribed in the corporal experience of an untouchable Dalitness? Is death, then, a gift for a community to come? Did Rohith's death embody the lack or a failure of an anti-caste community, located and positioned from an outcaste ontology, especially in modern spaces in this country?

Can (caste) death be one's own? As births are never treated as fatal accidents, deaths, too, are never incidents of choice. Perhaps, there is nothing in caste that transcends one's death from birth. Defiantly, Rohith's departing note is about the life of death as an incident of choice and a lack of choice. It is a gift—that communities give and take—where death defies and refutes one's own birth and becomes an open call for a *movement* to come. Perhaps Rohith's movement taught us in an Ambedkarite sense that 'the battle is in the fullest sense spiritual … it is a battle for freedom', which exceeds the sacral as well as the secular logic of the social as such.

A COUNTER-SPACE AND A COMING TIME?

When not given a proper burial, where his body was taken away and burnt on a pyre in haste, his kith and kin decided to have a Buddhist death ceremony in an Ambedkarite fashion with his ashes. On his 27th

---

[1] Sasheej Hegde's 'The Gift of a Life and Death' (2016) purports that Rohith's life and death demands an answer from all of 'us'. Drawing from the works of Marcel Mauss, Jacques Derrida and Olly Pyythinen, he understands Rohith's life and death as a 'gift'. However, he states that this gift is challenged by an inherent sociality as well as transformative radicalism of thought and action. Hence, he forcefully argues that a pervasive sociality can constrict the idea of 'gift'. He asks can one transcend the limits of the frames of caste sociality in a lived sense, as a free-standing 'gift'.

birth anniversary (30 January 2016), around 8,000 people clad in white walked in silence from *Deekshabhoomi* (Ordaining ground: A Buddhist monument in Nagpur) to the Rashtriya Swayamsevak Sangh head-quarters at Nagpur in protest. Besides, Ambedkarite Buddhists received students throughout the train stations from Hyderabad to Delhi, when students travelled to Delhi to seek justice for Rohith. And on the 125th birth anniversary of Babasaheb Dr B. R. Ambedkar on 14 April 2016, Rohith's mother and brother—Ms Radhika and Mr Raja Vemula—converted to Buddhism in Bombay, thereby inaugurating another debate on conversion and caste. Perhaps death raises the question of community, sociality and fraternity much more intimately for the Dalit community as a social death precedes an eventual death.

Rohith's life and death seem to suggest that Dalitness is accepted and romanticized only if it remains socially dead. It threatens society if it rejects passivity, exits out of social death and exhibits a will to life. Rohith had signed off his death desiring *movement*—'from shadows to stars'. His death can be evaluated as a gift of death towards life. It is a call for a future; perhaps, for a coming community. This prophetic call could treat someone as 'a glorious being made of star dust'. This clarion call is against Brahmanic modernity as well as capitalistic modernity that seemingly offers closure to 'things' and reduces human beings to their immediate identity and nearest possibility. In that sense, his martyrdom, perhaps, raised the value of what it is 'to become'. It is a call for a community that values how one dies, rather than what one's birth is. It is a call towards a community of death, not birth—which is an exciting freedom from social death.

Rohith, as a phenomenon, today counters caste itself. His pro-phetic call to the future of a community has a resistant touch, an act of 'annihilation'—which unravels caste's direct, insidious violence and its chronic inalienable dishonour. It fashions a genealogy which integrates experience, understands social inheritances and anchors the living-present with a conscious community of memory. The fact that the *Velivada* at the University of Hyderabad—the Dalit ghetto—became a powerful memorial site, which increasingly threatens normalization and forgetting, is a serious space that rejects the neatness of a secular social space. Protests and gatherings still happen, in the face of brutal retaliation. Cutting across identities, faculty and students renew their struggles for justice every day. *Velivada* became a counter-space, where art and pedagogy in its more radical form present itself as politics. It incorporates the basic value of life—that anything is an inter-being of other things. Many students and faculty faced wrath in the guise of police action and institutional violence. Yet, the struggle itself became multifarious—therefore, more powerful—through its inter-subjective representative registers and presentations against an intertwining that is resourced by both the Brahmanic and capitalistic modernity.

REFERENCES

Hegde, Sasheej. 2016. 'The Gift of a Life and Death: Rohith Vemula and "Us"'. *Economic & Political Weekly* 51 (49, December): 28–30.

Henry, Nikhila. 2016. 'It's Official. Rohith Vemula Was Dalit'. *The Hindu,* 18 October. Available at: http://www.thehindu.com/news/national/andhra-pradesh/It%E2%80%99s-official.-Rohith-Vemula-was-Dalit/article14424041.ece (accessed on 26 October 2017).

Hutchens, B. C. 2014. *Jean-Luc Nancy and the Future of Philosophy.* New York, NY: Routledge.

Mondal, Sudipto. 2016. 'Rohith Vemula: An Unfinished Portrait'. *Hindustan Times,* January. Available at: http://www.hindustantimes.com/static/Rohith-vemula-an-unfinished-portrait/ (accessed on 26 October 2017).

News Minute. 2016. 'Abstract of Rohith's Rejected Sociology Paper: Discovering Caste Prejudices in Science Labs'. *The News Minute,* 30 January. Available at: http://www.thenewsminute.com/article/abstract-Rohiths-rejected-sociology-paper-discovering-caste-prejudices-science-labs-38343 (accessed on 6 August 2019).

———. 2017. 'A Year on, Rohith Vemula Case Held up by Confusion over Caste'. *The News Minute,* 17 January. Available at: https://www.thequint.com/india/2017/01/17/a-year-on-police-claim-rohith-vemulas-caste-uncertain-case-makes-no-headway-dalit-suicide-death (accessed on 26 October 2017).

Stahl, Gerry. 2017. *Marx and Heidegger* (eBook). Lulu.com. Available at: http://www.gerrystahl.net/elibrary/marx/marx.pdf (accessed on 27 October 2017).

Thirumal, P., and Carmel Christy. 2018. 'Why Indian Universities Are Places Where Savarnas Get Affection and Dalit–Bahujans Experience Distance'. *Economic & Political Weekly* 53 (5, 2 February). Available at: https://www.epw.in/engage/article/why-indian-universities-are-places-where-savarnas-get-affection-and-dalit-bahujans (accessed on 7 June 2018).

Vemula, Rohith. 2016. 'My Birth Is My Fatal Accident'. *The Indian Express,* 19 January. Available at: http://indianexpress.com/article/india/india-news-india/dalit-student-suicide-full-text-of-suicide-letter-hyderabad/ (accessed on 26 October 2017).

Chapter 2

Intra-subaltern Conflict
Dalit–Tribal Conflict in Odisha*

INTRODUCTION

The concept of subaltern has disturbed the doctrinal boundaries of contemporary discourses. The epistemic boundaries of various fields and disciplines such as Marxism, feminism, cultural studies, anthropology, political science, history, media, cinema and literature are being radically redrawn. The subaltern as a referent for the marginalized masses in history took its distinctive origin from Antonio Gramsci and the then political situation in Italy. As a theoretical venture, Subaltern Studies revises and extends the Marxian proletarian discourse as well as strengthens its positions based on post-structuralist concept of 'difference'.

This inbuilt dichotomous dimension enables Subaltern Studies to deconstruct all dominant discourses including itself. What I have argued here is that the Subaltern Studies in one way have challenged

---

* A few portions of the text from the article by Malik (2017) have been revised and reproduced in the section 'Tribal–Dalit Conflict in the Narayanpatna Block of Koraput District' with due citations. I also acknowledge the cooperation of the people of Narayanpatna during my fieldwork at Narayanpatna in December 2015.

the Marxian unilinear 'class contradiction', the Gramscian 'cultural hegemony' and the Eurocentric notion of truth, history and consciousness, but in another way it looks beyond the post-structural orientation. But, interestingly, it discovers the metanarrative theory in anchoring to the critical theory that is 'the narrative about narratives' of historical meaning, experience, consciousness or knowledge. It argues that the class consciousness, hegemony, subalternity exists everywhere at the micro-level, which is multipolar, fragmented, divergent and opposes anything that is totalitarian, including the subaltern itself. So the 'subaltern' as a category has created its own contradiction and antithesis which refutes the very notion of subalternity or subaltern consciousness as unilinear, which could pose binary opposition to the elite or dominant. The differences within the subaltern on various aspects reveal the fragments and conflicts among different subaltern groups. These intra-subaltern conflicts are the reality in contemporary India, and Odisha as a state is not an exception.

With the above backdrop, the chapter tries to explore the nature and dynamics of intra-subaltern conflicts over resource competition, community identity formation and ethno-cultural segregation in contemporary Odisha. The chapter is divided into four parts. The first part is the overall introduction to the problem. The second part deals with the theoretical framework, which includes discourses regarding intra-subaltern differences, conflicts and its critique. The third part discusses the conflicts between the tribals (STs) and Dalits (SCs) in Odisha, by considering three cases from Phulbani, Kandhamal and Narayanpatna. The fourth part explores the role of the Maoists and the state's response in these conflicts, followed by the conclusion.

THEORETICAL FRAMEWORK

Although Gramsci, in the *Prison Notebooks*, uses the term 'subaltern' as synonym for 'proletarian', he expands its scope by using it as a referent for any social groups outside the established structures of political representation. With particular reference to the marginalized rural peasantry of southern Italy, he says that these subaltern groups have no social and political consciousness and is predisposed to the dominant ideology. According to Gramsci, in every class-divided society, the hegemonic and the subaltern classes are always in a state of conflict. Thus, in a wider perspective, he uses the term *subaltern* to refer to the marginalized and oppressed groups anywhere in the world.

Edward Said draws on the Gramscian notion of 'hegemony' and the Foucauldian notion of 'discourse' in explicating how the 'Orient' is constructed in the imagination of the West. In a similar vein, the subaltern historians in India attempted to rewrite the elite versions of Indian historiography, giving the subaltern agency its own space, doing away with all misrepresentations. Gayatri Chakravorty Spivak has questioned this theoretical venture of the subaltern historians in the context of the problem of representing the voice of the gendered subaltern.

It also emphasizes the fact that the nature and structure of the subaltern consciousness vary from one social context to another, owing to the difference in their experience of capitalist exploitation and the subaltern responses to it. Frantz Fanon, too, has elaborated this point in *The Wretched of the Earth,* where he states that racial difference has intensified capitalist exploitation in colonial situations:

> Economic reality, inequality and the immense difference of ways of life never come to mask the human realities. When you examine at close quarters the colonial contexts, what parcels out the world is to begin with the fact of belonging or not belonging to a given race. (Fanon 2001: 61)

The theoretical position within the subaltern, that is, 'the difference' within the category as per context, experiences and exploitation vis-à-vis conflict in ethnic, caste, religious, material need-cum-resource-based competition, including political lines, is visible within the category. The 'consciousness' or the 'being' of subaltern as a 'category' is further divided with different magnitudes of deprivation, marginalization and exploitation, which have created unrest among different communities, which leads to intra-subaltern conflicts.

These intra-subaltern conflicts in India, in some cases, perceive one community, that is, Dalits, as the immediate enemy or competitors to other community, that is, tribals, though theoretically both belong to the subaltern or marginalized group. This kind of subaltern conflict is in some cases due to conflict of material interest, migration–cum–exploitation, religious belief, language, sub-caste and regional differences and in other cases due to state-sponsored 'divide-and-rule game', where all these fuzzy consciousnesses overpower subaltern consciousness.

In the case of India, this intra–subaltern conflict at both the macro and micro levels is a common phenomenon happening all over the Indian states, which falsifies not only Marx's classical theory of class struggle of two binary contradictory forces but also the Gramscian idea of subaltern and hegemony. Like other states, the state of Odisha is not an exception to such kind of intra-subaltern conflicts in the past and also in the contemporary period. The conflicts between the two subaltern communities (Dalits and tribals) in contemporary Odisha urge me to write this chapter, which disprove the grand notion of Eurocentric subalternity and reveal the multifaceted truth within the subaltern.

The contemporary state of Odisha has been experiencing a series of ethnic, caste, religious, resource-based and political conflicts. These conflicts are the products of different magnitudes of deprivation, marginalization and exploitation, which have created unrest among different communities and dissatisfaction with the state authorities. These experiences simply highlight the antagonism, aggression and resistance in a context in which the policy-making process and administration respond through violent means. It presents a complex picture of contemporary intra–subaltern conflicts between Dalits and tribals in Odisha.

The conflicts in the Phulbani block of Odisha (over electoral issues) in Kandhamal district (over religious and resource conflict issues) and in the Narayanpatna block of Koraput district (over land alienation and encroachment issues) come within the broader framework of competition to gain control over the material needs and natural resources or to protect the religious and political ideologies. The intra-subaltern conflicts essentially involve competition for material resources between the tribals (indigenous people) and non–tribals (Dalits or SCs) in Odisha. The growing insecurity among the tribals is due to the gradual alienation and loss of their resources, that is, *jami* (land), *jal* (water) and jungle (forest), to the 'non-tribals' (mostly Dalits, the liquor vendors and the immediate exploiters, in Marxist term, the 'petty bourgeois') who are mostly outsiders or migrants. This made the tribals of Odisha landless and compelled them to engage in an uncongenial relationship and violent conflicts with the Dalits, thereby creating insecurity for the latter.

Differences and Contradiction within the Subaltern: The Discourse

Spivak's intervention and the fundamental question that she raised regarding representation of the subaltern had a huge impact on the trajectory of Subaltern Studies. It can be presented in the following lines:

> The idea that subalterns inhabit an 'autonomous' domain has been persuasively critiqued. The subaltern has come to be seen as inextricably linked to elite discourse, even in resistance, allowing for the possibility of seeing Subalternity both as radically relational, and scrupulously singular, not easily flattened into class identity. (Spivak 1988)

To criticize the universal notion of subaltern as the Eurocentric idea, Dipesh Chakrabarty has rightly mentioned:

> The critique of elitism could hardly afford to ignore the problem of universalism/Eurocentrism that was inherent in Marxist thought itself. The age of multinational capital devolves on us this responsibility to think 'difference' not simply as a theoretical question but as a tool for producing practical possibilities for action. Clearly, this talk of 'difference' was gaining currency in the trajectory of *Subaltern Studies*. There was a feeling that our lives are no longer adequately representable through the unitary language of a particular political philosophy, that is, through some kind of a Hegelian synthesis that can contain and subsume all our differences with others and those between ourselves. (Chakrabarty 1995: 758)

Hence, there is a need to go to a Derrida or a Lyotard who was the philosopher of 'difference' and 'non-commensurability' for modern times. Instead of submitting to Eurocentric imagination, a powerful critique of 'post-Enlightenment rationalism' was considered essential.

Chakrabarty quotes the Chinese scholar Lydia Liu to problematize 'Eurocentric, metropolitan and bureaucratic systems of knowledge'. In the context of Chinese history, Liu comments:

> The critique of modernity has always been part of the Enlightenment legacy from the Romantics, Nietzsche, Marx, and Heidegger to Horkheimer, Adorno, Foucault, Derrida and even Habermas. (Liu 1993: 758)

Thus, the project's elementary objective of searching for an essential structure of subaltern consciousness was no longer acceptable to many of the subaltern historians. The relationship of *Subaltern Studies* to Michel Foucault's writings, which became crucial since the middle of the 1980s, ushered in a 'post-structuralist moment' in its career (Chatterjee 1999: 416). Subalternists came closer and closer to what Sugata Bose calls a communitarian mode of historical writing. They now celebrated the indigenous religious fragments as the quintessence of India and contested the 'cunning of post-Enlightenment modernity' as well as the hegemony of the modern state (Bose 2003: 135).

Partha Chatterjee's *The Nation and Its Fragments* (1993) particularly reflected the influence of postmodern or post-structuralist scholarship (Chatterjee 1993: 27). With the coming of Foucauldian and post-structuralist critiques of Marxism, there took place an 'intellectual bifurcation' within the project. While some members continued to write histories from 'below', others came close to a variety of post-Marxist positions. Addressing this rift, David Hardiman announced as early as in 1986 that 'the lack of any subaltern theory was a strength rather than a weakness' (Hardiman 1986: 290).

Thus, it marked a distinct shift within *Subaltern Studies* towards analysing modern regimes of power. The emphasis was no longer on subaltern protest or insurrection. The recent volumes of *Subaltern Studies* were paying greater attention to developing the emergence of subalternity as a discursive effect without discarding the notion of the subaltern as a subject and an agent. This strategy identified both the appearance and dislocation of subaltern agency in dominant discourses. Subalternity thus comes out in the contradictions of the working of power and it refers to that action without which the dominant discourse cannot exist.

There was a storm of protest and criticism against this new perspective. One central argument was that *Subaltern Studies* was deviating from 'a diffuse notion of resistance to a miasmic description of power'. According to Sivaramakrishnan:

> It was the project's quest for human agency among the comparatively powerless groups in society and its attempt to return dignity and purpose to the activities of the unknown poor peasantry in colonised worlds that earned it acclaim and admiration. Now the project was caught up in anthropologies that were not favorable to the description of subaltern agency. To theorize power subtly in terms of Foucault, it meant to locate power, not the subaltern's resistance, as the inspiring subject. It has been pointed out that such shifts in *Subaltern Studies* and their concurrence with postcolonial criticism followed the new agendas for historical anthropologies of culture. (Sivaramakrishnan 1995: 241)

Rosalind O'Hanlon critically engages with the nature of this reconstruction that was attempted in the subaltern project. She suggests that 'the problem of experience, which is disconnected from that of agency, might be more effectively considered without the notion of universal human subjectivities' (O'Hanlon 1988: 191). She seriously examines what she sees as the tension between the aspiration to locate a resistant presence and the need to care for difference and otherness in the figure of the subaltern. O'Hanlon advocates that the deconstructed subject of the Subaltern Studies project necessarily emanates from another subject, which the 'totalizing theory' of historical materialism had actually taken apart earlier.

In a similar vein, David Washbrook has confronted the subaltern notion of cultural difference. Washbrook speaks of a global perspective of politico-economic developments within which, he argues, the history of South Asia should be located. In his view:

> There is much exaggeration in such assertion of difference; as the new *Subaltern Studies* approach is 'structured by the increasingly

fashionable methodology of discourse analysis and resistance theory'.
(Washbrook 1988: 57)

Tom Brass makes a stern critique of its being decoupled from class and revolution. In his view:

> It is impossible to mark out the notional concerns and political course of *Subaltern Studies* without allusion to the means in which its discourse is shaped by the postmodernist project. The postmodern discourse thus undermines the role of 'the economic' and reconstitutes ethnic or gender-specific categories as cultural subjects. Under the impact of this methodology, Subaltern Studies approach causes 'the depeasantisation of tribals', which in turn allows the reification of the 'other'. (Brass 1991: 193)

For Ranajit Guha and others, what matters is not class differentiation, but rather the antagonism between the 'elite' and its 'state', on the one hand, and the 'popular masses', on the other. This is precisely why the projected subaltern groups include all sorts of subordinate people who remain outside of the purview of the 'elite'. As Brass cited the lines from Ranajit Guha:

> '[S]ubaltern' is employed 'as a name for the general attribute of subordination in South Asian society whether this is expressed in terms of class, caste, age, gender and office or in any other way.' The class position of the subject does not help in understanding these kinds of difference. In the subalternist discourse, class-consciousness fails to turn up because of the clash between ethnic, gender, religious or regional identities on the one hand, and class-based ideological forms on the other. In the process, the non-existence of class itself is claimed to be evident. (cited in Brass 1991: 193)

In his critique of the Subaltern Studies position that 'ethnicity' as a material difference takes up the ground that was earlier held conceptually by 'class', Brass calls our attention to the Naxalite movement in West Bengal in the late 1960s. Drawing on the research work of Duyker (1987: 111), Brass points to the active participation of the tribal population of the West Bengal districts of 'Midnapore' (later divided as

East Midnapore and West Midnapore in 1 January 2002), Birbhum and Bankura in the Maoist guerrilla movement. According to Brass, 'Such an approach undoubtedly sets in motion the dislocation of class struggle by ethnic struggle as the primary focus of Naxalism' (Brass 1991: 193).

Critique of the Contradiction

Vinay Bahl sharply reacts to the subalternist idea of differences derived from ethnic, religious, local, racial and gender identities. She particularly points to Dipesh Chakrabarty's statement that the subalternists seek to preserve the notion of 'difference' as the philosophical question of their times. *Subaltern Studies*, according to him, 'can only situate itself theoretically at the juncture where we give up neither Marx nor "difference"'. Bahl suggests that Subaltern Studies should come back to its original position of creating an emancipatory politics. Differences are not inert. Hence, what deserves closer attention is what she calls 'operations of differences'. People's harmony must not be undermined for reinventing differences (Bahl 2005: 100).

Bahl gives the example of the Dalit women in India citing Gopal Guru's writings. In Guru's words:

> As modern research has shown, numerous differences can be observed within the same *dalit* caste-group between women and men, between grassroots level and educated employed women, between regions and languages. Differences are also discernible in the dalit women's fight against global forces, their demand for equality, their battle against *Hindu* fundamentalism, their ability to go beyond caste and regional identities, their reliance on the state for their empowerment, and their struggle against state policies of liberalization. (Guru 1995: 2548)

Bahl asks: Can we understand the intricacies of such issues? And the struggle of Dalit men and women across India by seeing Dalits as ethnic group, a 'community', a caste or a collection of primordial values? John Beverley, one of the main founders of the Latin American Subaltern Studies Group, has critically engaged with the theory of subalternity. Like the subalternists in South Asia, he is also keen to have a 'politics of difference' in a world threatened by the new order of globalization and facing homogenization in the name of economic development and progress. While focusing mainly on contemporary Latin American cultural studies, Beverley argues that:

> This globalized world privileges the interests of the corporations over individual expressions. Therefore, the question is to protect and hear individual voices, especially of the subaltern groups. The formation of a power base through a combination of these voices would continue to attend individual expressions but would not become institutionalized. (Beverley 1999: 38)

Beverley criticizes *Subaltern Studies* and says that Subaltern Studies unwittingly repeats the same hierarchical and hegemonic systems. To get out of the problem of negative definition, Spivak wants *Subaltern Studies* to reproduce 'a subaltern subject effect', not the subaltern. But over time, this 'subject effect' is also the outcome of a method of dislocation that challenges the binaries like 'inside/outside, modern/ traditional, colonial/native, subaltern/dominant'. Thus, in spite of efforts to deconstruct the hegemonic categories of people and the nation, Beverley explains:

> The tensions generated by these binaries are played out within the exist- ing dominant discourses. This 'deconstructive/reconstructive' process is the 'double urgency' of Subaltern Studies which needs a 'counter- hegemonic politics of people' that would be possible through a 'cultural politics of difference'. (cited in Ray 2007: 14)

Regarding the non-existence of subaltern unity and the difference within the subaltern project, Vinay Bahl critically observes:

> The myth of subaltern unity is promoted by the Subaltern Studies (SS) by emphasizing only the subalternist nonmaterial culture (i.e. subjectiv- ity, values, consciousness and identity). They have failed to consider aspects of the material culture which includes among other things political power, political institutions, clothes, food, furniture, living and working conditions, housing, technology and financial systems, trade and the impact of all the above on people's lives. What is left out is how human agency produces material culture while people interact

socially with other people and within specific social and material conditions. (Bahl 2005: 52)

Subaltern Studies, maligned from its arrival, continues to be contested even today as a historical project and a strategic practice. Debate still goes on. As I have to halt somewhere between the unity and differences of the subaltern consciousness, I think it is pertinent to end up the debate with some critical observations by Rajat Kanta Ray:

> Do the subalterns have a vision of the brave new world? On the subalternists' own admission, no. Desperately seeking to show that localized diversionary politics, articulated through 'the discourses of kinship, caste, religion, and ethnicity', is not to be confused with the backward, they take refuge in the fond notion that every time the subalterns rise up in rebellion, they seek to destroy hierarchy. Kinship would reproduce patriarchy, religion would reproduce authority, and caste would reproduce hierarchy, if those happen to be the bases of insurgency … The debates between the Marxists and the Subalternists as to how to conduct the people's struggle against capitalism is of little interest to mainstream liberal historiography. As far as the liberals are concerned, modernity produced civil society long before it established capitalism … and there is no other way of life but the civil way. (Ray 2007: 14)

DIFFERENCES AND CONFLICTS WITHIN THE SUBALTERN: SELECTIVE STUDIES FROM ODISHA

The resurgence of community conflicts over resources in the contemporary world has provoked renewed debate among social scientists about the nature and significance of community conflict in contemporary societies (Ambagudia 2015: 41). Such conflicts are conspicuous in India in general, and Odisha in particular. Conflicts over resources are apparently linked to the nature of the Indian society that is seen as the complete grid of inequality, discrimination, deprivation, exploitation, marginalization and social exclusion. The experience of different magnitudes and levels of impoverishment and the attainment of different stages of social, economic and political developments by different communities lead to the emergence of conflicts (Bardhan 2005: 185).

Different communities compete for scarce natural resources they need or want to ensure their livelihood. Such competition for use and access to resources results in violent conflicts.

Regarding the inter-community conflict, Ambagudia argues:

> The tribal society heavily depends upon two major sources of production, that is, land and forest, which are described as 'twin pillars of Adivasi economy'. Their relationship with the two, especially with the former, is something like their 'philosophy of life'. The tribals have an inherent and inalienable right over land and forest. Denial of such rights to natural resources or any attempt to dilute their profound relationship with land and forest certainly leads to the generation of inter-community tensions and violent conflicts. (Ambagudia 2010: 61)

Access to natural resources has become the site for competition and intra-subaltern conflict. Such competition creates inter-group inequalities and generates the feeling of 'relative deprivation', thereby leading to the occurrence of potential conflicts among different communities. Competition for use and access to resources results in violent intra-subaltern conflicts or conflict between two marginal groups. Conflict gets accentuated particularly if the resource is scarce and the claimants to the resource are many. Homer-Dixon linked the idea of resource conflict with environmental degradation. He argued that 'environmental degradation generates simple scarcity conflicts, group identity conflicts, and relative deprivation conflicts' (Homer-Dixon 1991: 105).

The changing relationship between different communities in contemporary societies within the broader framework of assertive identities and material survival is the prime factor behind these intra-subaltern conflicts. Scholars have been engaged in understanding contemporary community conflicts in the context of ethnicity and defined in terms of religion (see Brass 2003; Varshney 2002). However, social scientists have paid little attention to the study of contemporary community conflicts between the tribals (STs) and non-tribals, especially Dalits (SCs) in India in general and in Odisha in particular. During the last decade, there have been major conflicts between the tribals and Dalits in Odisha which are intra-subaltern in nature. Among these intra-subaltern conflicts between the tribals (STs) and Dalits (SCs) in Odisha, three case studies, from Phulbani, Kandhamal and Narayanpatna, have been discussed in the following paragraphs.

Dalit–Tribal Conflict in Bisipara Village of Phulbani Block

Bishnu Mohapatra and Dwaipayan Bhattacharyya in their electoral study in the Bisipara village of the Phulbani block of Kandhamal district in Odisha, in 1995, have highlighted the intra-subaltern ethnic conflict in the district. Regarding the Dalit (Pana)–tribal (Kandha) conflict in Phulbani over the electoral–political issues, Mohapatra and Bhattacharyya have mentioned:

> We take politics here in a broad sense of the term involving conflicts over political, economic and cultural resources, the reproduction of the old and the creation of new solidarities, fight against indignities and, above all, achieving new political agency. (Mohapatra and Bhattacharyya 1996: 160)

Bisipara: A Brief Profile

Bisipara is a village in Phulbani tehsil in Kandhamal district of Odisha. The village comes under Bisipara Panchayat. It is located eight kilometres towards South from district headquarters and three kilometres from Phulbani, at 200 kilometres distance from the state capital, Bhubaneswar. As per the Census (2011):

> The total population of Bisipara Village is 1001 and number of houses are 270. Female Population is 49 percent. The total literacy rate of the village as per the 2011 census is 76 percent, out of which male literacy is 85 percent and female literacy is 66 percent. The Scheduled Caste population is 16.8 percent and the Schedule Tribe population is 9.4 percent.

It is a small village in Phulbani block. The social profile of the village could be broadly categorized as the khandayats (a warrior caste), the Panas (Dalit or scheduled caste) and the Kandhas (a scheduled tribe). This apart, there were also a few Brahmin families. Though the Kandhas in Bisipara are fewer in number than Panas, the Kandhas are in a majority in the area around Bisipara, followed by Panas and the khandayats.

The Intra-subaltern Conflict in Bisipara Village

In their study on Bisipara village, Mohapatra and Bhattacharyya have referred to the tension between the Panas and the Kandhas in the past. As they mentioned in their writings:

Subsequently, in all political meetings and deliberations that we had the opportunity to attend the growing difference between the two communities was made the central theme of discussion. We knew beforehand that since March 1994, violent clashes between the Kandhas and the Panas took place in certain areas of the constituency. Now we were witness to how these issues were reconstructed and fed into the available forms of political mobilisation just on the eve of the election. (Mohapatra and Bhattacharyya 1996: 161)

Here, it is important to present a brief anatomy of the tension to comprehend the nuances of the changing relationship among the various communities and classes in the constituency. For these reasons I have indented the paragraph from Mohapatra and Bhattacharyya's *Economic & Political Weekly* article published in 1996. The article highlighted:

According to an official report, the immediate cause for the *Kandha-Pana* conflict was the entry of a *Pana* youth into a *Shiva* temple in the village of Khudutentuli on January 14, 1994. The *adivasis* took an exception to this action and organised their own people to purify the temple. The *Panas*, according to the same report, adopted an aggressive posture which enraged the *Kandhas*. Two days later, the *adivasis* retaliated by attacking and damaging the houses of the *Panas* in the same village. A week later another incident worsened the situation. This time the *adivasis* of a neighboring village of Ringibadi objected to the cutting down and carrying of bamboo by the Panas of Nandini village. The *Panas* felt humiliated and retaliated by assaulting the *Kandhas*. These isolated incidents soon led to full-scale mobilisation on both sides. The first murder took place on February 20, 1994: a *Pana* youth was killed in the village Linepada. By the end of June, the number of people killed rose to 18, a few hundreds were injured in group clashes and a large number of *Panas* fled from their villages and took shelter in Phulbani town. (Mohapatra and Bhattacharyya 1996: 162)

On 6 April 1995, the first large-scale Kandha mobilization happened in Phulbani town. Nearly 5,000 Kandhas, mostly from Linepada, Khajuripada and Phulbani blocks, marched in a rally from Kaladi village, led by a Kandha youth, Lambodar Konhar. As Mohapatra and Bhattacharyya have mentioned in their article, the main slogan in the rally was:

Jamhi Pana tamhi tamhi hana hana
Pana sasana chaliba nahi
Jadi chaliba nia jaliba

(Mohapatra and Bhattacharyya 1996: 162)

(Wherever you find a *Pana*, kill him.
Panas' domination will not be tolerated.
If it goes on, there will be fire.)

Lambodar Konhar and 15 others called on the collector in his office and submitted a memorandum, addressed to the president of India, with the demands of immediate preservation of the Phulbani assembly and parliamentary seats for the STs: renaming Phulbani as Kandhamala district; unconditional release of 27 Kandhas detained during the disturbances: taking strong actions against Panas; proper utilization of funds meant for social and economic development of the Kandhas and so on By the end of July, Phulbani witnessed a series of such mobilization by both the Kandhas and the Panas, often resulting in violent clashes and loss of lives. It was the intervention of the military police which ultimately brought the violence under control.

This incident concerning a Pana's entry into a temple brings to focus the politics of domination in Phulbani. F. G. Bailey, in his *Politics and Social Change*, describes: 'the victory of the Panas in Bisipara in securing the right to enter into the village temple in the face of severe opposition from the "clean" castes as late as the early 1960s' (Bailey 1963: 50).

This time, the opposition from Kandhas to their entry was a rude shock to the growing economic and political power of the Panas because the Kandhas' view that Panas in Phulbani are all exploiters. Prejudices against the Panas, both from the clean castes and the Kandhas, were startling and not always vindicated by the ground reality (Mohapatra and Bhattacharyya 1996: 162).

There are various ways in which the conflict between the Panas and Kandhas can be explained. First, according to some, this conflict was a product of a factional fight within the Janata Dal. To some others, the conflict was a reflection of the genuine grievances of the Kandhas in the district. Yet, to some others, the clashes were essentially of a competitive nature whereby two marginal groups found themselves locked in a battle over scarce resources. And, finally, according to some, the political–economic development, coupled with the concrete relations of power at various levels, created the conditions for such conflicts.

The bone of contention in the disputes between the two communities was the share of local power and the question of status in the village hierarchy. There is a local saying that '*Kandha* is the king and *Pana* is the minister'. Traditionally, the Kandhas of the area were indeed the chieftains, the local rajas, who were served by the Panas. The latter group played the mediating role between the Kandhas and the outside world.

This role of a linkage paid off well and made the Panas an indispensable part of the local hierarchy. In the past, Panas were given land as a reward for their service to the Kandhas. It is likely that this subordination of the Panas without effective resistance to it offered the system some sort of stability. However, the abolition of untouchability, reservation of jobs and electoral constituencies in post-colonial period made Panas less and less dependent on the old order. New institutions helped this caste to attain a new-found mobility. As the Kandhas, unlike Panas, were tied to the privileges of the old order, they were not sufficiently motivated to make use of the new avenues for mobility. In recent years, the pre-eminence of Panas in the area is seen by the Kandhas as a subversion of this old order. This change is a major source of resentment as far as Kandhas in Phulbani are concerned.

Bailey analyses two disputes, one between khandayats and Panas in Bisipara and the other between Kandhas and the Panas in Baderi. In the words of Bailey:

> Unlike in Baderi, where the *Panas* after their initial protest against the *Kandhas* conformed to the existing hierarchy, the *Panas* in Bisipara

continued their effort to challenge the supremacy of the *khandayats*. Bailey attempted to explain this variation by focusing on the respective structures of the villages and on their connection with the external world. (Bailey 1963: 51)

In 1995, in Bisipara as well as in many other villages, the conflict between the Panas and the Kandhas assumed a critical significance as both these communities draw their strength from their association with the external world. As Mohapatra and Bhattacharyya have remarked:

> This time, in particular, one of the main objectives of the '*Kandha*-activism' was to exercise domination by participating in the larger sphere of politics. Given their majority in the area, election offered them an instrument as well as an opportunity to legitimately put forth their claims over the *Panas*. (Mohapatra and Bhattacharyya 1996: 160)

This reveals the truly marginal character of the Panas who exploited all available opportunities for their betterment. They did not see their future in the old 'Kandha-dominated' social hierarchy. For them, the future was outside this order and in the larger arena of politics. In contrast to the Kandhas, the Panas were quicker to pick up the idioms of this politics, its rules and benefits. Their erstwhile contacts with the outside world as mediators, brokers and middlemen, their proximity to the administration, their familiarity with the market rules, their occasional role as moneylenders and, finally, their knowledge of Oriya (unlike the Kui-speaking Kandhas) materially put them in a better position in the village society. At the same time, these are the very people who continue to occupy the lowest rung in the caste order.

The reaction of Kandhas and upper caste Hindus to Panas' new-found assertiveness was predictable. The Kandhas suffered from a feeling of loss, and the upper castes felt threatened. While Panas think that it is their industriousness and adaptability that were responsible for their betterment, but the Kandhas frequently refer to the 'treacheries and low cunning of the Panas'. The upper caste Hindus share the same view as that of the Kandhas, albeit in a more articulate and prejudiced way. The upper caste views the Panas are great exploiters; they loot the illiterate Kandhas and disrupt the moral order of the village. That is, the increase in the Panas' political and economic power had been at the expense of the Kandhas.

It was only during the violent days of 1994 that the Kandhas could reclaim vast areas of their land from the clutches of the Pana moneylenders. By re-establishing their occupancy rights, the Kandhas sought to reiterate their social supremacy. It is the fusion of the land question, moral and cultural issues, and crave for political power which transformed the Kandhas' hatred towards the Panas into violence and led to the protracted intra-subaltern conflict.

Dalit–Tribal Conflict in Kandhamal District

Although the existing literature considers the conflicts between the tribals and Dalits as the manifestation of communal violence (i.e., Kanungo 2008, 2014), the present study looks at the conflict by going beyond the religious dimension and links it with resource utilization and material conflict, which argues that the socio-economic competition came to be transformed, over time, into communal conflicts between the Hindu and the Christian communities, and that it has much to do with the increasing influence of the right-wing Hindu forces such as the Bajrang Dal and the Sangh Parivar. In this study, it has been asserted that the Kandhamal conflict, though having a religious flavour, primarily emerged between Kandhas (tribals) and Panas (Dalits), which is intra-subaltern in nature. Before analysing the Dalit–tribal conflict in Kandhamal, it is necessary to have a brief look on the study area, the Kandhamal district in terms of its historical, social and demographic profile.

Kandhamal: A Brief Introduction

The British captured this area in phases from 1830 to 1880 by subjugating some hill chiefs. The present Kandhamal district was an integral part of Boudh from time immemorial until 1855. The British named this newly annexed territory as Kandhamal. These areas remained under the control and administration of the British until India attained her independence. Kandhamal remained a tehsil from 1855 to 1891, and it was administered by a tehsildar under the direct control and supervision of the superintendent of the Tributary mahals of Cuttack. When the new province of Orissa was formed in 1936, and Ganjam was merged with Orissa, from the Madras presidency, Kandhamal became a subdivision of Ganjam. In the wake of the amalgamation of the princely states with Orissa in January 1948, Boudh and Kandhamal constituted the new district of Boudh-Kandhamal, with its headquarters at Phulbani. Balliguda subdivision was added to Boudh-Kandhamal district on 1 January 1949. With the secession of Boudh from Phulbani district as a separate district, only Balliguda and Kandhamal subdivisions remained with Phulbani district, which was later rechristened as Kandhamal district in June 1994. It is surrounded by Boudh district in the North, Rayagada district in the South, Ganjam and Nayagarh districts in the east and Kalahandi district in the west. As per Census 2011:

> Total population of the district is 7,31,952 (1.11% of Odisha's population). The male population is 3,59,401 (49.1%). Female population is 3,72,551 (50.9%). The sex ratio of the district is 1000:1037. Total literates in the district are 4,07,383 (65.12%) among which 2, 39,270 (78.41%) are male and 168,113 (52.46%) are female. The Kandhamal district is one of the tribal districts of Odisha, 16.89 percent are dalit (SCs) and 51.96 percent are tribals (STs). (Census 2011)

The Intra-subaltern Conflict in Kandhamal

The historical anecdote provides the contested ground of the emergence of the intra-subaltern conflicts between the tribals and Dalits in Kandhamal. Bauman has well described this Kandha–Pana historical relationship:

> Exploring the historical relationship, it is worthwhile to note that both *Kandhas* and *Panas* were living together before the debut of British and missionaries in the district. The British entry led to the discovery of the *meriah,* (human sacrifice) practiced by the *Kandhas.* In this practice, *Panas* acted as the broker of supplying *meriah* children to the *Kandha* community. This is due to the fact that the *Kandha* tribals never use

their progeny as *meriah*. The *Kandhas* believed that the goddess Earth *(-Taru Pennu)* would only accept the *meriahs* if they were bought with a price. They also emphasized that victims from their own community were not procurable. (Bauman 2010: 78)

In this context, Swaro states that:

The agents, mainly *Panas*—a clever and business like people—lived with the *Kandhas* and cheated them in all possible ways, sometimes purchased but more frequently kidnapped the children (from outside plains) whom they sold to the *Kandhas* for human sacrifice. They occasionally (even) sold their own offspring without any hesitation. (Swaro 1990: 131)

Even Boal has described the Kandha–Pana relationship via meriahs:

There are two basic prerequisites for the *Kandhas*: (i) that the *meriah* must have been bought with a full price by the free will of the seller, whether middle men or parents; and (ii) that the sacrifice must be voluntary, that is, with the victim neither bound nor offering the least resistance. (Boal 1984: 53)

So the process of exploiting Kandhas by the Panas started long before the British rule in India. After the British made their debut to the district, they started rescuing meriahs from the houses of the Panas as well as tribal villages and initiated the conversion process with the rescued meriahs. Simultaneously, the Panas faced numerous challenges regarding the supply of meriahs. When it became impossible to supply meriahs to tribal villages, they came closer to Christianity and embraced the Christian religion.

Subsequently, the dynamics of the conversion process started amongst the Panas. Meanwhile, this process contributed to the initiation of hating the Christian Panas by the Kandhas as they discarded their old religion. After becoming Christians, the Panas started exploiting the tribals in the form of grabbing their land with the help of the British administration. This was one of the instrumental reasons of conflict between them. The Kandhas had been seeing the total landscape as their own and they had given some land to the Panas to live and supply meriah as per requirements. This kind of relationship took the shape of what Kanungo called a 'king–subject relationship' (Kanungo 2008: 17) between Kandhas and Panas because the Kandhas, the original inhabitants of Kandhamal, due to their control over land, perceived themselves as *rajas* (kings) and the migrant Panas from the coastal plains as their *prajas* (subjects) (Kanungo 2008: 17).

The process of land grabbing and exploitation of the tribals by the Dalits accentuated even after independence, through different processes. This uneasy relationship became even worse in independent India, when there was a bloody clash between tribals and Dalits during February–June 1994. This conflict occurred due to the need to gain control over and access to political, economic and cultural resources and to fight against indignities. These two competitive social groups found themselves locked in a battle over scarce resources. 'The *Adivasis* saw Dalits' participation and increased power in the larger politics as a potential threat to their "moral economy"' (Mohapatra and Bhattacharyya 1996: 162). The tribals perceived that by producing fake tribal certificates on the basis of knowing the Kui (Kandha tribe's language), the Panas were diminishing the benefits of state resources, and they felt 'relatively deprived' of using the state resources. In other words, this conflict emerged to avail the benefits of different types of affirmative policies meant for the tribal communities.

The conflict between the Kandhas and Panas is reinforced by the increasing socio-economic gap between these communities. Considering the socio-economic problem as the main reason for the recent Kandhamal violence, the Justice Sarat Chandra Mohapatra Commission in its interim report stated that the violence in Kandhamal was the result of concentrated discontentment prevailing among people since long ago. Conversion, re-conversion, land grabbing, lack of maintenance of land records and issuing of fake certificates were mainly responsible for the outbreak of the conflict. The interim report stated that the perception, threat and reality of marginalization and deprivation have engendered a conflict situation in Kandhamal, which has facilitated feelings and expression of mistrust, division and resentment between the Kandhas and the Panas. This has led to the existence of social conflicts because the Kandhas have the feeling that the Panas has deprived them of desired or accrued social benefits, rights and entitlement. The interim report of the Sarat Chandra Mohapatra Commission, which was submitted to the Odisha government on 1 July 2009, has revealed the following:

> Source of the violence is deeply rooted in the land disputes, conversion, re-conversion and the fake certificate issues. Suspicion among the Scheduled Tribe and the Scheduled Caste of Kandhamal is the main cause of the riots with the tribal suspecting that *Panas* (dalits) were capturing their land through fraudulent means. Therefore, the government should immediately take steps to remove differences between the communities. (Mohapatra 2009: 1)

The Kandhas (tribals) always saw the Panas as traitors, exploiters and grabbers of benefits meant for the tribal communities. Though Odisha land legislations prohibit the transfer of tribal land to non-tribals, a large amount of land has been grabbed by the Panas by producing fake tribal certificates using their knowledge of Kui language. Laws have been enacted, repealed, amended and enforced, but all failed miserably to check the transfer of tribal land to non-tribals in Odisha (Ambagudia 2010: 62).

Nevertheless, it must be recorded that the Justice Mohapatra Commission's interim report did not mention anything about the role of the much-debated Hindu groups in the entire process of the recent conflict. Different political parties also maintained a similar position. For instance, speaking at the National Integration Council meeting on 13 October 2008, in New Delhi, Odisha Chief Minister Naveen Patnaik stated that the Kandhamal violence was a manifestation of the 'conflict of interest' between Dalits and *Adivasis*.

A high-level team of the Odisha Biju Janata Dal, which visited the affected area, linked the tensions with the land disputes and credit system, and ruled out any connection with the Hindu forces (*The Hindu* 2011: 2).

But it can be deciphered that Hindu forces have succeeded in exploiting the tense situation and mobilizing the Kandhas (tribals and Hindus) against Panas (Dalits and converted Christians). Therefore, it has been transformed from the resource competition and intra-subaltern conflict of the Kandhas and the Panas into an inter-communal conflict between the Hindus and Christians.

The religious dimension of the argument in the context of the Kandhamal conflict cannot be totally overlooked, as Laxmanananda Saraswati stated:

> You are just burning tires. How many Isai houses and Churches have you burnt? Without *kranti* (revolution) there will be no *shanti* (peace). Narendra Modi has done *kranti* in Gujarat, that's the reason why *shanti*'s there. (Prasad 2008: 23)

On 6 September 2008, Apurvananda Maharaj at the Vishwa Hindu Parishad's (VHP) *Shradhanjali Sabha* (condolence meeting) announced that 'Attack on Swamiji is the same as attacking Hindu religion. All saints and sadhus need to counter attack unitedly otherwise India will be converted into a Christian nation' (Prasad 2008: 23). Again, the supporters of the VHP at the *Shradhanjali Sabha* of Laxmanananda Saraswati in Chakapada, Phulbani, promised to wipe out Christians from Kandhamal district. In short, Hindu forces are working as what Brass terms as 'conversion specialists' (Brass 2003: 32; Froerer 2006: 54). The Hindu forces just exploit these complex socio-economic intra-subaltern tensions at the local level into the simpler, broader and more potent language of inter-communal conflict (Froerer 2006: 54).

Tribal–Dalit Conflict in the Narayanpatna Block of Koraput District

Land, the most viable resource for sustaining tribal life, is under threat because of continuous land alienation and encroachment in tribal areas of Koraput district (Odisha) in general and Narayanpatna in particular. Amongst the encroachers who alienated tribal land, the non-tribes and migrants Dalits from coastal areas of Odisha and Andhra Pradesh are prevalent with other Hindu upper castes and landlords. The land laws preventing the sale of tribal land to non-tribals remain in paper. Through the Narayanpatna conflict (land movement), the tribals have been able to take their land back from the clutches of 'hooch traders' (especially the Dalits, locally called 'Sundhis' or local liquor vendors), landlords, what was rightfully theirs. Therefore, the Narayanpatna land movement (2009–2014) between the tribals and non-tribals (especially Dalits) has generated an intra-subaltern conflict which is very similar to the above two case studies of Bisipara and Kandhamal. Before analysing the intra-subaltern conflict between tribals and Dalits in Narayanpatna of Koraput district, it is very important to have a look at the social–demographic picture of Narayanpatna.

Narayanpatna: A Brief Profile

Narayanpatna block in the Koraput district of Odisha is located in the valley between the hills of Potangi and Laxmipur blocks on two sides, the plains of Andhra Pradesh on the third side and the vast tracts of river-irrigated agricultural lands of Rayagada district on the fourth side. A region inhabited by tribal populations consisting of Kuis (in majority), Praja and Jatapu, it remained isolated until recent times. Similarly, the population of Narayanpatna block in the Koraput district stood at 43,575 with 9,560 families. Among them the below poverty line families were 8,517 (89.46 per cent), with 82 per cent *Adivasis* (81.58) and 7 per cent (7.13 per cent) of Dalits (Census 2011: 49).

Narayanpatna is inhabited by 16 tribal communities, including Kui, Praja, Jarka, Matia, Doria and others, of whom the Kandhas are numerically predominant (www.koraput.gov.in). The Kandhas called themselves as Kui because they speak the Kui language and the name Kandha was given to them by outsiders. The tribal/*adivasis,* who constitute more than 80 per cent people of Narayanpatna block, are mixed with Dalit communities such as Mali, Dombo, Forga, Paiko and Rilli (Patnaik, Routroy and Sharanya 2009: 2). Dominant castes such as Sundis and Brahmins are numerically small but are powerful and influential (Patnaik, Routroy and Sharanya 2009: 2).

Though the incursion of non-tribes has a long history, going back to the establishment of the *Narayanpatna Raj* centuries back, the Sundhis have entered the district after they were driven away from Coastal Andhra during the Srikakulam armed struggle in the 1960s. The Sundhis as well as a section of Dalits from the Dombo and Relli castes, too, have made money by exploiting the tribals and selling them liquor; they have joined hand with the migrants from Andhra Pradesh and unitedly exploit the tribals of Narayanpatna. The non-tribals are around 5,000 in number, and the ruling elite of Narayanpatna belong to this group. It was also clear that the identities such as that of landlord, liquor tender, moneylender and politician are not separate or mutually exclusive, but usually coexist in the member of the dominant classes of the region with a common identity in the eyes of tribals as 'exploiters'.

The Land Grab Movement and the Intra-subaltern Conflict in Narayanpatna

Since 1998, the poor and landless peasants of Narayanpatna, Bandhugaon, Simliguda and so on have organized themselves under the banner of Chasi Mulia Adivasi Sangha (CMAS) and fought back their tormentors the Sundhi–Sahukar–Sarkar (liquor vendors–land-lords–government) nexus (Patnaik 2009: 2). The Sundhis are mostly from the Dalit community, who are liquor vendors and exploit the tribals through liquor as bait. By intoxicating the tribals through liquor, the Sundhis (the Dalit liquor vendors) acquire their land. So, in the Narayanpatna area, the Dalits are the immediate enemy of the tribals, in comparison to the distant enemies such as contractors, politicians and the upper castes.

Even though the CMAS was working in the region since 1998, it was only in 2009 when its land and anti-liquor movement took a decisive turn. It reached a flashpoint in January 2009 when the tribals of Narayanpatna not only drove away the liquor traders (mostly Dalits) from their villages, but mobilized themselves in thousands to pursue them to their stronghold (Patnaik 2009: 2). Four thousand people went to Narayanpatna and destroyed liquor factories and wine shops, including shops selling foreign liquor.[1]

By late 2010, only two liquor shops were running in the entire region and that too in the block headquarters of Narayanpatna and

---

[1] Data collected in an interview with Mage Meleka of Podapadar village in Narayanpatna block during the fieldwork in the said block in the Koraput district of Odisha on 23 December 2015.

Bandhugaon, where state's armed forces are stationed.[2] In villages like Bhaliaput, *Mahua* trees, from which cheap liquor was produced, were destroyed under a political programme of CMAS and the Biplabi Adivasi Mahila Sangha, and not a single *Mahua* tree remained in the villages of Narayanpatna.[3] The prohibition for the sale and consumption of liquor was almost total by 2009.[4] The mass upsurge led to the fleeing of landlords and liquor traders from the region, leading to the collapse of this parasitic trade.

The success of the anti–liquor movement encouraged masses to intensify the land struggle. The CMAS led the reclamation of agricultural land from the Sundhis (Dalits), landlords and *sahukars* (moneylenders), which were tricked out from the tribals.[5] Within months, more than 3,000 acres of such land were recaptured and distributed among the landless tribals of the villages.[6] As a reaction to the growing tide of mass struggle, a '*Shanti* (peace) Committee' was formed by the landlords and liquor traders with the active support of the state administration on 4 May 2009 to counter the movement (Pradhan 2009: 2). After the successful culmination of the anti–liquor struggle and the intensification of the land struggle by 2009, the state repression on the people and their movement was also scaled up (Pradhan 2009: 2).

Although there are a large number of tribes (Kandhas) in the Narayanpatna area under Koraput district, there also live the non-tribes such as Brahmin, Kumuti, Sundhi, Paidi, Dombo and Relli. The people belonging to higher castes such as Brahmin and Kumuti and Dalit-Sundhi living in the area are privileged people, who have established economic and political sway over tribals. They are known mainly as contractors and landlords and known for exploiting and suppressing the tribes.

---

[2] Ibid.

[3] Ibid.

[4] Data collected in an interview with Pustono Hirleka of Jaliaguda village of Balipeta *Gram Panchayat* in Narayanpatna block during the fieldwork in the said block in the Koraput district of Odisha on 24 December 2015.

[5] Ibid.

[6] Ibid.

Sundhi, Paidi, Dombo and Relli castes belong to the Dalit community, who are hooch traders and do small businesses (Malik 2017: 89). Most of them are equally languishing under the supremacy of the high-caste people, where a few Dalits among them are busy in politics by duping the tribes and grabbing their lands. They are deriving maximum benefits out of the government services and welfare schemes. They are developed and involved in anti-tribal activities and liquor business.

The CMAS could not take necessary steps to resolve completely disputes existing between tribes and Dalits in the fight for lands in Narayanpatna. All non-tribes were attacked considering them as anti-tribes and exploiting group who are alienating their land. During such attacks on the non-tribes, the Dalits along with other the exploiting group lost their houses and property. Due to attacks on the villages of Podapadar, Egua Gumandi and Digua Gumandi under Narayanpatna block in 2008, all the families belonging to Paidi and Dombo castes (SCs and Dalits) had to leave their villages for elsewhere and some are living in eight colonies provided by the district administration in Koraput town. Some other Dalit families are living at the roadside without any shelter.[7] For this reason, the dispute between the exploiter and the exploited turned to be the dispute between the Dalits and tribes which turned into an intra-subaltern conflict. The government utilized the dispute prevailing between the tribes and Dalits and hatched a conspiracy to divide people on this line.

The situation has come to such a pass that if somebody is shot dead by the police, he or she will be either a tribal or a Dalit. The Dalits did not understand the gimmicks played by the government, and the moneylenders and did not come forward to resolve the problems through discussions with the tribals. The state's repressive apparatus has forcefully arrested the movement by putting the CMAS members in jail as Maoists and banning CMAS for being a Maoist frontal organization. Regarding the 'divide-and-rule game' played by the state

---

[7] Data collected during the interview with Dinai Bidika of village Podapadr in Narayanpatna block of Koraput district (Odisha) on 30 December 2015.

in Narayanpatna by exploiting Dalit–tribal conflict over land, Suratha Kumar Malik, in his article, has remarked the following:

> The tribal–Dalit divide was intentionally created by the exploiters with the help of the State, in order to be instrumentalized for the purpose of creating a mass base for a counter-revolutionary movement against the tribal land movement. The Narayanpatna movement was posed by the government as tribal–Dalit conflict and a threat to 'common people' and CMAS was posited as a terrorist, militant organization that was threatening to substitute chaos in the place of the existing 'peace'. (Malik 2017: 90)

CONCLUSION

The recent history of Odisha provides several cases showing that conflict is not an isolated phenomenon. Intra-subaltern community conflicts represent a complex picture in Odisha. The gradual alienation of the tribal resources has created the regime of marginalization, deprivation and dispossession, thereby creating insecurity among the tribals. This notion of insecurity led to the initiation of violent attacks by the tribals. The tribals are gradually losing their faith in Maoists because the state has consistently been hunting them and the Maoists failed to fulfil the objectives they had set for the tribals.

The tribals in comparison to the Dalits in the selective study areas were increasingly placed in a greater position of marginalization and exploitation and had constant threats to their existence, social status and value system. This position, which creates a sense of social deprivation and a constant fear of losing their identity, had created an atmosphere of apprehension by the tribal communities. They, at the same time, became more self-conscious and were very much aware of the differences between themselves and others, the distinction between 'us' and 'them'. Such identity and dominant assertions desire to transform the very sense of subalternity towards more fragmented subaltern communities, which leads to the sense of 'dominant community' of the higher castes—now redefined at every micro-level.

In pointing out the intra-subaltern conflict (tribal–Dalit conflict) in Odisha in recent times, the role of the Maoists cannot be neglected.

The Maoists started gaining the tribal support since the mid-1990s. By naming themselves the People's Guerrilla Liberation Army, the Maoists incorporated the tribals and trained people for violent activities. In case of Narayanpatna, the left-wing extremism was sympathetic towards the tribals while they were fighting with the Dalits (Panas) and other exploiters, and they played the same role in case of Kandhamal Dalit–tribal conflict. On the other hand, the Panas (Dalits) have converted themselves to Christianity to get release from the caste stigma and also to get material benefit and English education through the help of the Christian missionaries.

The 'politics of entitlement' and the competition for material well-being through identity aggregation lead to the emergence of intra-subaltern conflicts in Odisha. The fear of deprivation and an uncertain future is not only restricted to the protest of those excluded, it is also an important factor in the quest for greater community control of the means, livelihood, natural resources, that is, land and forest, and of course the conflict to gain hegemony which is anchored to the past and situated in the present.

The intra-subaltern conflicts between the tribals (Kandhas) and Dalits (Panas and other Dalit castes such as Dombo, Rilli in case of Narayanpatna) from the above three case studies have confirmed that 'the large subaltern consciousness' and the 'mega project' have been fragmented with the material reality, resource conflict, religious sentiment and owing to the political game played by the state and the dominant.

The conflicts (tribal–Dalit) amongst Phulbani, Kandhamal and Narayanpatna point to the larger questions of mobilization and struggle for material well-being. The intra-subaltern consciousness has become a daily feature and its scale of assertion has expanded to a great extent, and diverse communities are involved in more and more confrontation among themselves.

So, in case of Odisha, as found from the select studies, intra-subaltern conflicts have both pull and push factors. The material scarcity and resource conflict made the subalterns conscious of their community identities in one way, and in the other way, it is the state, Christian missionaries, Maoists and the Right-wing Hindu forces that play a dubious role to sharpen the conflict. Therefore, the nature of the intra-subaltern conflict manifests with different perspectives and colours, that is, in case of Narayanpatna it is 'tribal–Dalit conflict', it is 'communal riots' between Hindus and Christians in case of Kandhamal, or electoral conflict in case of Phulbani.

The state and upper castes try to escalate the conflict by playing a divide-and-rule game, creating hatred against each other within the subaltern (marginal) communities. Therefore, the ideological apparatus and the repressive apparatus of the state are playing their role to create the intra-subaltern conflict or conflict within the marginal group to arrest the revolutionary forces or to absorb the discontent of 'democracy', which is the greatest and most sophisticated project of the bourgeoisie dominant hegemonic forces to remain in power.

As far as the solution to the intra-subaltern (Dalit–tribal) conflict in contemporary Odisha is concerned, it can be suggested that it needs a long-term approach with strong political will and sensible administration to deal with the tribal issues. The struggle of tribals for justice and livelihood must be respected and protected, so that a greater subaltern consciousness may be built, which will also help to build a successful democracy.

REFERENCES

Ambagudia, J. 2010. 'Tribal Rights, Dispossession and the State in Orissa'. *Economic & Political Weekly* 45 (33): 60–67.

———. 2015. 'On the Edge of Scarcity: Understanding Contemporary Community Conflicts in Odisha, India'. *Conflict Studies Quarterly* 10 (January): 41–55. Available at: http://www.csq.ro/wp-content/uploads/CSQ-10.-Ambagudia.pdf (accessed on 10 July 2018).

Bahl, Vinay. 2005. *What Went Wrong with 'History From Below': Reinstating Human Agency as Human Creativity?* Kolkata: K P Bagchi & Company.

Bailey, F. G. 1963. *Politics and Social Change: Orissa in 1959*. Berkeley and Los Angeles, CA: The University of California Press.

Bardhan, P. 2005. *Scarcity, Conflict and Cooperation: Essays in the Political and Institutional Economics of Development*. New Delhi: Oxford University Press.

Bauman, Chad M. 2010. 'Identity, Conversion and Violence: Dalits, Adivasis and the 2007–08 Riots in Orissa'. In *Margins of Faith: Dalit and Tribal Christianity in India*, edited by Rowena Robinson and Joseph Marianus Kujur. New Delhi: SAGE Publications.

Beverley, John. 1999. *Subalternity and Representation: Arguments in Cultural Theory*, 25–40. Durham, NC: Duke University Press.

Boal, B. M. 1984. *The Konds: Human Sacrifice and Religious Change*. Bhubaneswar: The Modern Book Depot.

Bose, Sugata. 2003. 'Post-Colonial Histories of South Asia: Some Reflections'. *Journal of Contemporary History* 38 (1): 135–148.

Brass, P. R. 2003. *The Production of Hindu Muslim Violence in Contemporary India*. Seattle, WA: University of Washington Press.

Brass, Tom. 1991. 'Moral Economists, Subalterns, New Social Movements and the (Re-)Emergence of a (Post-)Modernized (Middle) Peasant'. *The Journal of Peasant Studies* 18 (2): 173–205.

Chakrabarty, Dipesh. 1995. 'Radical Histories and the Question of Enlightenment Rationalism: Some Recent Critiques of Subaltern Studies'. *Economic & Political Weekly* 30 (14): 751–759.

Chatterjee, Partha. 1993. *The Nation and Its Fragments: Colonial and Postcolonial Histories*. Princeton, NJ: Princeton University Press.

———. 1999. 'In Conversation with Anuradha Dingwaney Needham'. *Interventions* 1 (3): 416.

Dirlik Arif, Bahl Vinay, and Gran Peter, eds. 2000. *Situating and Rethinking Subaltern Studies for Writing Working Class History*. Lanham, MD: Rowman and Littlefield Publishers.

Duyker, Edward. 1987. *Tribal Guerrillas: The Santals of West Bengal and the Naxalite Movement*. New Delhi: Oxford University Press.

Fanon, Frantz. 2001. *The Wretched of the Earth*. (Penguin Classics). London, UK: Penguin

Froerer, P. 2006. 'Emphasizing "Others": The Emergence of Hindu Nationalism in a Central Indian Tribal Community'. *Journal of the Royal Anthropological Institute* 12 (1): 39–59.

———. 2010. *Religious Division and Social Conflict: The Emergence of Hindu Nationalism in Rural India*. New Delhi: Social Science Press.

Guru, Gopal. 1995. 'Dalit Women Talk Differently'. *Economic & Political Weekly* 34 (41–42): 2548–2550.

Hardiman, David. 1986, 15 February. 'Subaltern Studies at Crossroads'. *Economic & Political Weekly* 21 (7): 290.

Homer-Dixon, T. 1991. 'On the Threshold: Environmental Changes as a Cause of Conflict'. *International Security* 16 (2): 104–116.

Kanungo, P. 2003. *RSS's Tryst with Politics: From Hedgewar to Sudarshan*. New Delhi: Manohar Publishers and Distributors.

———. 2008. 'Hindutva's Fury against Christians in Orissa'. *Economic & Political Weekly* 43 (37): 16–19.

————. 2014. 'Shift from Syncretism to Communalism'. *Economic & Political Weekly* 49 (14): 48–55.

Liu, Lydia H. 1993. 'Translingual Practice: The Discourse of Individualism between China and the West'. *Positions: East Asia Cultures Critique* 1 (1): 160–193.

Mahapatra, B. 2008. 'Kandhamal Violence: Social Conflict and Economic Gap Led to Communal Hatred'. Available at: http://hotnhitnews.com/Socio_economic_factors_behind_communal_hatred_in_Kandhamal_by_Basudev_Mahapatra.html (accessed on 6 July 2018).

Malik, Suratha Kumar. 2017. 'Tribal–Dalit Conflict over Land: A Case of Narayanpatna Land Movement in the Koraput District of Odisha'. *Contemporary Voice of Dalit* 9 (2): 184–193.

Mohapatra, B. N., and D. Bhattacharyya. 1996. 'Tribal–Dalit Conflict: Electoral Politics in Phulbani'. *Economic & Political Weekly* 31 (2–3): 160–164.

Mohapatra, Sarat Chandra. 2009. 'Interim Report on Kandhamal Violence'. *Outlook*, 3 July, 1. Available at: https://www.outlookindia.com/newswire/story/conversion-reconversion-led-to-kandhamal-riots/662128 (accessed on 20 July 2018).

Office of the Registrar, General and Census Commissioner. 2011. *Census 2011*. New Delhi: Ministry of Home Affairs, Government of India.

O'Hanlon, Rosalind. 1998. 'Recovering the Subject: *Subaltern Studies* and Histories of Resistance in Colonial South Asia'. *Modern Asian Studies* 22: 189–222.

Patnaik, K. S. 2009. 'Narayanpatna Block in Koraput, Orissa under Chasi Mulia Adivasi Sangh'. *Radical Note and Sanhati*, 25 September, 6–18. Available at: Sanhati.com/Narayanpatna (accessed on 15 July 2018).

Patnaik, K. S., M. Routory, and Sharanya. 2009. 'India: The Narayanpatna Police Firing on Chasi Mulia Adivasi Sangh in Orissa: A Citizen Report'. *South Asia Citizens Wire*, 24 November, 1–4. Available at: http://www.sacw.net/article1244.html (accessed on 6 August 2019).

Pradhan, P. 2009. 'Police Repression of Adivasis in Narayanpatna (Orissa) Bhubaneswar'. *Public Union for Civil Liberties (PUCL)*. Available at: www.pucl.org/topic/dalit-tribal/2009/narayanpatna.html (accessed on 12 July 2016).

Prakash, G. 1994. 'Subaltern Studies as Postcolonial Criticism'. *The American Historical Review* 99 (5): 1481–1486.

Prasad, A. 2008. 'Kandhamal: The March of *Hindutva* in Tribal Orissa'. Available at: http://archives.peoplesdemocracy.in/2008/1012_pd/10122008_11.htm (accessed on 23 November 2014).

Ray, Rajat Kanta. 2007. 'Nationalism, Modernity and Civil Society: The Subalternist Critique and After'. Presidential Address. *Modern India Section, Indian History Congress, Sixty-Seventh Session*. March, 13–14.

Sivaramakrishnan, K. 1995. 'Situating the Subaltern: History and Anthropology in the *Subaltern Studies* Project'. In *Reading Subaltern Studies: Critical History, Contested Meaning, and the Globalization of South Asia*, edited by D. Ludden, 212–255. London: Anthem.

Spivak, Gayatri C. 1988. 'Can the Subaltern Speak?' In *Marxism and the Interpretation of Culture,* edited by Cary Nelson and Lawrence Grossberg. Chicago, IL: University of Illinois Press.

Swaro, D. 1990. *The Christian Missionaries in Orissa: Their Impact on Nineteenth Century Society.* Calcutta: Punthi Pustak.

The Hindu. 2011. 'Barefoot: Remembering Kandhamal' December 17, p. 2.

Varshney, A. 2002. *Ethnic Conflict and Civic Life: Hindus and Muslims in India.* New Delhi: Oxford University Press.

Washbrook, David. 1988. 'Progress and Problems: South Asian Economic and Social History, c.1720–1860'. *Modern Asian Studies* 22 (1): 57–96.

Chapter 3

Interrelations of Gender, Caste, Religion and State
Women's Centrality as Counter to Secular Sectarianism

Tarushikha Sarvesh

INTRODUCTION

This chapter deals with secular sectarianism at two levels—state secularism and society's secularism—taking cognizance of the supply side and demand side of the idea of secularism. The chapter discusses how the state organs seem to be promoting a sectarian outlook among the citizens of a secular state and also how the secular claims of social groups happen to be limited in their view of equality, justice, democracy and inclusiveness. Although this chapter draws social accounts mainly from the khap regions of Muzaffarnagar, it also takes into account other social realities concerned with the interrelation of gender, religion, culture and state.

The idea of a secular state and a secular society is being debated all over again in pursuit of a new definition from the neo-secular standpoint. Secularism as an idea as well as in practice continues to remain problematized. The Indian state and civil society are dragged into such a predicament when their secular beliefs and actions are questioned, situating gender at the centre of the idea of development, citizenship, democracy and justice, as it forms the base of every state and community. The demands by civil society for banning cultural systems such as khaps are indicative of short-sightedness of our civil society members and also of our society at large. Within the framework of demands of accommodation and representation, civil society and cultural/religious groups fail to see the complexities of various social phenomena. They end up being selectively secular in their approach. When the issues of women of minority communities, especially Muslim women, in India are discussed, it is said that voices should be raised from within or at the best they should be allowed to take their own decisions regarding matters of their community. At the same time, for cultural systems such as khaps, decisions regarding their community matters cannot be left to them to be resolved as they are labelled as archaic and feudal in nature. Similarly, from the perspective of Muslim community in India, the uniform civil code (UCC) is conceived as an attack on their religious autonomy, impeding their religious freedom. Also, there are many Hindu subgroups, be it The Hindu Women's Association of Kumbakonam or the All India Varnashram Samaj Sangh, which have been opposing UCC from the early years of independence. Therefore, it is believed that the deferment of the UCC was not only to accommodate Muslim sensibilities but to anticipate a strong opposition from orthodox Hindus (De 2017). Religious and cultural groups seem to have misplaced judgements on the issues of democracy, justice and human rights.

Nivedita Menon explains the previously mentioned situation through the analysis of the UCC. An analysis of the debates surrounding UCC, with respect to personal laws, shows how the struggles between the state and cultural communities actually end up veiling the focal issues as 'The UCC debate remains poised on the polarity of state and community, rendering invisible the axis upon which it turns, that of gender (Menon 1998: 3). It appears to be an apt and lucid argument, but when one takes cognizance of the existing social realities and the power dynamics in terms of state and religious communities, one can gauge the potential of an authoritarian state to oppress a particular community in the name of progressive feminism. This concern is visible among the Muslim community in India after the ban on the supposed practice of triple *talaaq* (divorce). Another concern arises from the accommodationist understanding of secularism in case of multi-religious and multicultural societies. In the process of ontological security and homesteading, cultural groups construct hegemonic traditions referring to those sources of social authority that seek to represent themselves as the true interpreters of a particular tradition (Kendall 2006), and any transgression or change for justice and democracy through state inter-vention is vehemently opposed. An understanding of this may help us know why and how communities or cultural groups try to assert their identity and the ways in which such assertions are accepted or rejected with populist claims in mind, making feminist ontology invisible.

The aim of this chapter is to look into the gender issues in the struggle for moral superiority and identity politics with a sectarian view about justice and secularism. The state's identity is also analysed here through the lens of conflict as well as from the points of 'convergences' with specific cultural identities. This also brings us to the question of state's own variant of sectarianism while claiming a secular identity. The study highlights how the two dominant identities—the identity of the nation-state and the identity of the cultural groups—are rendering invisible the issues of gender in the name of secularism and multicultur-alism. The chapter tries to lay bare the complexity involved in the rela-tion of state institutions with cultural systems like chaps. It seems that in the multiple individual struggles of state as well as various cultural communities, for identity and legitimacy, the real sufferers are always falling off the straight line of vision. These are the groups of people who need to be made visible through a meaningful secular strategy.

The approach to secularism needs to move beyond the two exist-ing formulations—the classical approach and the political–theological approach. The classical secularism aims to liberate the public sphere from domination of the sacred; and the political–theological approach addresses the 'problems of modernity within the context of a disguised dominance of 'the transcendence'—both these approaches suffer from a basic insufficiency in handling human rights issues' (Antic 2017). Neo-secularization calls for defining the 'scope of religious authority' in two ways: 'first, safeguard against violations of human freedom through the abuse of religious authority in various contexts; and second, as called for by feminist scholars in religion, eschew constructions of religion as only a constraint and the antithesis of freedom' (Reilly 2011).

The question arises as to how women are accounted for within the concepts of nation-state and citizenship in a society like India, which is surrounded by the ideas of multiculturalism and cultural pluralism. Another complexity occurs when cultural systems like chaps claim a separate status from the broad Hindu identity, similar to that of religious minority groups. The provision for minorities in Article 29 of the Constitution is also claimed by cultural systems like chaps of Jets, who come under the larger Hindu category and hence do not come within its purview. Jets of western Uttar Pradesh claim that they do not follow the Brahmanical Hindu religious system and that they are followers of Arya Samaj with a 'kabilaayi' (tribal) origin. Groups like Virashaiva, Lingayat or the followers of Brahmo Samaj, Prarthana Samaj and Arya Samaj are counted as Hindus of varying forms. Jats claim to be different in that they do not follow traditional Hindu rituals and customs like *terahavi* (feeding Brahman priests 13 days after someone's death) and dowry practice and are also against praying in temples, though they are often seen doing things against their own preaching. As their traditions are based on a different way of life and practice from that of Brahmanical Hindus, Jats demand that laws related to Hindus must be made more inclusive by including their demands of prohibiting *sagotra* (*sagotra* would mean clan endogamy. Among certain groups clan endogamy is prohibited as is the case among Jats.) marriages as well along with the already existing prohibition on *sapinda* (*sapinda* regulations means restricting the marriageable relationship to 5 degrees on the father' side and 3 degrees on mother's side. It is also mentioned in Hindu Marriage ACt, 1955.) marriages. Khap regions include Hindu Jats, Muslim Jats and Dalits among other inhabitants who follow the region's *gotra*-based (*Gotra* is clan with actual or perceived kinship and descent) social arrangement. Hindu Jats have been asking for long to include *gotra* also within the prohibited degree of relationships, which was rejected long ago in 1945 by the Bombay High Court. The court had declared same-*gotra* marriages legal, based on P. V. Kane's explanation of the vast and contradictory material on *gotras* in India. The khap culture's defiance of the law has been putting politicians and state representatives of high stature in a spot, as they seek the support of these groups during elections. On this, almost all the political parties seem to be united in silence (Sen 2010).

The chapter, in its first half, problematizes the understanding of the modern secular Indian state. It deals with various notions surrounding the Indian state tracing back from scriptural texts to ancient Indian history as well as the indigenous understanding of the state. The second half of the chapter discusses the difficulty in handling gender issues within the complex of gender, culture, religion and state. The chapter also discusses the lived experiences of women struggling between the law of the state and that of the khap—caught up between the claims of individual and collective rights.

INDIAN STATE AND ITS VARIOUS IMAGININGS

Bhudev Mukhopadhyay, a writer and intellectual of 19th-century Bengal, defined nationhood as *jatiyabhav* (national feeling). Bhudev's concept of *jatiyabhav* is a society-centric notion of nationhood, which asserted the sovereignty of culture/society, *swadeshi samaj*, and rejected the Western state-centric (and hence society-destroying) exclusionary notion of nationhood (Bhattacharyya 2010: 49). Another writer of Bengal Renaissance, Rajnarayan Basu, also had reservations about the universal notion of modernity and asserted that the forms of modernity have to vary between different countries depending upon specific circumstances and social practices (Chatterjee 1997: 8). These ideas resonate well with most of the critics of the modern Indian state coming from various cultural and religious backgrounds. The khap inhabitants along with other communities criticize the state laws because of courts' judgments protecting individual rights of women in matters of choice of partner, personal laws and inheritance laws as well as for making laws gender just through the latest judgments by the Supreme Court on sections 377 and 497 of the Indian Penal Code. Almost all the communities are of the view that gender-sensitive laws should be reconsidered as they are being misused, ignoring the fact that practically every law is prone to exploitation. It reveals a sectarian bias in gender terms against the laws promoting gender justice. Similarly, they stand united in sentiment against the laws for the protection of scheduled castes/scheduled tribes formulated to counter caste-based violence. The dominant cultural and religious groups, who otherwise claim a secular position, stand together against the issues calling for gender and caste justice or democracy within cultural and religious groups. This kind of gender and caste sectarianism is equally evident among the hitherto low-caste groups and minority communities. They seem to have *customized secularism* to appropriately use it according to their interests, belief systems, needs and political gains (Sarvesh 2015).

Historically also, it is evident that the early advocates of women's rights addressed the women's question in a similar way, which seems to have percolated down to the modern times and kept the problem intact (Chatterjee 2010). The nationalist elites came up with the solution on two realms: the outer material realm and the inner cultural realm. In the outer material realm, they portrayed that they were equal as citizens, like the British are in Britain; but in the inner realm, they said they were different from the British as being essentially spiritual. It was this inner realm in which women were thought to be remade as 'appropriately modern'—in line with their belief system, and the colonial state needed to be out of this realm (Chatterjee 2010: 17). It is believed that amidst all these complexities, the efforts of the modern nation-state to 'carve out a sphere of the state where only the values of statecraft will rule' (Nandy 1995: 37) put it in direct struggle for identity and legitimacy with various cultural groups within its boundaries and creates the 'hierarchy of citizenship' (Nandy 1995: 38). This struggle for identity and legitimacy between the modern Indian state and cultural groups creates further negligence and marginalization of the underprivileged sections of the society such as women, minority and Dalits. Hence, there is a need for making the idea of secularism more inclusive, in terms of justice, human rights and democracy, to counter both state and religious authoritarianism and also to accurately locate their points of convergence that are in opposition to the idea of deeper justice and democracy up to the level of gender–power relations.

The khap region throws open issues of particular significance on the interrelation of state, laws, citizenship, justice, collective rights and individual rights. In terms of the state and the cultural systems, what seems to taper off is the situation and place of women as dual members simultaneously—as citizens of the state and as members of the particular cultural community. Khap has become a metaphor to depict the harsh gender realities, but by using khap as a metaphor we commit the mistake of supporting the dominant simplistic meta narrative, which erases various other voices and counterclaims. It becomes a struggle for moral superiority—Hindu versus Muslim, urban versus rural, liberal versus orthodox, east versus west, khap versus all—without theorizing the complex and layered realities. It becomes an obstacle to the understanding of real causes of injustices and also eclipses the role of state machineries contributing to such injustices. The oversimplistic discussions about khap limit the larger concerns, which emanate microcosmic realities.

Khap inhabitants criticize the modern Indian state for its disaffiliation from its cultural roots and claim that in the pre-modern state system they enjoyed cultural autonomy. The pre-modern state gives an indication of a status quoist state, which came in favour of the haves or the propertied class 'against the combined attack of have-nots' (Sharma 1996: 56). There is also an indication that the three institutions—property, family and *varna*—put together played a role in the origin of the state (Sharma 1996: 53). The other notion of state in ancient times is similar to that of the Contract Theory spun around the 'need' for a state-like formation. This notion of contract is there in the Agni Purana, one of the sacred writings on Hindu mythology and folklore: '*Agni Purana* believes in the secular origin of kingship, origin and tribute being the basis of social contract. The king receives in return of protection, contributions from the people to support himself and his retinue' (Shastri 1943: 15–16). The rules of governance are mentioned in another sacred work called the Manusmriti (Manu's code of law), which says that the king should govern and provide justice to his people after acquainting himself with their customs and beliefs (Buhler 2004: 181–182). Today, when one sees people lobbying for the amendments in the Hindu Marriage Act, 1955, and the Hindu Succession Act, 1956, and its latest amendment in 2005, one can almost trace the construction of this political psychology in which state was expected to play an instrumental part in helping the dominant groups and gender maintain their status quo. The communities, which saw women as properties along with their wealth and land, find it difficult to see the state laws formulate the idea of human rights for the marginalized genders. The longue durée of patriarchy would suggest that while the erstwhile state systems helped them control their women and property, the modern state deprives them of this control over women. This creates a sense of alienation in the minds of patriarchal groups like khaps, which feel that the state is unfairly imposing its will on them.

In a representative democracy like India, the problems surrounding gender get further complicated in situations when state has to interface with the cultural organizations—as in the case of khaps. The difficulties faced by the state in addressing gender issues call for an analysis of the nature, form and historical aspects of the Indian state. The gender issues that need to be addressed are often camouflaged by the simplistic debates surrounding the idea of the modern Indian state. People have created these binaries of East and West, and anything Western connotes negativity in popular understanding. There is a view that the Indian state is a Europeanized state, which is the root cause of all problems occurring within its boundaries. It is believed that this kind of a modern state is alienated and imposed.

The complexity of the Indian state makes one halt and focus on the issues surrounding the making of the identity of the Indian state and the difference between the sense of nation in people's minds and on paper. The Constitution of India has guidelines on well-nigh all possible relevant issues for a healthy democratic society. At least it appears so on paper. Although the Indian Constitution and state machineries look very inclusive and sensitive towards various kinds of cultural groups within their boundaries, one needs to rethink and analyse how far this idea of inclusiveness has reached.

Before moving on to the analysis of the current situation and the handling of women's issues by the Indian state in its interface with the communities, it is imperative to try and grasp the various accounts of the ideas of state that exist and have existed. The perception of Indian state as colonial and Europeanized is guided by a simplistic understanding of influences of different time periods on the modern Indian state, ignoring the actual sectarian functioning of the state machineries at the ground level. It gives a glimpse of the fears and concerns of groups bearing the intersections of patriarchy, culture, religion, state and citizen through different time periods. The idea of a pre-modern and post-modern state (Kaviraj 2010) tells us about the divided vision for the state and the discontents with it. It also indicates the desire for an 'appropriately secular' state in accordance with their sectarian interests whose picture, though muzzy, is sketched through the criticisms of the modern state.

It is said that many third-world states are states only in name because of the segmentary nature of the society (Nelson 2006: 9). Nelson also mentions that the 'state sovereignty cannot exist where real authority exists with subordinate social units' (2006: 9). It appears that the modern structure of the state seems to be struggling for legitimacy from certain groups, which draw their authority and loyalty independently of the state (Nelson 2006: 9). It creates a struggle between the two dominant political units—the modern secular state and the cultural systems like khaps. The weaker voices, which could have been heard, seem to be further relegated to the margins in this struggle for legitimacy and supremacy even within the modern state structure with secular credentials.

Based on the political structure of khaps, the Jats of the region claim khaps to be one of the oldest forms of governance with traces of democracy. The procedure of calling a meeting for decision-making on any issue goes from one level to another in the hierarchy of Sarv Jatiya Khap, Sarv Khap, Khap, Thamba, Thok and Khandan. When the dispute within the thamba panchayat remains undecided, then khap panchayat is convened and so on to decide the matter; khap panchayat's decisions are made available to the minister of the khap, who makes an entry in the khap register.

The khap inhabitants, including the members of castes and communities apart from Jats, feel that the modern police and legal system is not well equipped to deal with such societies and disputes, as the modern legal system is too aloof and disconnected from the local cultural issues. On this basis, the Jats want the state to designate their panchayats as *lok adalats* (lok adalats are an alternative and non-adversarial system of dispute resolution held by state authorities and law courts). This will give a just conclusion to their process of legitimation, which seems to have been slightly eroded in the wake of the so-called modern state system and representative democracy. The opportunities provided by representative democracy also gave such groups a chance to be part of the state political system. The entry into the state political system gave them a chance to make their voice heard in the state assemblies and parliament. They could voice their concerns and demand the amendments in various Acts, which seem to be going against their caste and patriarchal interests. For example, a few representatives in Haryana demanded the amendment in the Hindu Marriage Act of 1955, the Hindu Succession Act of 1956 and the Hindu Succession (Amendment) Act, 2005. On similar lines, the khaps of western Uttar Pradesh have been lobbying for the amendments and inclusions in such Acts. They claim that the laws were not made according to the customs of the community and that justice could be meted out only when the communities' customs and ethics are to be taken into consideration. Here again, we see the resemblance with the Manusmriti, which mentioned that the laws should not be made in opposition to the customs of the community, clan or family (Buhler 2004: 182). Khaps need to be seen as a part of the phenomenon of how certain groups are resisting the modern state.

PROBLEMATIZING THE INDIAN STATE

The Indian state, it seems, is caught between the devil and the deep sea. Neither can such claims by cultural groups and territorial caste organizations be fully accommodated, nor can they be completely suppressed. It is explained by scholars that the modern Indian state, which is such a large democracy, could survive till now because it left the complexities and issues of accommodation aside without taking any strong action. This is reflected when Sudipta Kaviraj says, 'Indian nationalist state produced a new powerful imagination for itself which reconnected it to popular aspirations' (2010: 70). It could be said that the modern Indian state succeeded in sustaining itself because it always had safety valves intact to give vent to the protests. It is said that after the 1970s, the local representation in politics increased and the local vote-bank politics got a fillip (Kaviraj 2010: 72–73), and this in turn seems to have facilitated the convergence of the interests of the modern Indian state and the local aspirations.

When we look into the histories of certain areas and groups, we realize that certain groups of people or certain regions could never be completely subdued, whatever be the ruling body or type of state system. With respect to the Jat community of western Uttar Pradesh in north India, this stands true. These territorial communities could keep their separate identities of local governing unit through different time periods. During the Mughal king Akbar's rule, they negotiated their separate space and identity and took the rights to govern their area as per their terms and conditions, and also kept expanding their area as colonizers (Pradhan 1996: 95). During the British rule also, they could not be completely subdued (Stokes 1978: 15). Although the khap panchayats' functioning was restricted during the colonial period, they were not completely eliminated. After the independence, they again started convening their largest congregation of Sarv khap panchayats (meetings of all the clan councils. 'Sarv' means 'all' in Hindi), to discuss certain reforms and their way forward.

The coming of democracy and modern nation was coupled with attempts towards the rebuilding of the identity of clan councils like khap. Khaps started gaining visibility especially in the late 1980s and the 1990s, when Mahendra Singh Tikait, a *chaudhary* (headman) of a Jat clan, almost developed the khap areas into a 'village republic' in the late 1980s (Jeffrey and Lerche 2001: 102). 'The historical juridical autonomy of the Jats—and their independent police force—was revived in a Jat Kisan Raj (farmers' rule)' (Jeffrey and Lerche 2001: 102). The Jats also tried to control the activities of low-caste sections of the village (p.103).

The above-mentioned development created a situation where the modern state and the cultural organizations were locked in a battle for legitimacy and control. In this battle for control, both the parties—that is, the modern state and the dominant cultural groups—appear to be at loggerheads, but they in fact avoid crossing swords with each other. One of the views of the state of ancient times, whether in the Indian context or in Greek philosophy, has been that state is not something in itself but a unity of all its organs and machineries (Sharma 1996: 47). The state starts fumbling if all its organs do not work in tandem. If the judiciary comes up with a particular judgement but it does not get implemented at the ground level by different state machineries, the situation goes back to the status quo ante. This is what often happens in many parts of India.

In khap areas, what happens is that the state machinery—that is, the bureaucracy and the district court—seem to be playing out the regional and cultural role at times; on some occasions, though, they try to put the burden back on the khap to solve their own case by taunting them to be losing their characteristic and trademark strength. Sometimes, the administrators themselves are seen to be humiliating the khap members on the grounds that they are weak when they try to take refuge in the state police and administration. A few examples, which would represent this argument well, are as follows.

In May 2012, the Deputy Inspector General of Police (DIG) of Saharanpur, a district in western Uttar Pradesh, uttered incendiary remarks regarding the elopement of young couples. A person named Shaukeen, along with a few people from village Kaserwa Khurd (it comes under Adarsh police station), had come to appeal for the recovery of his daughter who had allegedly eloped. The DIG told him that a man should commit suicide if his daughter elopes or brings bad name to the family. It is believed that he was also heard saying that if his sister did something of this sort, he would either kill her or commit suicide himself. These remarks by the DIG were heavily criticized by the media, but such sentiments were revealed in most of the police handlings of such cases. In this whole situation, one can see that the act of elopement is projected as abduction. Elopement involves a certain amount of free will or choice of the boy as well as the girl, which is not appreciated by families and communities, especially when it comes to the choice of a girl. This is the reason why the case is pursued mostly on the lines of abduction, and the state machinery is used for 'recovering' the girl. Even when the police are aware of the fact that the girl eloped by choice, they make a case against the girl's partner, as is evident from many such incidents within and beyond khap regions as the sentiments against human rights in gender terms are shared by well-nigh every community. This idea can be traced back from the ancient texts that show that the state was supposed to prevent the forceful abduction of women (Sharma 1996: 58), and this is supposed to extend to elopements. This narrative also faces a threat of being co-opted or manoeuvred by authoritarian cultural and religious groups.

Other similar examples could be drawn from among the lawyers of the khap regions. The lawyers belonging to Jat community in these regions often share the same sentiments as that of the other people. Surrounded by the lawyers in the chambers of Muzaffarnagar district court, I, during my fieldwork, heard arguments such as: 'The present day legal practitioners and lawmakers are Indians but they should be called "Black British"'. These lawyers believe that the borrowed legal system and the conditions of the United Nations' Charter are not helpful in this country. They say that these laws further promote crimes and disturbances in the society. They believe that the social atmosphere and culture should be examined and the laws should be framed in accordance with the status quo. The lawyers also believed that crime has increased because of the annihilation of social systems and declining respect for elders.

The above-mentioned sentiment comes from the notion that the state has to take into account the subjectivity of the case, that is, the cultural context. It appears that this kind of sentiment comes from the notion, as discussed before, that dates back to the ancient Indian concept of the state and duties of a state as mentioned in the Hindu scripture Manusmriti (Buhler 2004: 181–182). In those times, the king was instructed to give judgments after enquiring into the laws of various castes, guilds, families and so on and also instructed to make laws that do not oppose the customs of countries, families and castes. In the Agni Purana, it is mentioned that since the 'pleasure of the public' is one of the main criteria of good government, the king is advised to rule neither with too much tightness nor with too much clemency (Shastri 1943: 19). When one sees through the idea of the ancient state, one gets a sense that 'pleasure of the public' and 'need of the state' actually mean the need to maintain the state for the propertied and wealthy class as a tool against the have-nots, in order to punish the have-nots for indulging in robbery or stealing of property and wives whenever they step out of line.

The above-mentioned point regarding the nature of the ancient Indian state needs to be pondered upon because in the present times also the state seems to be working for the 'pleasure' of that section of the society which is in a better position economically and socially. The state seems unwilling to take the risk of upsetting the dominant public or groups. In this process of convergence in the interests of state organs and dominant groups, the voices and welfare of the public on the margins get ignored. The groups on the margins typically happen to belong to the female gender, religious minority groups and the groups lowest in the order of caste system in India, namely, the Dalits. It is very much evident in the khap areas as well (Chowdhry 2011). The two dominant parties—one in the form of the state itself and another in the form of the dominant clans—seem to be struggling for control and authority with each other, but actually one can see the collusion between them against the reforms, which could bring benefits to others at the margins. They negotiate with each other to mutually derive the political and economic benefits, pushing aside the rights and interests of the weaker sections.

In the ancient times, the crimes committed were considered as crimes against individuals and state came in to punish the guilty; but in the modern legal system, the crimes committed are crimes against the state, as the state is not supposed to simply maintain the status quo. As stated earlier, any crime committed in the modern legal system is the crime against the state, which means that automatically the state becomes party with the affected people; but when crimes are committed against the weaker sections or against the people considered insignificant by the administration and political class, the state seems to be detaching itself instead of fighting on their behalf. This is very much evident in khap areas, where cases of crime and violations are rampant: examples are killing of women or young couple in the name of honour, or usurping the property of the Dalit, or the killing of a Dalit boy if he marries a Jat girl. The traditional settlement mechanisms are still assisting the dominant sections. This could be understood through the following case. A Dalit boy named Tinku of Kairana village had eloped with a Jat girl from the same village. Usually in such cases the matter is taken to the panchayat and the chaudharies of both the communities are called to decide upon the case. In this case, it was not followed. The girl's family did not approach the panchayat. They preferred filing a complaint against Tinku and his family, charging Tinku with abduction.

From the above example, what comes across is that a more neutral mechanism for complaining was used by the dominant party. The space of state and its organs is supposed to be more neutral, that is, supposedly free from the cultural or communitarian biases. Yunus Mohammad of the same village told me, *'Unhe ladki ko wapas laane se zyada us ladke ko barbad karna tha. Case chadhaana tha uspar jisse sarkari naukari na mil sake. Ye sab kuch to panchayat mein nahi ho pata.'* (The girl's family preferred to go to the police station instead of calling a panchayat because their intention was to ruin the boy's future by making a police case against him, which would spoil his prospects of getting a government job.) The open access to government jobs for the Dalit communities has been a constant concern of the dominant communities of the region (Chowdhry 2011).

The state machinery seems to be reluctant in giving protection to the affected parties. Here again, we witness the withdrawal of the state. The aims of the modern state and the legal system are envisioned as an assurance of safety and protection of the individual rights of the citizens and also as the uplifter of the downtrodden.

LOCATING THE DISADVANTAGES OF SECTARIAN APPROACH THROUGH LIVED REALITY OF WOMEN'S RIGHTS

Pierre-Joseph Proudhon's statement 'Property and society are completely irreconcilable with one another' comes alive in present times: on the one hand, laws are available for the protection of women's rights; on the other hand, those very laws bear the allegation of being the motivation behind the trivialization and breakdown of social bonds, especially related to women. This section juxtaposes the laws available for the protection of women's rights with the lived reality of the women's lives in contemporary Indian society. The failure in the successful implementation of those laws is not seen as the failure of the state in providing justice and human rights to women as citizens.

This is especially true of khap areas, where property is of paramount concern: The entire social set-up is crafted and structured around property ownership. Honour and identity are also measured with the yardstick of property ownership. Prakashchand of Bhonra Kalan village explains it well when he says, 'Dharti mata aur izzat sabse badi cheez hai' (land and honour are the most important things). Prakashchand is a 38-year-old unmarried man. This village has the highest number of unmarried men. It is believed that those men could not get married because of less property and lack of income sources. According to Vinod, a resident of Bhajju village, *'Jo log zamin bech dete hain unki koi izzat nahi karta. Zameen ko bech dena matlab ma ko bechna hai'* (those who sell off their lands have no honour: to sell your land is like selling your mother).

In the light of the previously mentioned points, this section analyses the reality of women's rights and their protection by juxtaposing the laws available for the protection of women's rights with the reality of the women's lives in contemporary Indian society.

The data sources for this section are field narratives, reviews of documents and interviews carried out among the members of the Jat community of western Uttar Pradesh. Acts, rules, legal documents and cases are also reviewed. Historical accounts, texts and scriptures and community-based proverbs and narratives have also been used in order to understand the political psychology of the khap set-up and the demands. Interviews with lawyers of the Allahabad High Court, Muzaffarnagar District Court in western Uttar Pradesh and Kanpur District Court in eastern Uttar Pradesh were carried out to understand the 'secular' legal realities. In-depth interviews and observations among the men and women of western Uttar Pradesh depicted a complex picture of the dialogues between the cultural laws and the present Indian legal system. Reports on women's rights and legal issues compiled by various groups and organizations have been consulted as well.

In the case of women's rights and their claims to resources, the first thing that has to be thought over is the conceptualization of the idea of women as humans first in their identification as members of both state and religious/cultural groups and need to be brought within the framework of a secular approach. When the idea of women as citizens and beneficiaries of human rights is understood thoroughly, the shortfalls in the achieving of such status for women become instantly visible on the part of both the state and the cultural communities. The 'invisible barriers' (Uyl 1995) that happen to be the subtle and out of sight hindrances in the attainment of full women's rights and protection can be made visible only by locating 'softer powers' that shape the lives of women, their sexuality and social and political image, as well as self-image (Uyl 1995). Location of such invisible barriers help in getting a clearer picture of why and how the rights of women get denied, even if we accept that the intentions of lawmakers have been largely good and in the best interest of the female population. It becomes necessary to figure out why gender-sensitive laws often fail in giving protection to women or in helping them gain control over resources.

The needs and conditions that hinder the attainment of full rights for women have to be recognized in their specific social realities. The laws are made as one solution for all, which is in some ways unavoidable, but what can be worked out is the implantation of those laws and also making or changing the interrelated laws for making the benefits a reality. The social realities of different women differ significantly: It would be imprudent to ignore the fact that women from different regions, castes and cultures have different paths to access the laws that are made for providing justice to them (Cross and Hornby 2002).

Citizenship is an abstract concept, which is why it is suggested that immense care must be taken to explain what it means in practice and what can be done effectively in the context of development interventions (Sever 2004). It is argued that citizenship should be understood as 'multi-tiered' and formed through many different positions according to gender, ethnicity and urban/rural location rather than seeing citizenship from the angle of 'uniformity' (Yuval-Davis 1997). The ways in which the division between the family/private and the political/public operate to exclude certain groups, particularly women, from citizenship have to be consciously and perceptively looked into (Yuval-Davis 1997). Most of the time it is seen that community, and not individual agency or voice, is essential to the sense of 'self' to women, and that is why even when women are given the role of decision-maker in the family, they happen to take decisions based on collective needs rather than individual interests (Bulbeck 1998).

This sense of 'self', where a woman thinks only for the good of her father and brothers, is a major obstacle in Indian society in claiming the property rights she is entitled to. The change in the idea of the 'self' of womenfolk, where it is seen as something to be sacrificed for the betterment of the family, can, in one way, be brought about through strong implementation of law and exemplary action taken in case of any failure to abide by the law. Work at another level, involving women from all social backgrounds, is needed where women can be aware of their 'self', apart from their religious and cultural identities, to make their cultures and religions less authoritarian, more democratic and infused with the values of human rights (Othman 2006).

There are several laws in India that stand helpless and mute in the face of such social realities where women do not claim their rights, as it would render them 'selfish, uncaring and individualistic in the eyes of the society' (Rao 2008: 4). The Hindu Succession (Amendment) Act, 2005, happens to be the most glaring case in point. The amendment to the Act revised the rules on coparcenary property and gave daughters of the deceased equal rights with the sons. This Act gives an impression of a revolutionary change, but the ground realities tell a very different story. The narratives and voice of women as well as men from Muzaffarnagar district bring out the grim reality of the use of the amendment to the inheritance law. There have been protests and demands against the changes brought about in the inheritance law in favour of women. The Hindu Succession (Amendment) Act, 2005, for example, is being alleged to be the potential cause of degeneration of the family value system. Chaudharies in khap areas of western Uttar Pradesh and other elderly men lament that such low moral values are being impressed on their social system by the legal system.

Om Prakash, 69, of Mundavar village at the residence of Baliyan khap's chaudhary in Sisauli, is of the view that wherever new kinds of laws have been introduced, the social fabric of societies has got destroyed. He says, *Jit bhi jageh naye naye niyam kanoon a rae se, samaj sab barbad hoge se.'* Another elderly man, Iqbal Singh, 70, of the village expresses, *'Izzat aur vajood ka aankalan parivar se hota hai aur agar ye sab kanoon ladki ko parivaar todne ko uksayenge to ladki ka hi nuksan hoga.'* (Honour and existence are measured through the status of the family, and if these laws motivate girls to break down families then it will be detrimental for the girls themselves.) Devendar Singh, the husband of Phugana village's 'Pradhan', whose village falls under Gathawala khap of Malik *gotra*, is known by the most popular designation of *Pradhan Pati* (Pradhan's husband who does all the work). He says, *'Ladkiyon ka sara mamla agar court hum par chhor de to sab kuch control mein rahega.'* (If the court leaves all the matter related to girls to us, everything will be under control.)

Young women themselves say that after they get married, the husband's family will meet their needs and therefore it is better to leave the parental land for their brothers' use. The idea of the subsumed self is quite evident and not much is being done to reform this understanding either by state or by the cultural communities. A 30-year-old man from Narottampur village (belonging to Baliyan khap) said that his sisters were not ready to take their share in property and agricultural land even when they were offered by the parents, as they did not feel the need of it and suggested that it would be better for the brothers if the land remained undivided.

The reality of the inheritance law is that girls end up getting nothing from either their husband's side or their parents' side even when provisions are available. The obstacles in property claims by women are, first, due to the social stigma involved in claiming their rights, and, second, due to the fact that equal share in father's property applies only if he dies intestate—that is, without making a will. 'Given the bias and preference for sons and notions of lineage, discrimination against daughters in inheritance through will is bound to remain' (Shukla 2005). The Steering Committee of the Planning Commission on Women's Agency and Child's Rights for the Twelfth Five Year Plan had also raised concerns regarding women's property claims through its Sub-group on Economic Empowerment of Women with focus on Land Rights, Property Rights and Inheritance Laws. It pointed out that ownership of land by women happens to be very low, that their right to inherit property exists only on paper and this right gets subverted in various manners (Planning Commission, Government of India 2011). This sort of circumvention of law keeps it away from being effective. It happens to mark merely a nominal existence by being there and yet not prompting any substantial change, owing to some major loopholes like the 'right to will' provision, which still exists unrestricted in the inheritance law even in its amended form.

The other reasons that the lawyers give as to why women are not able to claim their property rights, are that women are hardly able to access the laws and the legal system either due to lack of awareness or due to poverty or due to the complicated and inaccessible legal system. Narratives from certain other countries in Asia as well as South Africa point out the similar problem of accessibility of laws and programmes to the poor women and rural women (Cross and Hornby 2002; Sever 2004). A senior advocate of the Allahabad High Court gave a solution to the problem involved in the implementation of the amended inheritance law. He said with conviction that this law will work only when a rule is introduced with a provision that in cases where property is not given to the daughters (or in case the daughters do not claim their share of property), the state government takes over the property and uses it for women's welfare dedicatedly. He says with such rules people would be left with no choice but to give the girls their due share in the property. There is a danger of overemphasized state authoritarianism in this suggestion. Another senior advocate stated that this rule can also be easily bypassed. The girl's family would give the property in her name and then ask her to show on paper that she sold the property to a third party and this way the family can get it back from her through the third party. It was suggested that in such cases where the selling of property is taking place, the woman should get the market value or at least the circle rate fixed by the government and the money should appear in the girl's bank account. The lawyers argued that once women start getting a taste of financial power, it would not be very easy to take back the money or property from them. The originators of these arguments underestimate the force of authoritarian religious and cultural systems. To reckon with such forces and complex realities, the definition of secularism needs to be reworked in gender terms in a way that it neither lets the state become all-powerful and tyrannical nor lets the religious groups use their authority to curb women's and other genders' human rights.

Zillah R. Eisenstein has talked about the aforementioned nature of law when she argues that, 'Because law is engendered, that is, structured through the multiple oppositional layerings embedded in the dualism of man/woman, it is not able to move beyond the male referent as the standard for sex equality' (Eisenstein 1988: 42). She further says that the law names reality and at the same time it mystifies reality (Eisenstein 1988: 22). This argument by Eisenstein stands true in the case of banning of khaps in the wake of 'honour' crimes. The Law Commission was asked to look into the matter of honour killings and prepare a report. Law Commission's Report No. 242 was submitted to the law ministry in August 2012. The report was titled 'Prevention of Interference with the Freedom of Matrimonial Alliances (in the name of Honour and Tradition): A Suggested Legal Framework.' The report mentions that:

> The law proposed by the Commission under the title of Prohibition of Interference with the Freedom of Matrimonial Alliances Bill is intended to curb the social evil of the caste councils/*panchayats* interfering with and endangering the life and liberty of young persons marrying partners belonging to the same *gotra* or a different caste/religion. These offending acts imperiling the liberty of young persons marrying or intending to marry according to their wishes are being perpetrated in certain parts of the country in the name of honour and tradition. It is felt that such honour crimes can be effectively checked by prohibiting the assembly or gathering of such members of *panchayats* for the purpose of condemning the marriage and taking further action of harming or harassing them. (Law Commission of India 2012)

The understanding of crimes of honour as well as the proposed solutions appears to be too simplistic and futile in the effort of controlling such crimes. The banning of khaps appears to be more of a propitiatory gesture offering superficial solutions. Such tactless solutions only contribute to the worsening of women's condition. This fact came to surface loud and clear when Chaudhary Naresh Tikait (headman of Baliyan clan) said that if courts troubled them and misguided the womenfolk, then they would be forced to kill the girls in the womb itself. This also hints at the easy availability of pre-natal sex determination test facilities, despite a ban on it under the Pre-conception and Pre-natal Diagnostic Techniques Act. The driver of a cab service in Muzaffarnagar said that he had worked in a clinic nearby where such tests were conducted. He said that many people had started keeping the portable ultrasound machines, as no registration was required for them. On the analysis of such facts and in the wake of such solutions, Zillah Eisenstein's statement that law names reality and at the same time mystifies it (1988) is validated.

A multi-pronged approach has to be adopted in dealing with such crimes and mental set-up. One way would be to have a robust arrangement for the protection of young men and women in case they report threats to their lives from the community or family—something which is currently very badly handled. A local stringer narrated what he once heard at a police station. The police were trying to persuade a girl who had eloped to go back to her family by telling her, '*Ekkis saal ka pyaar chaar din ke pyaar se jyada bada hota hai*' (two decades of love that the family gave you holds more importance than a small courtship with a man). Another suggestion that was made by the lawyers at the Allahabad High Court in a conversation with me is that the new enactment for the protection against crimes of honour has to be similar to that of Indian Penal Code Section 304B read with Sections 113 and 114 of the Evidence Act, as is provided for dowry death cases. Apart from these provisions, efforts should be made to locate certain people from within the community who either condemn such crimes or have the potential of coming out of such mindset and civil society should try to work along with such insiders and discuss with them rather than imposing views and solutions from above. Research on the khap regions of western Uttar Pradesh shows that many such insiders are available, and working in their limited capacity towards social causes beneficial for women and other marginal communities.

There are various incidents that show how the sense of justice in cultural jurisprudence lacks sensitivity towards the realities of women, and if this kind of distorted *jatiyabhav* permeates, the state machineries, how perilous can it be for gender justice if the state gives in to the 'secular' multiculturalist demands. An incident of Shoron village of Muzaffarnagar district was narrated by Kanti, an elderly woman of about 80 years of age, and Chaudhary Rajpal Singh, about 70 years of age, taking pride in their justice delivery mechanism. A case was brought before the panchayat regarding the issue of claims on the pension of a deceased defence person from the village. The guidelines for defence pensioners clearly state in the Joint Notification of Family Pension that the widow in whose favour the pension has been jointly notified should report the death of her husband to the Pension Disbursing Agency and submit the death certificate for the commencement of the payment of family pension, and in cases where the wife is not alive the pensioner may nominate some other family member (Principal Controller of Defence Accounts [Pensions]). This legal provision in favour of the wives of defence personnel happens to be unacceptable to Jat community members of Muzaffarnagar.

When the above-mentioned case was brought before the khap panchayat by the deceased man's parents for justice, the clan council summoned the families, the deceased man's parents, and his widow's parents. The widowed woman, after her husband's death, had started living with her parents. The widowed woman's family did not turn up despite being called several times, as they believed that husband's pension was their daughter's right. Rajpal Singh and Kanti narrate the story further and describe how young men dragged the woman's parents all the way from their house to appear before the panchayat. Chaudhary Rajpal Singh says, *'Ladke gaye aur juttam jutii karte hue laye phir unko'* (Young men went and literally dragged them before the panchayat). The decision was taken to give share in pension to the deceased man's parents, and it was believed that the clan council delivered justice. Many such cases are solved in a similar manner even by elected gram pradhans, which reflect how the cultural mind steers into the state organs, systems and its mechanisms. Certain members of the Jat community believe that the Indian legal system is too alienated in consciousness from the realities and experiences of the culture and community, which makes it incapable of delivering proper justice.

Such simplistic sense of justice fails to take into account the complex realities of women's lives and conditions.

The aforementioned argument about the simplistic understanding of women's realities and rights gets reflected in matters of domestic violence as well. The complex realities and experiences of domestic violence are dealt with perfunctorily at three levels: first, the level of comprehension; second, the level of implementation; and third, the level of interpretations of the law available for the protection of women from domestic violence. The use and understanding of this law in particular brings out the flippant orientation and simplistic understanding of the social and legal agency with regard to women's everyday life experiences. The provisions of the legislation and the scope of their use and interpretations show a wide gap, reflecting a distance between the 'ideal' and the 'real'. The Protection of Women from Domestic Violence Act, 2005 (PWDVA 2005), 'covers those women who are or have been in a relationship with the abuser where both parties have lived together in a shared household and are related by "consanguinity", "marriage", or through a relationship in the nature of marriage or adoption' (Choudhari 2009: 7). In addition, relationships with family members living together as a joint family are also included, and even those women who are sisters, widows, mothers, single women or living with the abuser are entitled to legal protection under the legislation (Choudhari 2009: 7). The law also provides for the appointment of protection officers and registration of non-governmental organizations as service providers for providing assistance to the aggrieved person with respect to her medical examination, obtaining legal aid, safe shelter and other such services (Choudhari 2009: 8).

The report entitled 'Staying Alive: Second Monitoring and Evaluation Report 2008' on the Protection of Women from Domestic Violence Act, 2005, highlights and reaffirms the obstacles due to the simplistic understanding of justice in case of women (Lawyers Collective: Women's Rights Initiative 2008). The findings of the report on Protection of Women from Domestic Violence Act, 2005, as well as the lawyers' experiences depict the obstacles and gap in the Act's on paper in practice use and implementation. The report shows that there have been petitions filed in various courts challenging the constitutionality of the PWDV Act, 2005, with grounds that the Act, by providing relief only to women, is in violation of the constitutional right to equality. The report also highlights the issue of the qualification of the protection officers or service providers. The majority of the protection officers have BA, BCom or BSc degrees, and in some places they are appointed on independent contractual basis, whereas in most places the already serving government officials are given the additional duty of protection officers. This is because no educational qualification or specific requirements are mentioned in the Act, which makes it weak in its very foundation. It raises questions about the ability and training of the protection officers in dealing with matters of human rights specifically related to women and legal procedures. Lack of seriousness in the appointment of protection officers makes the law less accessible to the aggrieved. The report also shows that medical professionals hardly acknowledge domestic violence as a public health issue despite being a stakeholder in the PWDV Act along with police and judiciary. The issue of interpretation of 'shared household' is becoming another obstacle. Another issue is that domestic violence goes mostly unrecognized in cases of non-marital situations, that is, when siblings, parents or children are involved (Lawyers Collective: Women's Rights Initiative 2008).

Legal practitioners at the Allahabad High Court, as well as at Muzaffarnagar and Kanpur district courts, said that in most of the cases relating to women's issues, immediate retaliatory counter-cases are filed, which hinder and defer justice. The major obstacle in the attainment of women's rights and full citizenship and human rights is the lack of recognition and conceptualization of women's issues and rights through their lived experiences from the secular standpoint. The process of dispossession and the language of constraints regarding the attainment of justice for women in line with human rights and citizen rights ought to be identified for the better formulation and implementation of laws, policies and programmes. Measures taken for the implementation of laws and for spreading awareness regarding them need to be visualized keeping in mind the least resourceful. A network of civil society, alongside religious/cultural groups, including privileged and underprivileged women from various backgrounds and locations, needs to be built and approached extensively in order to understand the experiences in a detailed way: The detailed experiences would assist in finding the centrality of women and gender–power relations in the interrelation of religion, culture and state (Reilly 2011).

In places where large sections of the society—like women and other marginal groups—suffer voicelessness, one cannot simply call it a result of cultural patterning; rather it also has to do with the conscious or unconscious ignorance on the part of the state from recognizing them as political subjects. The idea of a patriarchal state seems true in a way that the state and its laws appear to remain largely inaccessible to the female population. When the complex and inaccessible state legal system and the law of the cultural systems overlap, it imposes marginality of multiple kinds on the weakest sections of people.

WOMEN SEEN AS CULTURE-BEARERS AND EXTENSION OF MEN

The way a community talks about its female members and the manner in which it portrays the 'other' women of other communities brings out the hidden sense of women being merely the extensions of men and cultural systems. The language used and the stories woven around women's identities reveal the existence of women as mere extensions. This line of thought is not restricted to the representation of oriental and occidental women but is a common practice of almost every community—even the lowest in the hierarchy maintains and promotes such perception regarding 'own' women and 'other' women.

The notion around the control of women's sexuality can also be seen when low-caste groups try to challenge the authority of upper castes in the region by mocking the female members of that community. Women are used as an object to mock another community: For example, Valmikis[1] mock the Jats by using the narrative from Sanskrit

---

[1] Valmiki is a scheduled caste also. It is considered to be an impure caste and is placed very low in the hierarchy of castes. This community claims to be the descendant of saint Valmiki, who had been a hunter and dacoit in his early years after getting lost in the jungle. Hindu epics refer to him as a Brahmin saint.

epics such as Ramayana, saying the Jat men who claim to be warriors and of superior race could not even control their women. They accuse Sita of having one of the two sons with Saint Valmiki while she had taken refuge in his ashram (hermitage). In the Ramayana, Sita is the wife of King Rama, and she is considered the Hindu model of the ideal chaste/holy woman. Here, through mockery of an upper-caste woman, the lower-caste men get the satisfaction of having abused the upper-caste men and their symbols, but in doing so it is the women who in reality end up bearing the brunt from both sides. The mindset of using women for the mockery of other communities or violent attacks on the women of other communities is also used by state representatives for vested interests to widen the already existing divide between communities, as is evident from many cases of communal violence and crime against women as part of hate crimes permitted indirectly by the state at times (Perry 2001). This mindset of using women to settle scores by men is prevalent all over the world and at all times (Green 2012).

In another example, a similar mindset is revealed—this time involving Jats and Muslims of khap area, where Jat men mock the women of the Muslim community. Jats forbid marriage even within the same *gotra* (same lineage clan), whereas Muslims can get married to even close relatives as part of the preferential marriage alliance. This is abhorred by Hindu Jats. Jat men jokingly say that in Muslim communities sisters are not born; only wives are born.[2] This kind of differentiation and stereotyping is done by one group to claim superiority over the other group (Ron Scollon 2012: 273). What remains out of sight, in all these

---

[2] In the khap areas, the Jat community is divided into two groups: one is the Hindu Jat group, the other is the Muslim Jat group. Apart from Muslim Jats, there are also Muslims who are not Jats. Hindu Jats are not too appreciative of the Muslim culture and its systems regarding marriages. Hindu Jats forbid marriage even within the same *gotra*, whereas Muslims do get married to close relatives. This is abhorred by Hindu Jats. Muslim community's presence is substantial in the region and they share the space with Hindu Jats who consider themselves as a superior race. Hindu Jats try to show that Muslims can never compete with them, though they are living in the same region where Hindu Jats' rules are mostly adhered to. Since Muslims' have different rules and whoever has different rules regarding marriages, Hindu Jats have a tendency to mock them. Hindu Jats also mock a form of South Indian preferential marriage allianace between a girl and her mother's brother.

claims of cultural/spiritual superiority and stereotyping, is the issue of the othering of the female gender as it is victimized and mocked from both the sides in their claims of superiority and probity. State machinery also uses such ideas, as is evident from the usage of the terminology of 'love jihad' in India. There are crimes against women in the form of human trafficking, forced prostitution and so on, but associating them with a particular community calls for the questioning of the intention of the state machinery. At times, feminism and the principle of women's equality with men are instrumentalized in justifying punitive actions against minorities and ethnoreligious communities (Reilly 2011). In India, the way in which the issue of triple *talaaq* was dealt with has made the Muslim community wary of the fact that the state might use any excuse to unnecessarily criminalize the Muslim men. The neo-secular approach warns against this phenomenon, but it also warns against the 'inimical impacts of some forms of multicultural politics and of trends towards the fusion of authoritarian or religious forces and state power in the Global South context' (Reilly 2011).

All these mockeries and counter-attacks, on the outside, give the appearance simply of an inter-group conflict. But this oversimplified reading of the issue actually camouflages the fact that it is one particular gender that gets humiliated and mocked from both sides—in attacks and counter-attacks alike: women. The issue of cultural antagonism overshadows the gender issue involved in this. The narratives of cultural antagonism take away the focus from the one-dimensional depiction of the female gender fixed around libidinal impulse and gratification. Women's pivotal position and gender–power relations in the interrela-tion of religion, culture and state cannot be overlooked and must be included in the idea of secularism.

LOCATING SECULAR SECTARIANISM AMONG SUBVERTING MARGINALIZED GROUPS

Norani Othman (2006) emphasizes the need to find a language of pro-test and resistance to religious and state authoritarianism to reclaim the space for substantive democracy and justice, but the lower-caste groups fail to find a language of protest in posing subversion to upper-caste ideas of purity and chastity of women. Dalit communities in the khap regions also portray women of their community as the purest while challenging the upper-caste concept of 'sati'. The word 'sati' has been used in several contexts for women, which gives it multiple meanings, and most of such interpretations of sati could be seen in the analyses of the Puranas such as the Srimad Bhagwat Mahapurana (Vyas 1940). Sati is a dated practice in India, practised primarily among the upper castes: The standard practice was that a married woman burnt herself by sitting on the pyre of her dead husband. Sati is also understood to be a very chaste and virtuous woman who performs all the duties, especially in the capacity of a wife, with immense honesty and loyalty.[3] Contrary to the popular images of sati, Dalits of the region project a completely different definition of sati. They claimed that their women were the real satis, that is, epitome of chastity. They said their satis were categorically unmarried and virgin, which make them the purest. Raju, a young man from village Narottampur Mazara, said, '*Humari sati asli sati hai. Jo shaadi karke pati ke sath mar jaye wo kaise ho gayi sati? Humari sati ganga jal jaisi hoti thi aur samaj ke liye kaam karti thi*' (Our sati is the real sati. The woman who marries and dies with her husband, how can you call her sati? Our sati was like holy Ganges water who worked for the society). Raju belonged to the Karaundhiya *gotra*. He had recently gone to worship the place of his sati, which was located in another village named Dhansani. These women did all the good social deeds and healed people by the power of their purity and goodness. They claim to trace their identity from these holy women and accordingly they have named their *gotras*. I could relate to an attempt by the marginal and lower-caste people to assert themselves against the dominant sections of the society. The marginal groups, through their conceptual construct of a parallel but different sati, have not only tried to resist the socio–cultural notions to be passed on to them through the dominant ideology, but have negotiated a conceptual–cum–social space for themselves. In this

---

[3] Discussion on *Sati* with Swami Parmananda of Shri Krishna Pranami Mandir, Ekadil in Uttar Pradesh, India. *Sati* as per Swami Parmananda's study and understanding is that woman who has the following seven qualities – *Satya* (truthful), *Dharma* (dutiful), *Lajja* (shame and modesty), *Madhur Vani* (soft and sweet voice), *Dhayrya* (patience), *kul ki maryada* (maintains dignity of the clan), *Pati* (husband).

process, they have also subverted part of the established view about sati. The notion of purity attached by the marginal and the dominant groups of this region to their own conceptual 'sati' is also at variance with each other. The subversion by the weaker sections in these societies through their concept of 'sati' is done through this variance. The Dalit sati is the true symbol of chastity, as she is not married—unlike the dominant caste's conception of a married sati.

This kind of subversion poses a complex problem regarding the tools and forms of subversion. In the above context, it is very essential to point out that the marginal groups, through the formation of their own sati (as different from that of the dominant castes), have inadvertently indulged in the propagation of stereotypes in so far as the concepts of sati, chastity and purity are concerned. In other words, the tool used to subvert the dominant castes' perception is the same as that used by the latter for years. Here, the Dharmasutras need a special mention. In this a radical take on women's issues by the Dharmasutra of Āpastamba is brought to light. Āpastamba presents a take on the tradition of Dharma that is divergent and contrary to the common assumption that the ancient Indian society was uniform and stifling under orthodoxy imposed by Brahmins (Olivelle 1999: xiii). Āpastamba's Dharmasutra is considered to be in favour of women to an extent as it talks about property rights of daughters (A 2.14.4; Olivelle 1999: 57) and joint custody of property after marriage (A 2.29.3; Olivelle 1999: 72), but here, too, the women are described as upholders of traditional lore, and Āpastamba tells his audience that they should learn some customs from women (A 2.15.9; 2.29.11; Olivelle 1999). The very ideals of hegemonic traditions have to be challenged, but using the same hegemonic language dissociates the protest from its purpose.

The above-mentioned varieties of defence happen to cause more harm to women's condition. They hinder the mobility of women and affect the psyche of the society at large. Even the subverting texts have used the patriarchal tools and methods to either protect the dignity of women or give them some visibility. Though such subverting texts in themselves, when read in the context of its space and the time period, could be appreciated, one should be aware that this kind of a defence of women's rights and visibility has negative effects in the long run.

We see this in the context of the khap group in particular, and Indian society in general. In the above-mentioned claims, the subverting definitions of sati emanate from the fact that women in general and low-caste women in particular have always been seen as polluted and polluting. The women from the lower castes have been the victims of exploitation by the upper castes. Such exploitations have also been ana-lysed and understood through textual narratives and legends (Lorenzen 1991: 49). That is why in the subverting claims portraying the sati of low castes or ex-untouchables as virgins—the purest and most holy figures—challenges the upper castes' version of a monolithic reality. Here we get to witness the claims, which do have the potential to undercut the dominant representation of reality.

The problem with such claims is that, though they appear to be constructive and favourable to the female members of the community, in reality they keep the women trapped in the same ideals of hegem-onic traditions—be it Brahmanical or other religious principles of purity/pollution, honour/dishonour; pride/shame and so on. Not just developing a new language of protest but also redefining the existing concepts is needed to change the perception of those ideals, responsi-ble for putting people in disadvantageous positions even on the broad secular canvas of claims and counterclaims. Without such dialogues, any demand for justice will remain sectarian and half-hearted, which could pose further problems for the group which remains at the margins cutting across all the identity groups: women. Similar sectarian under-standing gets revealed through the secular academic debates about who can give an authentic theory and who cannot authentically theorize the lived experience of different caste, religious and cultural groups or women of different communities (Sarukkai 2007). This creates a sectarian divide at the level of the ideas of justice, democracy, equality and inclusiveness. For whom will multiculturalism be advantageous and disadvantageous (Okin 1999) and what is the course correction needed in that kind of multiculturalism—these issues will have to be figured out keeping gender–power relations at the centre. Civil society and other concerned groups need to be careful about not dissociating the protest from its purpose, through the usage of either hegemonic language or symbols of hegemonic traditions.

REFERENCES

Aytac, A. M. 2017. 'Lifestyle and Rights: A Neo-Secular Conception of Human Dignity'. *Philosophy and Social Criticism* 43 (4–5): 495–502.

Bhattacharyya, H. 2010. 'Inclusion in Nationhood: Bhudev Mukhopadhyay's Concept of Jatiyabhav'. In *The Politics of Social Exclusion in India: Democracy at the Crossroads*, edited by H. Bhattacharyya, P. Sarkar and A. Kar. Abingdon: Routledge.

Buhler, G., trans. 2004. *The Laws of Manu*. New Delhi: Cosmo Publications.

Bulbeck, C. 1998. 'Individual versus Community'. In *Re-Orienting Western Feminisms: Women's Diversity in a Postcolonial World*. Cambridge: Cambridge University Press.

Chatterjee, P. 1997. *Our Modernity*. Rotterdam and Dakar: South–South Exchange Programme for the History of Development (SEPHIS) and Council for the Development of Social Science Research in Africa (CODESRIA).

———. 2010. *Empire and Nation: Essential Writings 1985–2005*. Ranikhet: Permanent Black.

Choudhari, V. R. 2009. *Commentary on Protection of Women from Domestic Violence Act 2005*. Allahabad: Premier Publishing Company.

Chowdhry, P. 2011. *The Political Economy of Production and Reproduction: Caste, Custom and Community in North India*. New Delhi: Oxford University Press.

Cross, C., and D. Hornby. 2002. *Opportunities and Obstacles to Women's Land Access in South Africa: A Research Report for the Promoting Women's Access to Land Programme*. Available at: http://www.gov.za/sites/www.gov.za/files/landgender_0.pdf (accessed on 9 February 2015).

De, R. 2017. 'No, the Uniform Civil Code Was Not Deferred Just for Muslims'. *The Times of India*, 30 September. Available at: https://timesofindia.indiatimes.com/india/no-the-uniform-civil-code-was-not-deferred-just-for-muslims/articleshow/60888706.cms (accessed on 6 August 2019).

Eisenstein, Z. R. 1988. *The Female Body and the Law*. Berkeley, CA: University of California Press.

Green, L. L. 2012. 'Sexual Violence and Genocide against Tutsi Women'. *Race, Racism and Law: Speaking Truth to Power*. Available at: http://racism.org/index.php?option=com_content&view=article&id=1317:rwanda01&catid=163:rwanda&Itemid=254 (accessed on 1 November 2013).

Jeffrey, C., and J. Lerche. 2001. 'Dimensions of Dominance: Class and State in Uttar Pradesh'. In *The Everyday State and Society in Modern India*, edited by C. J. Fuller and V. Benei. London: C Hurst and Co.

Kaviraj, S. 2010. *The Trajectories of the Indian State: Politics and Ideas*. Ranikhet: Permanent Black.

Kinnvall, C. 2006. *Globalisation and Religious Nationalism in India: The Search for Ontological Security*. Abingdon: Routledge.

Law Commission of India. 2012. *Prevention of Interference with the Freedom of Matrimonial Alliances (in the Name of Honour and Tradition): A Suggested Legal*

Framework. Delhi: Law Commission of India. Available at: http://lawcommis-sionofindia.nic.in/reports/report242.pdf (accessed on 30 July 2013).

Lawyers Collective: Women's Rights Initiative. 2008. *Staying Alive: Second Monitoring and Evaluation Report 2008 on the Protection of Women from Domestic Violence Act, 2005*. Available at: http://www.lawyerscollective.org/files/Staying%20Alive%20Second%20Monitoring%20and%20Evaluation%20report%202008.pdf (accessed on 9 March 2015).

Lorenzen, D. N. 1991. *Kabir Legends and Ananta-Das's Kabir Parachai*. Albany, NY: State University of New York Press.

Menon, N. 1998. 'State/Gender/Community: Citizenship in Contemporary India'. *Economic & Political Weekly* 33 (5): 3–10.

Nandy, A. 1995. 'An Anti-Secularist Manifesto'. *India International Centre Quarterly* 22 (1): 35–64.

Nelson, B. R. 2006. *Making of the Modern State: A Theoretical Evolution*. New York, NY: Palgrave Macmillan.

Okin, S. M. 1999. *Is Multiculturalism Bad for Women?* Princeton, NJ: Princeton University Press.

Olivelle, P., trans. 1999. *Dharmasutras: The Law Codes of Ancient India*. New York, NY: Oxford University Press.

Othman, N. 2006. 'Muslim Women and the Challenge of Islamic Fundamentalism/Extremism: An Overview of Southeast Asian Muslim Women's Struggle for Human Rights, Gender Equality'. *Women's Studies International Forum* 29 (4): 339–353.

Perry, B. 2001. *In the Name of Hate: Understanding Hate Crimes*. New York, NY: Routledge.

Planning Commission, Government of India. 2011. *Report of the Subgroup on Economic Empowerment of Women under Steering Committee on 'Women's Agency and Child Rights' for the Twelfth Five Year Plan 2007–12*. Delhi: Planning Commission, Government of India. Available at: http://planningcommission.gov.in/aboutus/committee/strgrp12/str_womagency_childrights.pdf (accessed on 10 February 2015).

Pradhan, M. C. 1996. *The Political System of the Jats of Northern India*. London: Oxford University Press.

Principal Controller of Defence Accounts (Pensions). (n.d.). *Guidelines for Pensioners*. Delhi: Principal Controller of Defence Accounts (Pensions). Available at: http://pcdapension.nic.in (accessed on 10 February 2015).

Rao, N. 2008. *Good Women Do Not Inherit Land: Politics of Land and Gender in India*. New Delhi: Social Science Press.

Reilly, N. 2011. 'Rethinking the Interplay of Feminism and Secularism in a Neo-Secular Age'. *Feminist Review* 97 (1): 5–31.

Ron Scollon, S. W. 2012. *Intercultural Communication: A Discourse Approach*, 3rd ed. Chichester: Wiley-Blackwell.

Sarukkai, S. 2007. 'Dalit Experience and Theory'. *Economic & Political Weekly* 42 (40): 4043–4048.

Sarvesh, T. 2015. 'Owaisi's Bihar Debut: Hindu Secularism versus Muslim Secularism'. *Firstpost*, 30 September. Available at: https://www.firstpost.com/politics/destined-to-fail-why-owaisis-secular-muslim-agenda-may-not-work-in-bihar-elections-2450020.html (accessed on 24 October 2018).

Sen, R. 2010. 'Same-Gotra Legal, Court Had Ruled 65 Years Ago'. *The Times of India*, 15 May. Available at: https://timesofindia.indiatimes.com/india/Same-gotra-marriage-legal-court-had-ruled-65-years-ago/articleshow/5932546.cms (accessed on 6 August 2019).

Sever, C. 2004, January. *Bridge Development–Gender: Gender and Citizenship: Overview Report*. Brighton: The Institute of Development Studies. Available at: http://www.bridge.ids.ac.uk/sites/bridge.ids.ac.uk/files/reports/Citizenship-SRC.pdf (accessed on 9 March 2015).

Sharma, R. S. 1996. *Aspects of Political Ideas and Institutions in Ancient India*. 4th rev. ed. New Delhi: Motilal Banarsidass.

Shastri, J. L. 1943. *Political Thought in the Puranas: With an Appendix Containing Complete Extracts of Verses on Polity*. Lahore: J. L. Shastri.

Shukla, R. 2005. 'Equality among Unequals: A Critical Look at Hindu Succession'. Infochange Women, September. Available at: http://infochangeindia.org/women/analysis/equality-among-unequals-a-critical-look-at-hindu-succession.html (accessed on 9 February 2015).

Stokes, E. 1978. *The Peasant and the Raj: Studies in Agrarian Society and Peasant Rebellion in Colonial India*. Cambridge: Cambridge University Press.

Uyl, M. D. 1995. *Invisible Barriers: Gender, Caste and Kinship in South Indian Village*. Utrecht: International Books.

Vyas, V. 1940. *Srimad Bhagavat–Mahapuran*, Vol. 1. Translated by S. S. Dev. Gorakhpur: Gita Press.

Yuval-Davis, N. 1997. Women, Citizenship and Difference. *Feminist Review* 57: 4–27.

PART II

Limits of Minority-ism

Chapter 4

Ghar Wapsi or Reconversion?

Samir Gandesha*

[T]here is no longer any homeland other than a world in which no one would be cast out any more, the world of a genuinely emancipated humanity.

—Theodor W. Adorno (1982)

Can there be any question that, today, from the United Kingdom to Turkey, the European Union to the United States itself, representative democracy is in an abject crisis globally? And such a crisis could be said to correspond to what Maurizio Lazzarato (2015) has recently called the transition to the 'authoritarian' phase of neoliberalism. Such a transition was, perhaps, most clearly revealed, appropriately, in the very birthplace of democracy, itself, with the seemingly irresistible pressure that the so-called Troika (the European Commission, European Central Bank and the International Monetary Fund) exerted on the Syriza government to turn its back on the Oxi! or 'No!' victory in the July 2015 Referendum, which posed the question as to whether

* I would like to thank Professor Franson Manjali of Jawaharlal Nehru University, New Delhi, and my colleagues at Simon Fraser University, Professor John Harris of International Studies and Professor Emeritus of English and Director of the South Asian Network for Secularism and Democracy, Chinmoy Bannerjee, for their extremely helpful comments on earlier drafts of this chapter.

to accept or reject the Troika's austerity conditions in return for subsequent tranches of bailout funding. Compare this to the bailout of the supposedly 'too-big-to-fail' financial institutions during the Wall Street meltdown of 2008. It was at this moment that neoliberalism ceased paying even symbolic obeisance to democratic procedures and principles and shifted gears, abruptly it would appear, in the direction of what is, in essence, the dictatorship of finance. It has caused even the most sanguine of defenders of the European project, such as Jürgen Habermas (2012), to speak of a 'post-democratic' European Union. This crisis has many distinct features that can be understood in both subjective and objective terms.

Objectively, the crisis has to do with the weakening of the sovereignty of a nation-state that is increasingly under pressure via the constellation of forces often referred to simply as 'globalization': deepening sovereign and private debt, increasing competition within the world market, the threat of capital flight, binding international trade agreements, currency speculation, tax avoidance and evasion, environmental degradation, and deepening and intensifying conflicts over ever scarcer resources and so on. In particular, what has come to the fore is the role of bond-rating agents and financial bankers in ever limiting the ambit of democratic-representative bodies and institutions. In post-referendum Greece, it has meant that the taxation function of the state is now directly administered by the Troika. This amounts to a clear reversal of the principle of 'No taxation without representation' that, in part, fuelled the Tea Party during the American War of Independence.

Subjectively, while the deepening of capitalist social relations and modernization more generally was said by a wide range of theorists from Marx and Weber to Habermas, himself, to lead to dissolution of particular identities and practices and to encourage secular forms of solidarity that would transcend these, it seems to have had exactly the opposite effect. Rather than a 'post-national constellation' in Europe, we see the rise and consolidation of particularistic 'imagined' communities and identities. There is a palpable tendency towards what Hobsbawm and Ranger (1983) call the 'invention of tradition' and the rise and hardening of ethnic and nationalist identities that are increasingly revanchist and exclusionary in nature. This was made especially clear by the recent referendum in the United Kingdom on 23 June 2016, which has led Britain to trigger Article 50 of the Lisbon Treaty and put it on course to leave the European Union. An important argument for the leave side was the imperative of re-establishing political sovereignty via the unaccountable and unrepresentative Brussels bureaucracy. The question of the unaccountable and unrepresentative nature of the British state itself, posed in the Scottish Referendum of September 2014 is scarcely raised. Psychologically, the rise of xenophobia can be understood as a tendency towards authoritarianism or the tendency to 'identify with the aggressor' (Adorno 2008; Frankel 2002; Gandesha 2016) in conditions of deepening social and economic crisis, conflict and, ultimately, insecurity.

In Europe, for example, we have seen the rise of right-populist and neo-fascist parties in response to the deepening crisis of income inequality and neoliberal austerity. In the United States, it has given rise to Donald Trump's Republican presidential nomination on the basis of an agenda of fear and loathing that would see a wall placed on the US' southern border with Mexico apparently to keep the 'murderers', 'rapists' and 'drug-dealers' out, funded by the Mexican government, as well as a ban on Muslims entering the country. Of course, the Sanders campaign—and the movement it helped crystalize—for the Democratic ticket was a countervailing tendency of no small moment.

India has by no means been immune to these same pressures and processes since its abrupt turn towards neoliberalism in the summer of 1991, although the process had been initiated in the late 1970s. It would be a mistake, nonetheless, not to place them within a *specific* set of historical and post-colonial forces and tendencies that differentiate it from the historically metropolitan regions (see, for example, Harriss et al. 2013). While globalization has affected emerging economies differently from 'advanced industrialized' ones, for example, it has promised a new global power bloc in the BRIC nations (Brazil, Russia, India, and China), whom globalization can be said to have benefitted at least in terms of growing investment in fixed capital, transportation and communications infrastructure and the like. However, in recent years, we have seen the fragility of such development, with the acute sensitivity of Russia and Brazil, in particular, to the volatility of commodity markets, energy in particular, and China's difficult road from an export- and capital-led model to one that is more oriented to domestic consumption.

In India, there has been much breathless talk of the so-called Gujarat model that has generated impressive rates of growth averaging something like 8.5 per annum from 2004 to 2012 (Hashmi 2014), but this itself has not been without its contradictions, including growing indebtedness amongst farmers and intensifying labour unrest in the cities culminating in the historical general strike of 2 September 2016, which saw between 160 and 180 million Indian workers take the streets. Indeed, in terms of 'quality of life indices' rather than misleading measures of rates of economic growth measured by gross domestic product output, Gujarat has trailed far behind Kerala, which was governed on and off between the Left Democratic Front and the United Democratic Front from 1957 to 2011.[1] But what has been more significant was the rise of Hindutva as a foundation for the rising fortunes of the Bharatiya Janata Party (BJP), the corresponding decline of a justifiably much-maligned Congress Party and a deep crisis of an already-divided Communist left in the rest of India with the partial exception of West Bengal. In fact, the authoritarian turn of the Indian state is nothing new, of course, and is not exclusively the preserve of Hindu nationalism but has deep and ignominious roots in the hegemony of the secular Congress Party, expressed most clearly in Indira Gandhi's imposition of the Emergency in a 21-month period between 1975 and 1977, during which time she ruled by decree and which included a mass sterilization programme overseen by her son, Sanjay. It also came again to the fore in the communalized violence of 1984 and the attack on the Golden Temple in Amritsar, the subject of much controversy recently. In essence, Indira Gandhi was killed by the very monster of Sikh extremism that she helped to create but found that, ultimately, like Dr Frankenstein, she was unable to control.

There are several reasons for the rise of Hindutva. While Hindutva has always been present on the Indian political landscape, the increasing

---

[1] See, for example, http://www.indiatomorrow.net/eng/-fact-sheet-that-explodes-myths-about-gujarat-development- (accessed on 13 September 2019).

assertiveness of political Islam or 'Islamism' since the late 1970s, corresponding with the Iranian Revolution of 1979, has provoked it to play an increasing role in public life. This is often lost sight of in the West, where the rise of militant Islam is understood almost exclusively as the foil to US global ambitions since the end of the Cold War. This is the gist of Samuel P. Huntington's (1996) simplistic 'Clash of Civilizations' thesis. What is additionally obscured is the fact that Islamism has its roots at the tail end of the Cold War with the US' mobilization, via the Pakistani intelligence service, of the Mujahidin, to bring down the Communist government of Najibullah and, ultimately, to drive out the Soviet forces (Mamdani 2004). Geopolitically, this has complicated the relationship between India, an erstwhile Soviet ally, and Pakistan, which has remained in a troubled and deeply contradictory way within the US's sphere of influence. In recent years, this problematic relationship has grown ever more complicated. It has exacerbated the violence that has existed since 1947 within the deeply contested region of Kashmir, part of the state of Jammu and Kashmir, the riots and pogroms of 1992, and the 2008 attacks in Mumbai by Lashkar-e-Taiba. Today, the Indian army is brutally asserting Indian sovereignty in this state against the will of a plurality of its residents. More specifically, the growing Islamicization of Pakistani society initiated under General Zia has, it could be argued, progressively undermined secularism in India by generating burgeoning support for Hindutva as a counter-force. This is, as it were, another kind of 'clash of fundamentalisms' (Ali 2003). It is important to acknowledge, however, that the drive of the Hindu Mahasabha and the Rashtriya Swayamsevak Sangh (RSS) for the establishment of a Hindu state long pre-existed the Islamicization of Pakistan. The mass mobilization of voters under the banner of Hindutva is as much a matter of a backlash against the implementation of the Mandal Commission's report on the 'Other Backward Classes,' as it is a response to the changing geopolitical situation.[2] In February 2016, the sensitivity of India's relation to Kashmir as a whole has come to a head with the detention of the Jawaharlal Nehru University Student Union President, Kanhaiya Kumar, and five other students for their slogans on Kashmir, amongst other things. And, significantly, charges were laid under a sedition law that was brought in under the British

---

[2] I thank J. Reghu and Shaj Mohan.

Raj to forestall the growth of the nationalist movement in the early 20th century.

It is in this sense that the Indian state can be understood not so much as *post*-colonial but rather as post-*colonial*. Many of the repressive laws that had secured the Raj were kept on the books, for example. The anti-sedition legislation that had been invoked against Kanhaiya was, itself, of British provenance and geared specifically to counter the Independence Movement. As historian Romila Thapur argues, Islamist and Hindutva organizations—such as the RSS, Arya Samaj, and so on—were always already equally present in the struggle against the British Raj. However, while the former, predominantly in the form of the Muslim League, found expression in the states of East and West Pakistan, the latter was frustrated, went through a period of dormancy, and then belatedly arrived on the scene in the late 1990s. Such an assessment is, however, debatable in that there seems to be evidence that Hindutva, whatever it claims today, was less concerned in the early days of the Swaraj, with opposing the *British* than it was to oppose the *Muslim League*. It would seem that a resurgent and militant Islam helped to nudge it from a state of latency into manifest political expression. Hindutva has been an authoritarian populist mobilizing ideology—one which has sought to mobilize the masses, however, in a subordinate and dependent manner (Mouzelis 1986)—enabling the BJP to cement its social base and, in particular, has helped Narendra Modi consolidate power first as chief minister of the state of Gujarat and, more recently, since 2014, as prime minister of the country. In a manner not unlike the Nazi's appropriation of certain elements of socialism (they were, after all, called the National *Socialist* German Workers Party), Hindutva could be seen as appropriating aspects of a left anti-colonial politics for what is, ultimately, a deeply reactionary, racist and quasi-fascist agenda. Incidentally, this is brought home by the fact that militant Hindus, both within India and in the United States, have thrown considerable support behind the Islamophobic and exclusionary politics of Donald Trump (Swan 2016). This must appear as especially cynical because, as Jawaharlal Nehru University historian Mridula Mukherjee has shown, not only were Hindutva organizations not involved in the Quit India Movement, they often sided directly with the British. For US foreign policy, it gestated in the neo-conservative form of the Project for a New American Century under the stewardship of William Kristol and Robert Kagan, but found rampant expression under Bush (and British policy under Blair). Such a programme entailed an aggressive and expansive foreign policy under the guise of human rights and women's rights as well as the 'Responsibility to Protect (R2P) which, taken together, could be understood—paradoxically as it turned out—as "humanitarian interventionism".' The latter was defended steadfastly by members of the belligerati, formerly left/liberal writers who became overt supporters of US foreign policy, figures such as Paul Berman, Christopher Hitchens and Salman Rushdie. After it was revealed that the claims that Iraq possessed weapons of mass destruction were baseless, the justification for invasion came to hinge upon the liberation of the Iraqi people from dictatorship and tyranny. Both the United States and the UK have done so, moreover, by mobilizing an ever more fearful population through overstating the threat of terrorism. The precedent had already been put into place by the Schroeder/Fischer government of Germany and the Clinton Administration in Kosovo in 1999. Now, the Chilcot Report has revealed that there were no justifiable grounds for war.

In the case of the BJP, such a rhetorical appropriation of certain aspects of left politics has to do with an 'anti-colonial' rhetoric of a certain sort that has gone hand in hand with the persecution of Muslim and, to a lesser extent, Christian minorities as part and parcel of re-imagining the nation as identical with an *erstwhile humiliated, downtrodden Hinduism*. Such a narrative of the domination of the Hindu nation first by the Mughal invaders from the north in the 17th century and, later, by the Europeans: the French, the Portuguese and the British in the 18th and 19th centuries. Again, the parallel with the post-Great War claim that Germany had been betrayed by its political leaders in the humiliation of the Versailles Treaty is striking. Before the election, as Pankaj Mishra (2014) has recently pointed out in a comprehensive and insightful piece in *The New York Times*, Hindutva projected a sense of long-time Hindu victimization, suffering and subordination to colonial rule, first by the Mughals and then by the Raj. The first sought to impose Islam on the original inhabitants of the subcontinent and the latter, Christianity, by aspiring to convert particularly lower castes and

Dalits with hopeful messages of the universality and equality denied to them under actually existing Hinduism. As Mishra (2014) states:

> Certainly, the ruling classes of wannabe superpowers have spawned a complex force: the ideology of anti-imperialist imperialism, which, forming an axis with the modern state and media and nuclear technology, can make Islamic fundamentalists seem toothless. One can only hope that India's democratic institutions are strong enough to constrain yet another wounded elite from breaking out for geopolitical and military manhood.

As much Hindutva may wish, however, to present such a picture of victimization, what psychoanalysis would call a form of paranoiac projection whereby the aggressor construes himself as victim, insofar as it suits its present political agenda, the historical record is much more complex. Christians have been on the subcontinent since at least the second century BCE, from the small colonies on the south-west coast, Goa and Kochi, established by the Portuguese, and in the areas surrounding Chennai such as Pondicherry, settled by French traders. As a rule, the British did not allow missionaries into the subcontinent until the third decade of the 19th century, though there were notable exceptions to it, such as William Carey and others.

Nevertheless, one could argue that this narrative plays a key legitimizing role today for Hindutva in general and the BJP in particular. An important dimension of the 'anti-colonial' agenda, defined not in socio-economic and political terms but in explicitly *cultural* terms, has been the controversial project led by the RSS and other Hindu fundamentalist organizations to 'convert' or 'reconvert' Hindus who were the supposedly targets of proselytizing Abrahamic religions as part and parcel of a process of colonization. In other words, the politics of Hindutva can be understood as a species of 'identity politics' where the agent of politics is not or no longer understood in terms of socio-economic class (or caste) but rather in cultural or linguistic terms. As Frantz Fanon (2005) argued in the context of African liberation struggles, such a definition of political agency opens the door to the substitution of native *post-colonial* for European *colonial* elites. Critics of the practice refer to it as 'conversion', while its advocates consider it to be a process of 'reconversion' or bringing wayward Hindus 'back into the fold'.[3] In other words, advocates of the practice refer to it as *Ghar Wapsi* or 'homecoming'.

My interest in this chapter is simply to clarify this semantic distinction. Critics of the practice of conversion claim that it entails either duress, coercion or a kind of bribery. And this claim itself is consistent with the pronouncements of senior Hindu priests who emphasize the manner in which there really is no place for other faiths in India, particularly Muslims and Christians. They must either convert or subordinate themselves totally and inexorably to the 'Hindu' nation. The equation here, as alluded to above, is of India with Hinduism as such: The Myth of India as the land of Hindus or 'Hindustan'.[4] This is a clear case of a monolithic account of the 'good life' or, what John Rawls calls a 'comprehensive' doctrine, being placed above 'right' or procedures by which competing accounts of the good life could be said to mutually coexist by forming an 'overlapping consensus' or agreement on the fundamental principles of public life that may, for example, be taken to be embodied in India's own Constitution, drafted by jurist and Dalit activist, B. R. Ambedkar, to which citizens of all faiths and creeds could commit themselves. Arguably, in a pluralistic democracy, the *good*—stipulating, for example, restrictive food practices such as the prohibition on the consumption of beef—can only take precedence on the basis of discrimination against minorities, who simply do not share such an account.[5]

---

[3] See Harris (2014). It could be argued 'Hinduism' as a 'religion' with a coherent doctrinal creed is comparatively young, the most recent religion in India it could also be argued that it is Hinduism that is enforcing a conversion *away from Home*.

[4] Although the etymology of Hindustan is Persian in provenance and simply refers to the Indus valley civilization, rather than a particular religion as such. Cf. Anderson (2012).

[5] This demonstrates family resemblances with ISIS's more extreme program vis-á-vis the Yazidi people (in fact, all 'Kuffar' or non-believers) of 'convert or die'. It is also reminiscent of Israel's recent constitutional redefinition of itself as a 'Jewish state' which transforms its Arab citizens into not just de facto but also de jure second class citizens. It is also similar to Turkey's prosecution of dissident writers and academics of their affronts to 'Turkishness' for daring to speak the truth about the Armenian genocide or for declaring their solidarity with the Kurds and the PKK (Kurdistan Workers' Party). It is also reminiscent of the Saudi refusal to countenance Shiaism as a legitimate form of Islam and as a consequence has led

For its defenders, many of whom eschew the term 'conversion'
and favour formal legal restrictions on the practice, as Modi himself
has done as chief minister of Gujarat, the phenomenon is referred to
as a form of genuine 'homecoming' (*Ghar Wapsi*) or a return to the
Hindu 'family' and, therefore, to an 'authentic' Indian identity. What
is suggested here is, in fact, an absence of duress or coercion and a kind
of hospitality and welcoming. For it is precisely by way of such a putative homecoming that one could be said to overcome the conditions
of one's own *estrangement*. In the language that Hannah Arendt uses in
her penetrating biography of Rahel Varnhagen, homecoming is the
way in which the individual becomes transformed from social *pariah* to
parvenu, stigmatized outsider, to *assimilated insider*. However, rather than,
as was the case with Varnhagen, who was a Jewess assimilating to a
predominantly Lutheran society in post-Revolutionary Berlin, Indian
Muslims and Christians, at least according to Hindutva, were returning to their own authentic community after spending time, like many
Hindu deities, saints and yogis, in the metaphysical wilderness. In this
register, it might be, strangely and counter-intuitively, understood as
very much in line with the kind of putatively anti-imperialist rhetoric
mentioned above: That after centuries of Mughal and British rule,
under which Hindus were compelled to convert to the dominant
Islamic and Christian *alien powers*, now India awakens as a *pakka* or
genuine Hindu nation. In the process it addresses its post-colonial
legacy by breaking with socialism and its ties to the now-defunct
eastern bloc. It engages in an aggressive process of modernization and
liberalization which has driven the dramatic rates of growth witnessed
over the past two decades, whose epicentre has been, at least so the
story goes, Narendra Modi's Gujarat. Yet, as Mishra (2015) points out,
such rates of growth—centering on resource extraction, cheap labour,

to the persecution of the Shite community, most recently dramatized with the
execution of respected Shia cleric Nimr al-Nimr. In a more benign but no less
pernicious form, in Canada it has led to a privileging of Old Stock Canadians over
recent immigrants and completely effaces the claims of the aboriginal inhabitants
of what they call 'Turtle Island' (North America) prior to colonization and settlement. Of course, the original version of this was the idea that the state's mission,
through residential schools, was to 'kill the Indian in the child' in order to foster
the assimilation and, indeed, extinguishment of aboriginal people as such, not to
mention their claims to the land.

and foreign capital inflows, rather than high productivity and technological innovation—have left virtually untouched India's 'shameful ratios', namely, that '43% of all Indian children below the age of five are undernourished, and 48% stunted; nearly half of Indian women of childbearing age are anaemic, and more than half of all Indians still defecate in the open'. It is finally in a position to cast off the oppressors' alien spiritual and religious chains. The idea of homecoming suggests a return from a condition of exile, estrangement and alienation to one of belonging, flourishing, a fulfilled life.

In what follows, I want to raise the question about the semantic distinction between 'conversion', on the one hand, and 'homecoming', on the other. At first glance, it would seem that the idea of 'forced conversion', on the one hand, and 'Ghar Wapsi' could not be further apart. While the former denotes coercion and duress, the latter seems to suggest a journey that could be said to entail a learning process, the attainment of a certain sort of self-knowledge or even 'enlightenment'. The question I pose, then, is: Is it possible to justify such a distinction?

In the Western philosophical tradition, as I have pointed out (Gandesha 2013), the narrative of homecoming is pervasive and has a profound ethical dimension, as previously mentioned. The centrality of homecoming to the Western philosophical tradition is perhaps most powerfully and evocatively manifested in the philosophy of Hegel. The becoming of Spirit takes the form of Spirit's 'homecoming', or return to itself through a process of externalization (*Entässerung*), loss, and *Erinnerung* (re-internalization). Hegel makes this clear when he says:

> …the other side of its Becoming, *History*, is a *conscious*, self-*mediating* process—Spirit emptied out into Time; but this externalization, this kenosis, is equally an externalization of itself. This Becoming presents a slow-moving succession of Spirits, a gallery of images, each of which, endowed with all the riches of Spirit, moves thus slowly just because the Self has to penetrate and digest this entire wealth of its substance…. But recollection, the inwardizing, of that experience, has preserved it and is the inner being, and in fact the higher form of the substance. (Hegel, 1977: 492)

It might be objected to here that while Hegel uses the language of home and homecoming, these are merely metaphors that have little, if any, bearing on the content of his actual arguments. This argument can be countered by carefully considering Hegel's use of terms. Key to Hegel's intention of showing the manner in which the norms to which Spirit commits itself to are its own historical forms that have been objectified and externalized insofar as they have been forgotten as such and now appear—as in his earlier use of the case of the 'positivity' of the Christian religion—to confront it as something strange or as alien. It is through the process of an act of interiorizing memory, or recollection (*Er-innerung*), that these objectified forms are brought or returned to itself as *heimlich* ('homely', familiar, comfortable). That is to say, now Spirit can be said to 'inhabit' these forms as the products of its own autonomous, and therefore rational, activity. It is thus that Spirit goes through a process of elaboration and externalization, mis-recognition, and, finally, recognition of the products of its world-transforming activity. In the process, the forms of normativity historically embodied in customary forms of practice initially apprehended as something merely external, heteronomous and irrational are ultimately revealed to be historical products of Spirit's own elaboration, or what Hegel calls the 'labour of the concept', that had gone their own way and become alienated and, ultimately, forgotten. The final recollection of those forms as available for rational justification is how we might understand what Hegel means by the reconciliation of substance and subject. It is through the reconciliation of substance and subject that the wounds of the modern world are finally healed (Gandesha 2013).

The Hindu equivalent, it could be argued, is the Ramayana, literally 'Rama's journey'. Like Homer's epic poem, the *Odyssey*, and Hegel's *Phenomenology of Spirit*, both of which it predates, the Ramayana charts the return home of Rama (the mortal incarnation of Vishnu) to the throne in Ayodhya, the city of his birth, which was rightfully his and his alone, after 14 years of exile. In the R. K. Narayan translation (1973), Rama's exile was a result of usurpation on the part of his stepmother Kaikeyi. She could be said to allegorize the usurpation and domination of Hindus by external 'alien' colonial powers. Nonetheless, like these other foundational texts of the Indo-European tradition, it presents the idea of exile as occasion for the attainment of self-knowledge. The idea of 'leaving home', of embarking on a journey that is as *metaphysical* as it is *physical*, *spiritual* and *corporeal*, is key to Rama's own spiritual and psychical development; it is central to Rama 'becoming who he is'. His time spent wandering in the wilderness makes Rama into the virtuous defender of justice that he, in fact, is. Much of the Ramayana's preoccupation with the themes of exile and homecoming are not only reflected in Rama's experience of exile and triumphant return home, but also through other characters, such as the monkey-king Sugreeva, who experience exile and destitution, and are saved by Rama. In fighting on behalf of Sugreeva against his powerful, impetuous brother, Bali, Rama actually liberates the latter, who finds himself blessed with a 'place in the highest heavens'.

Key to understanding such a homecoming is the very experience of exile itself. In a way that betrays a fascinating parallel with both Platonic philosophy, with its emphasis of reincarnation and the transmigration of souls, as well as an idea of justice defined as 'doing one's own work' that parallels the idea of dharma that we find in the Gita, and *Phenomenology of Spirit*, the Ramayana suggests the importance of the experience of exile (what Hegel calls the path of 'doubt and despair') for Rama's own self formation. Early on in the story, the Holy Man Viswamitra approaches Dasaratha, Rama's father, and asks that the young boy accompany him in the forest and help protect him. Dasaratha is deeply sceptical and fearful for the boy's safety, but eventually relents. The sage says:

> A seed that sprouts at the foot of its parent tree remains stunted until it is transplanted. Rama will be in my care, and he will be quite well. But ultimately, he will leave me too. Every human being, when the time comes, has to depart and seek fulfillment in his own way. (9)

Here, as in the Western philosophical tradition, as suggested above, there's an intimate connection between exile and the realization of human flourishing. In order to pass from consciousness to self-consciousness, from being-in-itself to being-in-and-for-itself, it is necessary for the self to lose itself by externalizing and alienating itself in the world and then, subsequently, finding or re-finding itself. In order to be truly at home in the world, one must take one's leave of it through a process of self-estrangement. Self-knowledge is grounded in a break with the familiar, the safe and the customary. So when, through the machinations of Kaikeyi, Rama's coronation is subverted at the eleventh hour and he is sent into exile, he remembers the noble words of the sage. He also remembers the fact that it was while on his journey with the sage in the forest that he had met Sita and inaugurated his career of battling the forces of evil in vanquishing Thataka (or Taraka). This very journey was the source of self-development, justice and wisdom. When his mother, Kausalya, begs him to take her with him into exile, he explains that her place is by her husband (and Rama's father's), Dasaratha's, side. He goes on to say:

> After living in the forests, I will come back—after all, fourteen years could pass like as many days. If you remember, my earlier stay in the forests with Viswamithra brought me *countless blessings* (emphasis added); this could be a similar opportunity again, for me. So do not grieve.

Ghar Wapsi, in the contemporary period, cannot be understood without reference to the Ramayana to which, it could be argued, it implicitly and explosively points. The latter, since the 1980s, had become part of the filmic imagination of India in the popularizing, made-for-television drama. *Ghar Wapsi* refers to his return home from his sojourn in the forest with Viswamithra and also foreshadows his ultimate return home—as Vishnu—to his rightful place in the heavens alongside of his bride Sita (Goddess Lakshmi). The *Ghar Wapsi* of wayward and benighted Christians and Muslims Specify or omit. Evokes Rama's own mythical *Ghar Wapsi* to Ayodhya. In fact, it could be said to repeat such a 'homecoming'. Advocates of the practice could, then, claim that it honours, in the most profound manner, those whom it welcomes 'home'.

If we understand *Ghar Waspi* in these terms—in terms of a less-than-innocent homecoming, a homecoming as the negation of alienation that entails the negation and incorporation of otherness of the *alien other*—then the distance between the two understandings of 'conversion' is perhaps not so great as would initially appear. In the West, the primordial text of its own self-understanding fundamentally addresses the problem of a return home (*nostos*), the *Odyssey*, which concerns itself with Odysseus' 10-year journey home after the Trojan war that also lasted 10 years. Yet, as Horkheimer and Adorno (2007)famously argue in *Dialectic of Enlightenment*, this homecoming, far from being an 'innocent' one culminating in meaning and fulfilment, entails a terrible, brutal violence. It does so into two distinct ways. First, in order to survive a menacing external nature—as symbolized by the various dangers he confronts in the Cyclops, the Sirens, the Lotus-eaters, Scylla and Charybdis and so on—Odysseus, in order to survive, must turn the prospect of that very violence against himself and against his own men. Rather than propitiating the gods from without by a sacrificial offering, Odysseus does the work of enlightenment (rationalization) by internalizing such sacrifice by renouncing the impulse to enjoyment as is so stunningly exemplified by the Sirens episode in which he has himself tied to the mast so he can hear the seductive song while the men have their ears stopped up with wax to prevent this in order to keep working. He does not work and can enjoy, albeit repressively, aesthetic pleasure; the men, however, in order to work must be denied such pleasure altogether. And, upon returning home, the aggression that built up by virtue of precisely such an introverted sacrifice is visited with terrifying force on the suitors (and the maids who have been seduced by them) who have taken over Odysseus' Ithaca home, and eat and drink freely of his 'substance'. The treatment of those 12 of 50 maids of Odysseus' household who consorted with the suitors are forced to clean up the blood and gore that Odysseus, Telemachus and their men have left in the wake of their settling of scores with the suitors are taken outside and hung. It is described in the following terms:

> With that, taking a cable used on a dark-prowed ship
> he coiled it over the roundhouse, lashed it fast to a full column,
> hoisting it up so high no toes could touch the ground.
> Then, as doves or thrushes beating their spread wings
> against some snare rigged up in thickets—flying in
> for a cozy nest but a grisly bed receives them—
> So the women's heads were trapped in a line,
> nooses yanking their necks up, one by one
> so all might die a pitiful, ghastly death…
> They kicked up heels for a little—not for long.
>
> (Homer, trans. Fagles, pp.453–54)

CONCLUSION

The opposition between *Ghar Wapsi* and forced conversion cannot be maintained because the very notion of homecoming conceals a hidden violence. With the attempt to reclaim the site of the Babri Masjid, such violence bursts to the surface and becomes open for all to see. The question then arises as to why the rise of the rhetoric of *Ghar Wapsi* now at our historical moment? As suggested, at the outset is the passage to the authoritarian phase of neoliberalism. Such a phase corresponds to what Christian Marrazi (2010) calls the 'violence of financial capitalism'. For Lazzarato (2015), such a transition corresponds to the shift from the governance of the institutions of the state to a form of governance by debt. It entails what he calls the 'making of indebted men' (Lazzarato 2012). And an indebted man is a man responsible, as an individual, for his debt and is therefore constituted by guilt. So important is this transition that Lazzarato makes the rather startling claim that the capital–wage relationship has given way to the relationship between the creditor and the debtor. What could be the possible relation to *Ghar Wapsi*? Allowing for the obvious differences of the role of finance and liquidity in Western economies, one may speculate that for Modi's neoliberal project, *Ghar Wapsi* can play a key role in bringing wayward 'Hindus' back within the fold, not simply for purely religious and cultural reasons, but for socio-economic ones. As both Max Weber (2002) and Walter Benjamin (2004) insisted, one must not discount the economically rational role of religion itself, and not just of Puritanism. The putative 'return' of wayward Christians and Muslims to Hinduism is not simply part of a bulwark against a supposed Islamic threat (from both without and within), but can also be regarded as their re-inscription into a distinctive economy of spiritual debt or dharma, of doing the work to which one is assigned. If the politics of debt lie at the heart of an authoritarian turn of neoliberalism, and if the universalizing pretentions of globalization are always articulated in local and regional conditions, then in India such an authoritarian turn bears, at least in part, the name of *Ghar Wapsi*.

Be this all as it may, a final question that must be posed is the following: If *Ghar Wapsi* appears to ultimately undermine the secular foundations of the Indian state by the implication that only those who, as it were, return to the Hindu fold can authentically be considered to be Indian, to what extent would such a conclusion remain within the ambit of what Perry Anderson (2012) calls the 'Indian Ideology'? This is the idea that the Independence Struggle led by Gandhi and carried through by Congress was a secular and unifying force. That the Congress Party alone laid a legitimate claim to manage the contradictions between antiquity–continuity, diversity–unity, multiconfessionality–secularity. That with its fall from grace dating back to Indira Gandhi's invocation of the emergency and the debacle of 1984, the rise of the BJP represented, then, a clear break with this legacy. Or, could it be that the BJP simply has made explicit what was already implicit in the Hindu character of the Congress and its project?

REFERENCES

Adorno, T. W. 1982. 'The Wound Heine'. In *Notes to Literature*. Translated by S. W. Nicholsen. New York, NY: Columbia University Press.
———. 2008. *Lectures on Negative Dialectics*. Translated by Rodney Livingstone. Cambridge: Polity Press.
Ali, Tariq. 2003. *The Clash of Fundamentalisms: Crusades, Jihad, Modernity*. London: Verso Press.
Anderson, Perry. 2012. *The Indian Ideology*. Gurgaon: Three Essays Collective.
Benjamin, Walter. 2004. 'Capitalism as Religion'. In *Selected Writings Volume I*. Cambridge, MA: Belknap Press.
Fanon, Frantz. 2005. *The Wretched of the Earth*. New York, NY: Grove Press.
Frankel, Jay. 2002. 'Explaining Ferenczi's Concept of identification with the Aggressor: Its Role in Trauma, Everyday Life and the Therapeutic Relationship'. *Psychoanalytical Dialogues* 12(1): 101–139.
Gandesha, Samir. 2013. 'Hegel's Homecoming of Spirit'. *Contours: Journal of the Institute for the Humanities* 4. Available at http://www.sfu.ca/humanities-institute/contours/issue4/issue4_p5.html. (accessed on 20 August 2019).
———. 2016. 'Identifying with the Aggressor: From the "Authoritarian to the Neo-liberal Personality"'. Lecture presented at the Freud Museum, London.
Habermas, Jürgen. 2012. *Crisis of the European Union: A Response*. Translated by C. Cronin. Cambridge: Polity Press.
Harris, Gardiner. 2014. '"Reconversion" of Religious Minorities Roils India's Politics'. *The New York Times*. Available at: https://www.nytimes.com/2014/12/24/world/asia/india-narendra-modi-hindu-conversions-missionaries.html?_r=1 (accessed on 6 August 2019).
Harriss, John, Stuart Corbridge, and Craig Jeffries. 2013. *India Today: Economy, Politics and Society* Cambridge: Polity Press.

122 | Samir Gandesha

Hashmi, Sameer. 2014. 'Can India's Economy Model Itself on Gujarat?' *BBC News*, 5 May. Available at: https://www.bbc.com/news/business-27257790 (accessed on 6 August 2019).

Hegel, G.W.F. 1977. *Hegel, Phenomenology of Spirit.* Translated by A. V. Miller. Oxford, UK: Oxford University press.

Hobsbawm, Eric, and Terrance Ranger, eds. 1983. *The Invention of Tradition.* Cambridge: Cambridge University Press.

Homer. 1996. *The Odyssey.* Translated by Robert Fagles. New York: Viking.

Horkheimer, Max., and T. W. Adorno. 2007. *Dialectic of Enlightenment.* Palo Alto, CA: Stanford University Press.

Huntington, Samuel P. 1996. *The Clash of Civilizations and the Remaking of World Order.* New York, NY: Simon and Schuster.

India Tomorrow News. 2014. 'Fact Sheet That Explodes Myths about Gujarat Development'. Indiatomorrow.Net. Available at: http://www.indiatomorrow.net/eng/-fact-sheet-that-explodes-myths-about-gujarat-development (accessed on 13 July 2019).

Lazzarato, Maurizio. 2012. *The Making of Indebted Man: An Essay on the Neo-Liberal Condition.* New York, NY: Semiotext(e).

———. 2015. *Governing by Debt.* New York, NY: Semiotext(e).

Mamdani, Mahmood. 2004. *Good Muslim, Bad Muslim: American, Cold War and the Roots of Terror.* New York, NY: Harmony Press.

Marrazi, Christian. 2009. *The Violence of Financial Capitalism.* Cambridge, MA: Semiotex(e) Books.

Mishra, Pankaj. 2014. 'Modi's Idea of India'. *The New York Times,* 24 October. Available at: https://www.nytimes.com/2014/10/25/opinion/pankaj-mishra-nirandra-modis-idea-of-india.html (accessed on 20 September 2019).

———. 2015. 'Narendra Modi: The Divisive Manipulator Who Charmed the World'. *The Guardian,* 9 November. Available at: https://www.theguardian.com/world/2015/nov/09/narendra-modi-the-divisive-manipulator-who-charmed-the-world (accessed on 20 September 2019).

Mouzelis, Nicos. 1986. *Politics in the Semi-Periphery: Early Parliamentarism and Late Industrialisation in the Balkans and South America.* London: Macmillan.

Narayan, R. K., trans. 1973. *Ramayan.* London: Penguin.

Swan, Jonathan. 2016. 'Hindu-American Emerges as Trump Mega-Donor'. *The Hill.* Available at: https://thehill.com/homenews/campaign/288377-hindu-american-emerges-as-trump-mega-donor (accessed on 6 August 2019).

Weber, Max. 2002. *The Protestant Ethic and the Spirit of Capitalism and Other Writings.* London: Penguin.

Chapter 5

Understanding the Analytics of Uniform Civil Code (UCC) and Pasmanda Frame

Afroz Alam

Three decades after the intense communal mobilization against the Shah Bano judgment in 1985, the ghost of Uniform Civil Code (UCC) is again back with much vigour and energy not only to deliver electoral gain to right-wing political parties, but also to preserve the shaking sanctity and the privileges of higher castes among both Muslims and non-Muslims. The issue of UCC got inflated when Shayara Bano challenged the constitutionality of Section 2 of the Muslim Personal Law (Shariat) Application Act, 1937, which recognizes the validity of polygamy, triple *talaq* and *nikahhalala* (a practice of temporary new marriage with a will to divorce as a pre-condition to remarry the old husband). The issue became highly politicized when the Bharatiya Janata Party (BJP)-run central government argued in the Supreme Court with an affidavit that polygamy, triple *talaq* and *nikahhalala* are not the essential practices of Islam. While the All India Muslim Personal Law Board (AIMPLB), while assuming itself as the voice of entire

Muslims, submitted an affidavit to the court that justified polygamy, instant triple *talaq* and *nikahhalala* as Islamic and cannot be altered.[1]

It must be argued that all laws, including personal laws or UCC, are political contraptions. Ironically, despite having the plethora of personal laws in India, it is only Muslim personal law which has always been made the subject of political exploitation. In fact, the very submissions are political in character, which will ultimately end in fomenting the communal passions of the people and will eventually benefit the right-wing political parties to spike their conservative agenda of preserving the high-caste privileges. The whole debate revolves around personal laws versus civil code without bothering about whose rights are represented in either of these two alternatives and who should speak for change on behalf of whom. It is argued, and rightly so in certain contexts, that high-caste privileges are strongly entrenched under the rationale of Islamic sanction, which is not self-evident.

A full-fledged and highly publicized opposition with communal fanfare was launched by the AIMPLB, other related organizations and Ulemas against UCC by arguing that it is against Sharia and thus unacceptable to the Muslim community. Interestingly, AIMPLB has launched signature campaigns to prove its legitimacy to speak on behalf of entire community.[2] Nevertheless, it would be misleading to accept that the resistance to UCC by the so-called Muslim organizations is Islamic in character. It must be noted that the opposition to UCC is based on assumptions and apprehensions about the possible anti-Muslim character of the law and that too without raising the epistemological questions as what ought to be the meaning, nature and content of the so-called UCC. Rhetoric and counter-rhetoric were at play to keep the issue alive without bothering about its relevance and the invisible cost.

Do Muslims need the existing personal laws? On the one hand, constitutional provisions regarding freedom of religion, minority rights and cultural preservation are invoked to justify the continuance of existing

---

[1] Affidavit submitted by AIMPLB is available at http://barandbench.com/wp-content/uploads/2016/09/Counter-affidavit-in-Shayaro-bano.pdf

[2] The format of the signature campaigns of AIMPLB could be seen at AIMPLB's website at http://www.aimplboard.in/for-gents.php

personal laws. The most important is the argument that Muslims are a homogeneous mass and thus united with one voice in defending the existing personal laws without any change. Any interference in the existing law will be treated as threat to the very existence of Islam.[3] On the other hand, while taking advantage to this fierce opposition, the Hindu right-wing organizations including the BJP and the Rashtriya Swayamsevak Sangh, which are classically known as great conservative forces, turned themselves progressive overnight by emphasizing the need to bring UCC in the name of gender justice and in the process earning the attention of Hindu community by negatively portraying the defiance of such Muslim groups as anti-progress, anti-women and finally as anti-India. Muslims are stereotyped as a conservative force which does not believe in the unity and integrity of India.

In my considered opinion, the right-wing forces, present in both the communities and mostly having the background of high castes, are working in consensus to keep the religious wedge issues alive to preserve their existential relevance. The diverse interests and opinions of various other groups on UCC and Muslims personal laws are tactfully marginalized by creating hype around the threat to religion. In this chapter, I aim to put forward four propositions. First, Muslims are not monolith social groups but are divided along many cross-cutting lines of identity. Therefore, it would be wrong to argue that all diverse groups within Muslims in India are having uniform view on the much-hyped questions of UCC and Muslim personal laws. Second, due to intense disagreements within and between these social groups, it is difficult to develop consensus on something called Uniform Islamic Code that may deal with the personal matters such as marriage, divorce, inheritance, maintenance, adoption and polygamy in clause-by-clause manner. Third, in the absence of a uniform and codified Islamic law, the very hypothesis of existing Muslim personal laws being subscribed by all the diverse groups within Islam and doing justice to every section of Indian Muslims appears a chimera and thus becomes indefensible. In this regard, I explored Pasmanda's frame on UCC using three tools: first, surveying Pasmanda literature, interviewing Pasmanda activist, and taking notes from the field trip to Pasmanda-dominated regions in

---

[3] See the affidavit submitted by AIMPLB.

Eastern Uttar Pradesh. Fourth, given the diversity of opinions, interests and cultural practices among Muslims, one can go with two-way solution: first, to preserve the cultural autonomy of diverse Muslim groups, a reform must take place in the existing Muslim personal laws in the light of egalitarian principles of the Quran; second, to preserve the individual autonomy, the existing Special Marriage Act should be reformed on broader lines to work as civil code uniformly for those who seek relief in their personal matters through the application of this law. In a word, there must be a choice available to those who disagree with their religious personal laws.

MUSLIMS OF INDIA: SECTARIAN VERSUS MONOLITH

Politically and even otherwise, Muslims in India are approached as a single monolith community against the socially diverse character of other religious communities that are largely and deeply divided on multiple lines. The monolith generalization of the community is often drawn from the shared faith, fundamental acts of worship, marginality and external polarity. Nevertheless, Muslim community, like all other religious communities, is heterogeneous and divided along cross-cutting lines of sects, sub-sects, class, caste, region, topography and languages.

In India, the sectarian divisions are strongly visible in terms of them being categorized as Shia and Sunni. The division is not only social but also there are much-nuanced differences in the principles and practices of Shia or four schools of Sunni jurisprudence (Hanafi, Maliki, Shafi and Hanbali) and their sub-sects such as Wahabi, Ahl-e-Hadith, Deobandi and Barelvi, but also the cultural pattern of each of these categories do not match with what is stated as monolith Islamic. Apart from this, there is miniscule presence of Ahmadiyas and Sufi sects. Taking 'class' as a tool, Muslims could also be categorized in terms of high-, middle- and low-income and status groups with mutually exclusive interests and deprivations. The diversity among Muslims along linguistic lines could also be easily verified and so are the regional variations from Kashmir to Kanyakumari and from across the countries and continents. Most significant is the division among Muslims on the lines of caste with similar experiential positioning and hierarchical ranking. The segmentation of

Muslim community could be seen in three caste locations: Ashraf (high caste), Ajlaf (Shudra) and Arzal (Ati-Shudra/Dalit).

In a nutshell, if we look closely, the religious identity is of secondary importance in the socio-cultural and economic life style of these diverse groups with conspicuous lacking of uniform community sentiment as Muslim alone. There are differences on many practical and ritualistic aspects of their faith, including what ought to constitute an essential aspect of Islam and what not. The variations in terms of marriage, divorce, inheritance, succession could easily be noted as there is no consensus on the uniform principles of Islamic law. In many cases, the disadvantageous sections among different groups are unaware of the fact on what is called Islamic and therefore easily influenced by Ulema and local imams that too without verifying their Islamic sanctions as per the Quran and Hadith.

To put it simply, the exclusive reliance on symbolic Islamic code in personal matters raises questions of which Islamic model is to be followed since Islamic society has been split, not only between orthodox, revivalist, modernist and secularist reactions to the idea of UCC, but also between various denominations, sects, sub-sects, castes and gender.

MUSLIM PERSONAL LAWS: A COLONIAL CONSTRUCT

It is often claimed that the existing Muslim personal laws are derived from the Islamic sanctions. But nobody raises the question whether the so-called Islamic sanctions of the existing Muslim personal laws are Quranic in character or only the interpretative outcome of those humans who command Islamic jurisprudence and thus raise the possibility of narrow or broad interpretations based on their preferred selection, exclusion and silences. In this regard, first, we must note that most of the Muslim personal laws outlined by different schools of jurisprudence were not Quranic but were developed through human judicial reasoning (*Ijtihad*). Second, the existing Muslim personal law in India is the byproduct of colonial master plan of Warren Hastings in 1772, which promised that with respect to 'inheritance, marriage, caste and other religious usages, or institutions, the laws of Koran with respect to Mohametans, and those of the Shaster with respect to the Gentoos, shall be invariably adhered to' (Cohen 1996: 26). The British replaced the Islamic law pertaining to criminal matters with the Indian Penal Code, 1860, the Criminal Procedure Code, 1899, and the Indian Evidence Act, 1872, without any significant opposition.

Interestingly, the Muslim Personal Law (Shariat) Application Act in 1937 was the net outcome of orthodox Muslims' negation of Hindu customary practices among the newly converted Muslims such as Khojas, Vohras, Mensons (Jain 1987: 617–618) as well as distinct customary practices in Mapilla Muslims of South India and Cutchi Memons regarding inheritance and succession. There is also a claim made by Danial Latifi who viewed that the Muslim Personal Law (Shariat) Application Act was enacted to improve the status of Muslim women by restoring the custom-eroded right due to them under the Muslim law (Latifi 1972: 106–107). As the statement of objects and reasons of the Act point out: 'The status of Muslim women under the so-called customary law is simply disgraceful. All the Muslim women's organisations have therefore commended the customary law as it adversely affects their rights. They demand that the Muslim personal law (Shariat) be made applicable to them.'

Another noted development in 1939 was the Dissolution of the Muslim Marriage Act based on Islamic law of the Maliki School, which is comparatively more liberal than the Hanifi School as far as the right of Muslim women to obtain a divorce is concerned (Gani 1988: 18–19; Mahmood 1976: 59–61). This Act was heavily opposed by the followers of Hanifi School of Muslims.

Ironically, the saner voices among Muslims who champion the cause of reform in existing Muslim personal laws are often ignored to artificially perpetuate the Islamic sanctity of these laws. A. A. A. Fyzee is one of such voices. Fyzee, a noted scholar of Islamic jurisprudence, while discoursing on the Shariat Application Act, 1937, stated that the so-called Muslim law in India is not a law of divine command but a piece of legislative enactment by the British. He, in fact, insisted upon reform in the existing Muslim personal laws to remove the gender anomalies and argued that Muslim personal law cannot be considered as Sharia because Islam is not the state religion, judges are not Muslims and there is no caliph to enforce Sharia (Fyzee and Faidi 1970).

Thus, we need to deconstruct the submissions of so-called Muslim organizations claiming *triple talaq* as legal and Islamic and cannot be disclaimed. Is it Quranic, the prophetic, some caliphs or the opinion of certain Islamic jurist? If there is anything clearly stated in the Quran, then all other authoritative sources appear meaningless. And the Quran clearly states that divorce is a process which is procedurally spread over at least three months. Divorce is not about the momentary utterance of the word 'talaq' three times in one go and that too without witnesses. Likewise, it is also the case with polygamy. In the Quran, polygamy is predicated upon the welfare of orphans but consciously removed in Sharia as a necessary condition without prescribing the reason. The most important part is the subjectivity of fair treatment to all wives, which is difficult to measure, and therefore having multiple wives was denied impliedly.

Given this context, it is flawed to justify the existing personal laws in the name of Quranic sanctions. It is now strongly articulated by many social groups within the fold of Islam in India that the agenda of UCC and Muslim personal laws has nothing to do with Islam rather it is linked with exclusive power relations between Ulemas and the community as well as Ashrafias with Pasmanda. It is due to this intra-power politics that four boards have been set up for each section of Shia and Barelvi ulama and one each by some Sunni and Shia women. This is certainly a great challenge to the authoritative claim of the AIMPLB's largely Deobandi ulama, to speak on behalf of entire Muslims (Sikand 2005). At the same time, AIMPLB has failed to address the Pasmanda question as this body mainly Ashrafia in character has been consistently indifferent to the need and interests of these marginalized communities within Muslim fold. Let us explore the Pasmanda frame on the subjectivities of UCC and Muslim personal laws.

PASMANDA MUSLIM FRAME AND POST-MINORITY POLITICS

Ajlaf and Arzal are together known as Pasmanda, a Persian term denoting 'those who have fallen behind'. The term is used to highlight the shared sense of deprivations and socio-economic marginality among lower-caste Muslims. In public sphere, the first-ever articulation of Pasmanda frame got shaped when Ali Anwar documented the caste-based experiences of lower-caste Muslims in Bihar in his seminal work *Masawatki Jung* (Anwar 2000). The frame gets strengthened when Masood Falahi's book *Hindustan Mein Zaat-Paat Aur Musalman* appeared in 2006 (Falahi 2006). Falahi's work has clearly demonstrated how the higher-caste Muslims and Ulema worked hand in hand to perpetuate the notion of *kafu* (rules about possible marriage relations between groups) as Islamic through the selective interpretation and re-interpretation of Islamic texts. Later, Khalid Anis Ansari through his regular scholarly interventions sharpened the Pasmanda frame.[4]

Pasmanda scholars have argued that the term Muslim is not inclusive rather exclusive in character to denote only Ashraf Muslims. It was highlighted by Neshat Quaiser who argues that the term Muslim 'is meant—for several centuries—Islamic and a ten to fifteen per cent of the total Muslim population at any given point of time representing the "high-caste culture" and being the sole repository of Islamic glory' (Quaiser 2011). The politics in the name of Muslim is only an 'elite Muslim restorational politics' (Quaiser 2011). Neshat Quaiser raises questions on the intentions of higher-caste Muslims such as: Are these *Muslims* really *concerned* with communal riots or general backwardness of Shudra Muslims? Hasn't the aggressive Hindutva communalism provided them with an opportunity to make their presence felt more prominently and make assertions to recover some of the lost *location* in whatever forms possible? (Quaiser 2011). For him, this situation has produced two things:

> Firstly, the location of religion has assumed the role of a battleground for assertion of the religious identity for more power where the conflicting religions are engaged in fighting their battle. And this in turn is made out to be a battle for survival concealing internal differentiations of all types within the warring religious groupings and marks the danger of social solidarities taking place on lines that would reinforce the existing modes of domination. Muslims with *location* have once again got new strengths—*all* Muslims with new connotations—for whom

---

[4] See Khalid Anis Ansari's blog: http://khalidanisansari.blogspot.in/ (accessed on 16 August 2019).

they now speak afresh [...] Like the textual religion, communalism has created a new homogenous community of Muslims that does not otherwise exist in reality, but on the surface, this image has been successfully reproduced. Those who speak for the Muslims do so from a vantage position of the *location*. The voice of the location-less people has been hijacked and re-presented to benefit others. Secondly, what is disturbing is the *location*-less speaking the language of their Muslim detractors. There are others who do not belong to the *location* yet they speak from the vantage position of that location, which in turn further strengthen the cause of the Muslim high caste/class elite. This has created an *incorporated location*, a lure for homogeneity. Is it a case of victims internalising the categories of their own oppressor? Or, is it a tactical move—ways and means to negotiate with the given situation, on the part of the *location*-less people? (Quaiser 2011)

Let us look at the core arguments of Pasmanda scholars. First, both Ajlaf and Arzal Muslims are socially and politically disenfranchised by the Ashraf in organizations such as madrasas and personal law boards, representative institutions and departments, ministries and institutions that claim to work for Muslims (minority affairs, Waqf boards, Urdu academies, AMU, Jamia Millia Islamia and so on). Second, Pasmanda Muslims are not treated as Muslims, rather still as a part of Shudra and Dalit categories of Hindu and therefore undergo similar humiliation, disrespect and violence on caste grounds on a daily basis. Third, the Pasmanda frame challenges the notion that Indian Muslims on the whole are an oppressed community. It is argued that it is Pasmandas who bear the maximum brunt as they are made powerless and subordinate not only at the hands of state but also by its own dominant group, Ashraf. Fourth, the so-called Muslim politics and Muslim issues are in actuality the part of Ashrafia politics in India to secure their interests at the expense of Pasmanda Muslims. Fifth, Ashrafia politics often termed as Muslim politics will never take up the bread-and-butter concerns of Pasmanda Muslims, who constitute about 85 per cent of the Indian Muslim population and come primarily from occupational and service *biradaris* (co-fraternity). Khalid Anis Ansari argued that:

The notion of 'minority' and 'majority' communities in India—read primarily in terms of religious identity—is of modern origin and linked with the emergence and consolidation of a hegemonic secular nation-state project. In this sense, while 'secular' nationalism becomes the locus of legitimate power and violence, Hindu and Islamic nationalisms become the sites of illegitimate power. The seemingly epic battles that are constantly fought within this conceptual framework—around communal riots or 'Hindu'/'Islamic' terror more recently in the post-9/11 world—have been instrumental in denying a voice to subordinated caste communities across religions and in securing the interests of 'secular', Hindu or Muslim elites respectively. In this sense, the pasmanda articulation has highlighted the symbiotic nature of majoritarian and minoritarian fundamentalism and has sought to contest the latter from within in order to wage a decisive battle against the former. (Ansari 2013)

Interestingly, Pasmanda Muslims often identify themselves with Ashraf in terms of a cherished notion of being Muslims, but the same is rarely the case with Ashraf Muslims who treat Pasmanda as 'other' and Pasmanda regularly experience caste-based humiliation and disrespect in their daily life. Ali Anwar says 'There is a bond of pain between pasmanda Muslims and the pasmanda sections of other religions. This bond of pain is the supreme bond ... That is why we have to shake hands with the pasmanda sections of other religions' (Anwar 2000).

Now we can see that Pasmanda Muslims are getting organized against the caste-based discriminations and trying to find common cause with similarly placed low-caste groups in other religions with a punch-line, '*Dalit-Pichda Ek Saman, Hindu Ho Ya Musalman*'. They argue that:

We are not setting the Dalit/Backward Caste Muslims against the so-called ashraf Muslims. Our movement is not directed against them. Rather, we seek to strengthen and empower our own people, to enable them to speak for themselves and to secure their rights and justice ... We welcome well-meaning people of the so-called ashraf background ... who are concerned about the plight of our people to join us in our struggle. (Ansari 2013)

Pasmanda intellectuals argue that Pasmanda *Tahreek* (movement) is all about attaining social justice by means of bringing constitutional and democratic changes in terms of deepening the existing affirmative action policies, adequate representation of Pasmanda Muslims in political parties, state support for cottage and small-scale industries, democratization of religious institutions and interpretative traditions and so on. Ansari argues that Pasmanda *Tahreek* is all about a struggle for a post-minority politics which aims to democratize Indian Islam in the long run by triggering a process of internal reform.

In this backdrop, there is a need to assess the representative character of AIMPLB. In all estimation, AIMPLB represents a very limited section of Indian Muslims and remained a self-appointed body to speak on Muslims questions. Even the largest sections of Muslims are excluded from it including Pasmanda. Pasmanda Muslims remained marginalized not only in AIMPLB but also in most of the so-called community organizations such as Jamiat Ulema-e-Hind, Jamaat-e-Islami Hind, Muslim Majlis-e-Mushawarat, Milli Council and the Markazi Jamiat Ahle Hadees and so on. All these organizations are dominated by A*shrafs* and thus hardly put forward the issues of lower-caste Muslims.

Falahi's *Hindustan Mein Zaat-Paat Aur Musalman* documents serious instances of caste-based discrimination within the Jamaat and the problematic intellectual positions, especially with regard to casteist interpretations of *kufu* (prescriptions for ensuring suitability and compatibility of spouses in marital alliances), of various theologians connected to the organization. Indeed, the absolute domination of Jamaat by Savarna, male Muslims exposes the limits of the radical sociality that is being hailed as the unique feature of Maududian theopolitics.

FIELD OBSERVATIONS: FIVE *TAKIAS*

Recently, I had the opportunity to visit five peripheral-cum-ghettoized places exclusively inhabited by the Ajlaf (Dalit) Muslims in three districts of Eastern Uttar Pradesh, namely Ballia, Azamgarh and Mau. I am referring here the distinct endogamous religious mendicant classes who are broadly identified as Faqirs with eight divisions such as *Sain, Jogi Faqir, Jalalia, Zinda Shahi/Shah Madari, Chishti, Qalandari, Pakhiya,* and *Rifai* and use several other caste nomenclature such as *Shah, Alvi, Saain, Qadri, Syed* and so on. The distinguishing part of their identity is their linkages with various Sufi traditions. They live in at the outskirt of the city often known as *Takia. Takia* is a place where saints used to take rest and instruct the people but now a *Majar* or *Dargaah* of that saint is established and yearly *Urs* are organized in his memory by *Faqir* castes.

Historically, *Faqirs* were wandering *Dervesh* teaching Islam and living on alms but a lot has changed now. I have picked up three *Takias* from Ballia district, namely Ujiyar, Ratsar and Rasra, and one each from Mau and Azamgarh (Saraimir). During my field visit, I noted that there are very few families who are involved with their traditional occupation of begging and being attached to Sufi shrines. Many have changed their occupation and engaged as landowners, cultivators, fruit vendors, daily-wage landless labourers, motor mechanics, tailors, grave diggers, white washers and *muazzins* and imams in their own mosque. They are also found driving autos, cycle rickshaws and taxis. Some started small set ups of poultry, betel and tea shops and some breed sheep, cattle and goats. There are some who run medium-range businesses such as readymade garments and transport. I have also found there are good number of people who are employed with government jobs, particularly in police, teaching and private firms in bigger cities and living a decent life. Socially, despite the upward movements of certain people belonging to *Faqir* castes, they are still subjected to stigma of being *Faqir* and often treated as *Achhoot* and impure Muslims by the high-caste Muslims. Economically, they are the most marginalized and deprived communities. They are educationally backward.

While interacting with elders, youth, women in these five *Takias*, I found that they practice core principles of Islam such as believing in one God, Prophet, *Namaz*, *Haz* and *Roza* but differ immensely in their cultural practices. Some of them have argued that they are more Islamic than any other sects, caste and groups within Islam as they say that they attend mosque, read the Quran on a regular basis and pray five times each day. It is argued with a sense of proud by some youth that

> Islam plays a central role in our life and we can die for it. But there were many who were of the view that our religion is important but so is our self-respect. We are not treated as Muslims by our fellow Muslim *biradaris* (Ashraf) despite our belief in Allah and Rasool.

Surprisingly, there were many who do not know at all that there are sectarian differences within Muslims rather they treated their way of life as the sole Islamic and few who knew were least bothered about the sectarian differences. But in total I observed that they were largely *Sunni Barelvi*.

When I asked about the recent debates on UCC, surprisingly, very few have heard about it. And those who have heard about this did not know what is this all about. Interestingly, they did not bother to know what 'UCC is' or 'what AIMPLB is' as they suspended the whole talk that these are merely the business of those who have enough bread to eat at home. For them, the most important thing is how to earn, eat and live every day. They are largely dependent on their local imam/Qazi to know the details of Islamic principles about marriage and divorces. Inheritance has bothered them little as they have hardly enough property to transfer or inherit in *Virasat* (legacy). They are largely endogamous and monogamous. All the disputes related with personal matters are resolved through their local community panchayats.

While interacting with local imams in their mosques, I came to know about the similar generic call that it is against Sharia and Islam and nothing less and nothing more. Yes, these local imams did show their reverence to AIMPLB, but when I asked about the affidavit submitted to court, they were able to say only this that it is all about triple talaq and blaming the court, government working against Muslims, Islam and all Muslims should be united. The response was more rhetorical and less substance as the local imams themselves were not aware what this whole debate is all about.

An Interaction with Ayaz Ahmad, a Pasmanda Activist

During my fieldwork I met Mr Ayaz Ahmad, a Pasmanda activist and working as Assistant Professor of Law at Glocal University, Saharanpur. I asked him about how does a Pasmanda look at the question of UCC? Is the existing personal law only a garb to preserve and protect the castiest and patriarchal privileges of *Ashrafs*? He argued that:

If I reflect from the vantage point of Pasmanda, question of UCC is raised to create the binary of Hindu versus Muslim in order to entrench both identities as a monolith whole. This entrenchment of communal identities is aimed at suppressing caste fault-lines. The suppression of caste fault-lines is necessary to hold on to the privileges accumulated under Brahmanical social order. Thus, demand for UCC helps the Savarna to consolidate its dominance over the Bahujan under the garb of Hindu identity and opposition of UCC helps the Ashrafiya to consolidate its dominance over the Pasmanda under the garb of Muslim identity. However, UCC is not the exclusive strategy of constructing the binary of Hindu versus Muslim. It is deployed in combination with various other cultural symbols which mark out the caste ridden diverse populace into two hostile groups. The most prominent among them are Aligarh Muslim University and Banaras Hindu University (Muslim modernity versus Hindu modernity), Muslim Madarsa Education and Hindu Sarasvati Education (Muslim culture versus Hindu culture), Muslim Sufis and Hindu Yogis (Muslim Spirituality versus Hindu Spirituality) Muslim League and Hindu Maha Sabha (Muslim Politics versus Hindu Politics), Muslim Personal Law versus Hindu Personal Law, Muslim Secularists and Hindu Secularists (Jinnah versus Gandhi), Muslim Fundamentalist and Hindu Fundamentalist (Iqbal versus Savarkar), Muslim Liberal and Hindu Liberal (Maulana Abul Kalam Azad versus Pandit Jawahar Lal Nehru). All these oppositional symbols can be ontologically understood by replacing the expression 'Muslim' by 'Ashrafiya' and 'Hindu' by 'Savarna'. Similarly, the question of UCC can be understood in the dialectic of (religious) identity formation and invisibalization of (caste) identity and the need for their continuous reproduction through hostile binaries.

The question of protection and preservation of patriarchal privileges of Ashrafs in the garb of existing personal law is only partially answered by above analysis as this question goes to the very root of caste system. As explained by Dr Ambedkar in his paper titled 'Castes in India: Their Mechanism, Genesis and Development', patriarchy constitutes the core of caste order. Unlike hostile religious identity which is only a symptom of caste structure rather than the cause of it, patriarchy is the central pillar of the caste system itself. Therefore, patriarchal privileges of Ashrafs are not just protected under the garb of personal laws rather the garb of personal law itself is created by the patriarchal foundations of Ashrafiya identity! Hence, patriarchy is the base on which Ashrafiya privileges are laid down and existing personal laws only partially support them. Naturally, Dr Ambedkar underlines gender injustice or patriarchy as the chief mechanism of the origin of caste in India.

To my question, is the opposition to UCC an outcome of 'higher-caste' consensus than Islamic, Ayaz responded thoughtfully and argued that:

> Both position of and opposition to UCC is an outcome of 'higher caste' consensus across religious categories rather than pious allegiance to constitutional principles or Islamic tenets as it is made out to be. Neither the constitution mandates creation of UCC nor does Islam oppose such a system as the very idea of UCC in practical terms is non-existent in both Constitutional an Islamic jurisprudence. The main reason for demand of UCC by Savarna and its opposition by Ashrafiya is clear from the answer to first question. Both functions go on to support caste order.

While answering my question, will there necessarily be an unavoidable conflict between secular UCC and religious separate laws, he says that

> [N]o, there need not be any real conflict between secular uniform civil code and religious separate laws as the former cannot come to life without accommodating the later. In fact, the existing secular uniform civil code in the form of Special Marriages Act does exactly the same although in a very bias and unscientific manner.

To the question whether it is possible to develop a civil code without affecting the core values of Islam and cultural autonomies of 'minorities within minorities', he confidently voiced:

> Yes, it is very much possible to develop a civil code without affecting the core values of Islam and cultural autonomies of 'minorities within minorities' if this question is approached from the vantage point of gender justice and justice to people with different sexual orientation. If civil code is to be utilized as hegemonic tool of dominant groups belonging to any category which is inherent in all exercises of law making, then such a possibility is impossible to imagine, hence futile to explore.

Ayaz Ahmad straightforwardly came to Pasmanda position on UCC and MPL (Muslim Personal Laws) debate by arguing:

> The Pasmanda identity has emerged in opposition to minority politics as the later failed to fulfil the aspirations of the former. It is similar to the emergence of Bahujan identity which was formed in opposition to majority politics for materially similar reasons. Pasmanda identity is relatively young and its arrival is actively resisted by the Ashrafiya proponents of minority politics, in the present context by manufacturing an opposition to UCC. Thus, opposition to UCC through conservation of regressive laws and practices along with hegemonic symbols as discussed earlier continuously obstruct the articulation of Pasmanda concerns. In any case, answer to earlier questions makes it evident that the UCC debate has no substantive objects to achieve apart from its role as consolidator of communal identities. Further, the question of gender justice if any can be addressed within the framework of existing personal laws provided that sincere efforts for reforming personal laws are made and it is not utilized to sustain Hindu versus Muslim binary to sub-serve Brahmanical agenda of hierarchical social order. Keeping this background in mind, the Pasmanda position on UCC debate would evolve firstly, to open up maximum space for its expression, secondly to root Pasmanda position in ethical concerns of inter-sectionality.

CONCLUDING REMARKS

UCC has become a communal term. The mere invocation creates divide between the communities, scholars and so on. Even during Constituent Assembly Debates, the idea was dropped in the name of religious freedom. Only politics has been played but no academic exercise. We are constantly moving forward in post-colonial secular India, and thus the resistance to pressing reforms in personal laws appears meaningless. A common, modern and secular Special Marriage Act of 1954 has already given all Muslim couples the option to register their marriage under Act. Similarly, Muslim Women (Protection of Rights on Divorce) Act, 1986, empowered criminal courts to enforce some of the rights generally available to divorced women under the Islamic law. There is a need of reforms within personal laws to reconcile with gender justice norms of civil code without disturbing the broader framework of Islam and at a time when the political climate of the country is more conducive than counterproductive. The most radical and progressive law of Islam of the past cannot be a regressive law for today. Reform is certainly needed, but what would be the nature of reform? The problem lies in not only the non-codification of Muslim personal laws but also the absence of officially recognized Sharia Court which ultimately result into the administration of personal laws cases by the state courts based on the Indo-Muslim judicial precedents which often produces constitutional and humanitarian crises. Is UCC the magic alternative? The answer is purely dependent upon whose interests would be represented in the new UCC. The extreme barrier against the concern of equity across genders is not solely the personal laws but the cultural preferences and pressures of and on the women to follow customary rules without questioning the marital decisions, unilateral talaq, property disentitlement, polygamous inequity and temporal maintenance in the court of law.

In fact, the plurality within Muslim community has also been deliberately ignored and side-lined to serve the designs of privileged groups of both Muslims and non-Muslims. The invocation of religious-cum-emotive issues such as Ram Mandir, UCC, Urdu and so on is being looked upon with distaste among the Pasmanda scholars. They are of the view that these issues are often circulated to keep the development concerns and aspirations of Pasmanda Muslims at bay. The heterogeneous character of the Muslim community bars them to have unitary interests when it comes to personal laws. In fact, overemphasis on Islamic personal laws and Islamization is only to reinforce the caste distinctions.

The divergent lines are strongly drawn across the castes, classes, factions, sects and sub-sects among Muslims. In cultural realm, the dominant groups even refuse to recognize the marginalized sections as dignified Muslims. The varied personal codes have been culturally personalized by the dominant groups to arbitrarily maintain the idea of *Kafu* for marriage as well as uniquely diverse cultural practices such as divorce, maintenance, inheritance, adoption of child, polygamy and so on. Similarly, the so-called personal laws are being constantly reworked in familial domain to bypass the so-called Islamic laws and thus giving primacy to the internal dynamics of kinship, caste, class and gender. Therefore, what is essentially Islamic has rarely been at threat than what is portrayed as Islamic without having any congruence with the core principles.

Interestingly, the 'fear psychosis' regarding UCC is inflated writ large by the subtle means of 'Ashrafia consensus'. It is mendaciously depicted as 'Islamic consensus' to perpetuate the 'hierarchical marginality' of Ajlafs (OBCs) and Arzals (Dalits) who will eventually benefit, if a rationally sensible civil code is adopted without disturbing the egalitarian essence of Islam. Thus, the proposition of a 'uniform civil code' should not be easily suspended if it aims to challenge not only 'patriarchal bias', which is grossly un-Islamic, but also the habit of the dominant caste to maintain an exclusive and discriminatory personalized civil code.

Importantly, a common legal platform needs to be created for civil issues that are common across religions/communities without sacrificing 'legal pluralism'. The designs of the 'orangish yellow colour' party need to be questioned, whose only purpose is to create unbridgeable chasm between the religious groups in the name of UCC. Be that as it may, the right wing should not be allowed to create the UCC blueprint as they are more serious in politicizing the code than in its secular rationality, rather a multidimensional task force needs to be put in place to arrive at an all-inclusive platform.

I aim to argue that if we ultimately go with the utilitarian value of 'cultural autonomy' for minorities in the majoritarian world, a similar autonomy should be accorded in favour of those individuals and groups within minorities who, for any reasons, want to seek remedy from the state and judiciary as a citizen of the country.

REFERENCES

Ansari, Khalid Anis. 2013. 'Muslims That "Minority Politics" Left Behind'. *The Hindu*, 17 June. Available at: http://www.thehindu.com/opinion/lead/Muslims-that-minority-politics-left-behind/article12076617.ece (accessed on 6 August 2019).

Anwar, Ali. 2000. *Masawatki Jung*. New Delhi: Indian Social Institute.

Cohen, Bernard S. 1996. *Colonialism and Its Forms of Knowledge: The British in India*. Princeton, NJ: Princeton University Press.

Falahi, Masood Alam. 2006. *Hindustan Mein Zaat–Paat Aur Musalman*. Mumbai: Ideal Foundation.

Fyzee, A. A. A., and A. A. A. Faidi. 1970. *The Reform of Muslim Personal Law in India*. New Delhi: Nachiketa Publications.

Gani, H. A. 1988. *Reform of Muslim Personal Law: The Shah Bano Controversy and the Muslim Women (Protection of Rights on Divorce) Act, 1986*. New Delhi: Deep & Deep Publication.

Jain, M. P. 1987. *Indian Constitution Law*. Bombay: N. M. Tripathi.

Latifi, Danial. 1972. 'Change and the Muslim Law'. In *Islamic Law in Modern India*, edited by Tahir Mahmood, 106–107. Bombay: N. M. Tripathi.

Mahmood, Tahir. 1976. *An Indian Civil Code and Islamic Law*. Bombay: N. M. Tripathi.

Quaiser, Neshat. 2011. 'Locating the "Indian Muslim" Mind: An Incomplete Conversation'. *History and Sociology of South Asia* 5 (49): 49–68.

Sikand, Yoginder. 2005. 'India: Patriarchy and Sectarianism: Explaining the Dissensions in the All-India Muslim Personal Law Board'. Available at: http://www.wluml.org/node/1876 (accessed on 6 August 2019).

Chapter 6

Resisting Minoritization
Postcolonial Muslim Politics and Indian Democracy*

Mursed Alam and Seema Ahmed

The 'Muslim question' and the political response of the Muslims to their minoritization in India have been pestering issues for Indian democracy. Although the Indian Constitution has provided the Muslims with various political and religious safeguards, the rise of right-wing forces and the communalization of Indian society and the various organs of the state have often rendered Indian Muslims to the status of sub-citizens/subalterns, which has serious consequences for Muslim identity and political discourse in India. Political theorists have identified two broad frameworks for analysing Muslim political response in India: the Muslim homogeneity perspective and the secular heterogeneity perspective. While the former, a la Iqbal Ansari, Syed Shahabuddin view Muslims as a single political unit and Muslim

* The chapter hugely benefitted from the suggestions and comments by Abdul Matin, PhD scholar at School of Social Sciences, Jawaharlal Nehru University. It also owes a lot to Dr Anindya Sekhar Purakayastha and Mosarrap H. Khan. All the shortcomings, however, are due to the authors.

politics as legal–constitutional way of securing minority rights, the secular heterogeneity perspective, in its various versions put forward by Moin Sakir, Asghar Ali Engineer, Mushirul Hasan, Imtiaz Ahmed views Muslim politics as another version of communal politics peddled by Muslim political and religious elites in trying to unite the Muslims under the broader category of the *Millat* (community to shield their political ambition and practice anti-democratic and communal politics). Both these perspectives, however, identify, whether positively or negatively, the invocation of identity politics of the Muslims in India. However, there have also been calls for a change in the political demands of Muslims, emphasizing instead on the issues of employment, education and political empowerment. While the attempt for a separate Muslim party has not gained ground, there have been calls for forging a broader coalitional platform with other subaltern groups and minorities. Is such a political imaginary mere theoretical exercise, or is it implementable practically? What are the impediments that are hindering the possibility of such an alternative? The present chapter proposes to investigate these issues with a focus on Muslim politics in West Bengal which has been less analysed in the discourses on Muslim politics in India. Building on works such as *Muslim Political Discourse in Postcolonial India: Monuments, Memory, Contestation* (Ahmed 2014), *Being Muslim in South Asia: Diversity and Daily Life* (Jeffrey and Sen 2015) and *What Ails Indian Muslims* (Jal and Ali 2016), we would analyse the 'Muslim question' in 21st-century India to make a case for broad-based coalitionary politics.

WHAT AILS INDIAN MUSLIMS TODAY

The question of minority rights, and especially that of the Muslims, has been a controversial issue since independence. The partition and the communal frenzy surrounding the partition, pre- and post-1947, found the Muslims who preferred to stay in India in a peculiar situation. They are accepted as the formal citizens of the newly established country, but their allegiance to the nation was held a suspect (Pandey 1999). The Constituent Assembly debates emphasized that the Muslims in India have to prove their loyalty to the nation. Mere preference to stay on was not enough; they must give 'practical proof' of their declaration of loyalty, as the Home Minister Vallabh Bhai Patel said (Ali 2016: 44). The Muslim employees were viewed as the 'fifth columnists'' and the secret spies of Pakistan. A secret circular ordered the authorities not to employ the Muslims in any sensitive post because that might compromise the security of the nation (Ali 2016: 45). Such an attitude of the administration and the general feeling prevailing in the country were not favourable for the development of the community. The situation was compounded by lack of able leadership from Muslim community who could guide the community for their socio-political and economic betterment. The partition ensured that those who demanded Pakistan, mainly the upper class and upper caste Muslims who feared that their political opportunity would be compromised in an undivided independent India, went to Pakistan leaving behind a mass of people who did not have the necessary political will and expertise to organize and lead the community. Maulana Azad was more of a scholar than a politician and he failed to rise to the occasion to lead the community. The Indian Union Muslim League, too, lost the legitimacy after Pakistan was created.

Given such a situation, the Muslims in India, except the few privileged upper class and upper caste Muslims, constituted the significant portion of the underdeveloped and lagged behind in almost all the socio-economic and political indicators compared to other communities. That the situation has not changed much even after 70 years of independence speaks a lot about Indian democracy and the failure of the community leaders to secure the group rights for the community. The Government of India appointed various committees to assess the socio-political and economic condition of the Muslims in the country, such as the Gopal Singh Commission, the Misra Commission and the Sachar Commission. Based on such commissions and the various studies done by many scholars, we would first like to point out the issues concerning the Muslims in India today.

Zaheer Ali (2016) has aptly catalogued the problems before the community in the 21st century, some of which he considers as 'peripheral' and some other as 'real' in the sense of deserving serious attention on the part of the community leaders and the government. Among the issues he considers peripheral are the minority status of the Aligarh Muslim University, the Status of Urdu, Vande Mataram Controversy, Muslim Personal Law and so on. There can be objections to such a binary characterization of issues concerning Muslims as 'peripheral' or 'real', and a case can also be made about the significance of the issues Ali characterizes as 'peripheral'. However, it also needs to be mentioned that those issues are 'peripheral' in the face of utter socio-political and economic deprivation of the Muslims in India. They also do not concern the Muslims in India uniformly, for example, although the question of Urdu might be an emotive issue for the North Indian Muslims, it is a non-issue for the Muslims in West Bengal who mostly speak Bengali. The 'real' problems before the community, as Ali thinks, are as follows.

Security of Life and Property

Independent India has been witness to not infrequent outbreak of riots in which the major casualty has been the Muslims, and pogroms such as Gujarat 2002 under the watchful eyes of the administration have seriously compromised the security of the Muslims in India. Studies show that the riots break up in areas where the Muslims are comparatively well off in terms of business and trade and in areas where they have significant presence in terms of numbers. This proves that the target of the riots is to dispossess the Muslims of whatever economic support they have and also to consolidate Hindu vote against the Muslims where they are sizeable in numbers and thus creating problem for the Hindu right to come to power. Apart from the riots, there have been numerous cases where innocent Muslims are falsely framed in various terror-related cases, many rot in the jail without trial and come out after 10 or 15 years as social and psychological wrecks. Hasimpura-style fake encounters are not uncommon, and the recent killing by police of eight alleged Students' Islamic Movement of India activists in November 2016 in Madhya Pradesh in a case of jail break, which seems to be fabricated, shows the grave injustice when it comes to the question of Muslims in India. For the police, terrorism has a religious colour, and the media trial of Muslims whenever a bomb blasts, even when in a mosque, continues unabated.

Economic Exclusion

That the Muslims in India are economically worst off and are poorly represented in public services is hardly a new fact. However, the anti-Muslim stance was there right from the start. In 1948 the secretary of the Home Ministry issued a letter addressed to all the secretaries asking them to be cautious about the Muslim employees, 'It is obvious that they (Muslim employees) constitute a dangerous element in the fabric of administration; and it is essential that they should not be entrusted with any confidential or secret work or allowed to hold key posts' (Ali 2016: 44–45). And this circular continued to be in force until 1969. The Sachar Committee Report points out how the Muslims are even denied loans by government and private banks to start a business. Such discriminations and official impediments keep the Muslims economically backward and hinder the creation of a strong middle class. The Gopal Singh Commission made it clear that the percentage of Muslims in elite jobs such as the Indian Administrative Service had gone down to 3.2 per cent while scheduled castes (SCs) were 9.9 per cent; in the Indian Police Service, Muslims were 2.7 while the SCs 9.8 and in the Indian Foreign Service, Muslims were 3.37 per cent while SCs were 16.48 per cent. The comparison with SCs makes the picture perhaps clearer. The Sachar Committee Report also pointed out the same anomaly. Table 6.1 shows the exclusion of Muslims from public jobs in various states in the country.

The Sachar Committee Report points out that 94.9 per cent Muslims living below poverty line do not get food grain and in rural areas 60.2 per cent Muslims do not own land.

Political Exclusion

That the Muslims have the right to live here, but not to rule, seems to be the norm. The 16th Lok Sabha has only 22 Muslim members, the lowest since independence. And in the state Legislative Assemblies in the 12 states in which Muslims have significant presence, the number of Muslim members has been well below the percentage of their population. Such glaring incongruities militate against the idea of representation of all groups in a functioning democracy.

Table 6.1 *Muslim Representation in Government Jobs in Different States of India*

S. No.	Name of the State	Muslim Population (%)	Muslim Employment (%)
1	Andhra Pradesh	9.2	8.8
2	Assam	30.2	11.2
3	Bihar	16.5	7.6
4	Delhi	11.7	3.2
5	Gujarat	9.1	5.6
6	Jharkhand	13.8	6.7
7	Karnataka	12.2	8.5
8	Kerala	24.7	10.4
9	Maharashtra	10.6	4.4
10	Uttar Pradesh	18.5	5.1
11	Tamil Nadu	5.6	3.2
12	West Bengal	25	4.2

Source: Jal and Ali (2016: 48).

Educational Backwardness

According to the Sachar Committee Report, the literacy rate of the Muslims in 2001 was 59 per cent, which is well below the national average of 65 per cent. At school level, 25 per cent of the Muslim children are not enrolled or dropped out; in undergraduate level, 1 out of 25 and in postgraduate 1 out of 50 students are Muslims (Jal and Ali 2016: 50–53). Different reasons can be put forward for the educational backwardness of the Muslims. However, there is no denying the fact that a vicious circle of poverty and educational backwardness works in a circular way to prevent the educational achievement of the Muslim children.

MUSLIM POLITICAL RESPONSE

What has been the Muslim political response to such discrimination, subordination and minoritization? After the independence and up to the 1970s, Muslim political response has been viewed as 'self-protective' and 'defensive'. However, as Hilal Ahmad says, during this time the Muslims in India engaged in the politics of minority rights focussing on educational and cultural issues such as the protection of Urdu and the minority status of Aligarh Muslim University. In and after the 1970s, the crisis of the Indian state and the rise of Hindutva politics under the mobilization of the Vishva Hindu Parishad and other Sangh affiliates threw up some radical Muslim political leadership such as the Imam Bukhari and others. The attempt has been to mobilize the Muslim community for the protection of the Babri Masjid, the Muslim Personal Law and other issues.

Instead of discussing the specificities of Muslim politics, let us see how Muslim politics has been viewed by the scholars and activists and what other alternatives are now being thought of. Scholars of Muslim politics in India have approached the issue from various perspectives. But, as Ahmad points out, these approaches can be classified under two broader perspectives: the homogeneity and heterogeneity perspectives.

Muslim Homogeneity and Legal–Constitutionalist Approach

The legal–constitutionalist approach to Muslim politics hinges on two basic points. First, there is one homogeneous Muslim community with certain common interests. Although the Muslim community is linguistically, socially and culturally varied, it is religion which provides a basic logical unity to them, and they are bound together by common concerns. Second, these common concerns or interests are provided and protected by the Constitution. So, the politics the Muslim community can do is the politics of rights, demanding the implementation of their constitutionally sanctioned rights. India has adopted an India-specific secularism which is suited for Indian social life. It not only respects all religions but also keeps an equidistance from all religions. At the same time, it guarantees the religious freedom for the minorities and also comes up with protective discrimination policies for various backward groups. However, the problem with the Indian political system is the concentration of power. There is not adequate representation of different sections in various institutions, which impedes the proper functioning of these institutions to achieve their objectives. The dominant group often resorts to measures which threatens the very foundation of the Indian state. The Muslim community, which exists as religious community, realizes that it is by political action alone that it can secure its constitutional rights. Thus, the religious community is transformed into political community, especially at times of crisis as a reaction to the 'external pushes'.

Heterogeneity Perspective: Marxist, Modernist-Secular, Social Assimilationist Approach

All such approaches—Marxist, modernist-secular and social assimilationist brought under the category of heterogeneity perspective—highlight the internal diversity of the community and hold that the homogeneity thesis is invented by Muslim elites to mobilize the Muslim masses for their own political gain. Moin Shakir holds that the Muslim elites, both the religious elites and those associated with various secular parties, come from the upper class and upper caste, whereas the Muslim masses are basically economically backward. The Muslim elites are well integrated with the bourgeois capitalist system of India and are enjoying its benefits. This class analysis of the Indian Muslims leads Shakir to propose that the politics the poor Muslims should follow is not the elitist politics which only reproduces the capitalist/bourgeois system, but the politics of emancipation for the poor masses. Mushirul Hasan, speaking from a modernist-secular perspective, holds that Muslim community is highly diversified, and the idea of a single Muslim community was invented in colonial India by the colonial authority and the Muslim separatists. He finds a link between colonial and postcolonial Muslim politics in the sense that the Muslim elites invoke and use the idea of *millat*. He contrasts this minority politics or the politics of minorityism with the commitment of the secular Muslim intelligentsia to the Nehruvian ethos of secularism. He talks about the role played by individuals like Maulana Azad, Dr Ansari, Md Habib and organizations like Aligarh Muslim University, Jamia Millia Islamia in upholding the secular and democratic nature of India and employing a secular frame of analysis.

Imtiaz Ahmed looks at Muslim politics as a result of Islamization in the Muslim community which happened in response to the Sanskritization of Hindu community. In the face of a rising fear of Hindu communalism, Islamization emerged as a legitimate and viable political response. Imtiaz says that there have been two kinds of Muslim political responses in postcolonial India: They act as a political pressure group either using their demographic dividend for political demands and/or supporting a national political party. Imtiaz suggests a 'third way' which consists of aligning with the other marginalized sections of other communities and work on a common platform. This, he thinks, can lessen communalism.

DALIT–MUSLIM ALLIANCE

On the political front, the strongest criticism of the North India-centric Muslim politics comes from the Pasmanda Muslim politics, which holds that the Muslim upper caste leaders, by creating a binary of Hindu–Muslim, actually denied the internal caste oppression within the Muslim community and talk about the Pasmanda politics of the lower caste Muslims. There have been, in recent times, calls for a Dalit–Muslim alliance. Muslims and Dalits both face the brunt of Hindutva politics, and the recent attacks of the cow vigilantes on the Dalits in Gujarat and the participation of the Muslims in the organized protest of the Dalits in Una, Gujarat, has thrown up a possibility of a Dalit–Muslim alliance. Owaisi, the leader of AIMIM, has called for such an alliance. However, does such an alliance have a practical feasibility, and if so can it sustain the momentum after the moment of agitation is over? Can there be a genuine share of interests beyond the 'temporary marriage of convenience'. In an article, Faisal Devji (2016) has analysed the possibility of such an alliance. There has been, he thinks, a 'virtual absence of an autonomous Muslim politics' which leaves it open to be 'deployed by and against others'. The kind of politics Muslims practice in their name has been 'unable to move beyond local and state arenas' and the politics of clientage practised by the Indian Union Muslim League in Kerala is feasible only in a fragmented political scene. The recent

Lok Sabha Election (2014), too, has shown that the Bharatiya Janata Party, with its huge majority, can completely bypass the Muslims. Thus, pointing out the loopholes of Muslim politics based on religious identity he writes:

> ...the 'Muslim community', whatever else it might be, does not and cannot exist as a political entity except in a negative sense, as the alleged victim of prejudice or hostility. This is due not simply to its divisions of caste, class, sect and language, which after all characterise all communities, but rather the very effort to unify it religiously even if in the broadest and most tolerant way. If anything, the quest for Muslim unity on religious grounds takes Hindu nationalists rather than Dalits as a model, but this only makes a Muslim politics impossible, given the unequal status of the two communities. (Devji 2016)

He talks about the Dalit example which, instead of focussing on religion or faith, focuses on caste identity. But the Muslim community, saddled with the minority identity, is deprived of politics and is bound to focus on issues of identity. He thinks that Muslim community is an anti-political category by definition, although religion can be an empowering political weapon for a majority for sustaining its dominance; for a minority, however, it can often be damaging. Thus, he talks about a Muslim politics of caste:

> But to make a Muslim politics possible, the 'Muslim community' has to be destroyed, since defined as a religious minority, it has not only failed either to protect or advance its members politically, but, as the 2014 elections showed, made even its vast numbers irrelevant to India's electoral arithmetic. If a Dalit–Muslim relationship is to be anything more than a temporary marriage of convenience, therefore, the 'Muslim community' must be broken by caste just as its Hindu version has been. Only by including Muslim low castes into the system of reservations, for instance, might new political interests and alliances be created, with other Muslim groups also being freed to work out a political future of their own. This seems to be the direction of low-caste Muslim politics emerging during the post-Mandal period, especially in Bihar with the All-India Backward Muslim Morcha and the Pasmanda Muslim Mahaz. (Devji 2016)

However, whether such an alliance is possible beyond Bihar and Uttar Pradesh, or can the Dalits and Muslims come together nationally or for that matter in other states? Let us discuss the matter with a focus on Muslim politics in West Bengal.

MUSLIMS IN WEST BENGAL

According to the 2011 Census, Muslims in West Bengal constitute 27.1 per cent (including a minor section of Urdu-speaking Muslims) of the total population of West Bengal. The Muslim community in West Bengal is differentiated in terms of class, caste, linguistic and sectarian affiliations. Although Muslims are distributed in all the districts of West Bengal, the ministry of minority affairs during the United Progressive Alliance regime recognized Murshidabad and Malda as the minority-intensified districts in West Bengal. However, a majority of the Muslims are economically worse off and are engaged in agriculture and other low-wage daily works and in informal sectors. Many also migrate to the metropolitan cities such as Delhi, Bombay and other parts of India for work.

GOVERNING THE MUSALMAN: THE LEFT AND THE MUSLIMS IN WEST BENGAL

Traditionally, the Muslims in West Bengal rallied behind the Left Front since it came to power in 1977. The land reform and other people-centric policies of the Left Front benefitted the Muslim masses too, and they supported the Left. However, they did not vote the Left en masse as the Congress hold in Malda and Murshidabad was still intact. However, the class-centric politics of the Left failed to give any importance to community or caste issues in West Bengal, neither did they try to create leaders from the community who could represent and act as pressure group or otherwise for the community. The Sachar Committee Report pointed out the loopholes of the class politics of the Left, and the Muslim community started to realize that even the Left, which used to flaunt its secular credentials, has only perpetuated the minoritization of the Muslims in West Bengal. Although the Left could keep the communal forces at bay with its class-based politics; it, however, did not help much as it kept the Muslims in the lurch. As one respondent said, 'The Left is much like the BJP and would not do much for the Muslims. And the reason for this is that the Left has been a party of the Brahmins who came from East Bengal.' Of course this is misconstrued, but this also gives an indication of the frustration of the Muslims with the Left Front. After the Sachar Committee Report, the Left Front tried to redress the problems of the Muslim community by coming up with certain urgent measures such as the establishment of Aliah University, other backward class (OBC) reservation for Muslims, establishment of English madrasas and so on. However, it proved to be very late.

POST-SACHAR MOBILIZATION: SUBALTERN MUSLIM POLITICS AND THE MAMATA REGIME

After the Sachar Committee Report, the Muslim community woke up to its degrading situation. And the Muslims, from the religious leaders to the academics, started openly criticizing the policies of the Left government. The opposition, too, was quick to highlight the issue and started taking the dissenting voices on the board.

The Trinamool Congress came to power in 2011 toppling the Left regime and riding on a promise of 'poriborton' or change. It was helped in that regime change by the civil and non-civil actors such as Maoists and other subaltern groups. The Trinamool Congress government also made a lot of promises to the Muslim community, that it would do for them what the Left has never bothered to do. At times, the Trinamool Congress government does look like foregrounding a coalitionary politics under the leadership of Mamata Banerjee, who brought in identity politics and community issues, such as the issues of the Motua community, the Adivasis and the Muslims by openly interacting with these community leaders. The socio-political churning and the subalternization of politics, as Ranabir Samaddar has talked about, have also paid Trinamool back.

As for the Muslims, Mamata's strategy has been to fall back on the religious leaders and secure the Muslim votes. After she came to power, she announced 'imam bhata' (a monthly allowance) for imams and muajjins (persons who discharge some religious duties in the Muslim society), would don the hijab in election campaigns, would be shown as praying in her election posters and would openly advocate the issues of Muslims in the rallies organized by Muslim. She also came in contact and developed the majars (Sufi shrines), such as the Furfura Sharif in Hoogly, the Pathor Chupri in Birbhum, the Haldibari majar in Jaipaiguri. During the religious festivals at these shrines, the Trinamool leaders such as Firhad Hakim and others from the minority cell would be present looking after various facilities for the ordinary Muslims who would visit in thousands and for whom Mamata thus appeared to be a 'nijeder lok' (a dear one). Apart from that the Bengali daily *Kolom*, edited by Ahmed Hassan Imran, the Trinamool candidate to the Rajya Sabha from West Bengal, which addresses the issues concerning the common Muslims, also garners support for the Trinamool Congress. With these, she seems to have captured the imagination of a significant portion of the Muslim masses. As one respondent said, 'Before Mamata nobody gave the Muslims any respect.' Another respondent, although he is critical of Mamata, said, 'She is better than the Left.' However, although a significant portion of the Muslims voted for the Trinamool Congress, it cannot be said that the community turned en masse to it as in the 2014 elections, the Trinamool Congress failed to win a single seat in Malda, and in Murshidabad the Congress could manage to hold on to some of its seats.

PITFALLS OF THE POLITICS OF THE GOVERNED

Mamata's strategy of governance has been to take on board few religious leaders and to tap on the identitarian issues of the Muslims. The religious leaders seem to operate as a pressure group coming to negotiations with the government on various issues thought to be concerning the community. Gudavarthy (2012) has shown some of the pitfalls of the politics of negotiations as theorised by Partha Chatterjee as the 'politics of the governed' or as 'political society'. Building on him, we want to point out the limitations of such politics involved here:

1. Politics of negotiation and operations of the pressure group are contingent upon the context and the willingness of the ruling regime to concede to the demands. If in a different context the ruling authority wants, it can completely disregard such pressure groups.

2. There is the danger of the resistant subaltern bodies getting appropriated by the ruling class. They are often appropriated by being brought within the fold—they can protest and demand; but that has to be under the banner of the ruling party. Mamata's strategy seems to be the same. After Razzak Molla left the Left Front, he floated his own party, Bharatiya Naybichar Party (BNP), which sought to work for the Muslims, Dalits and other backward communities. Siddiqullah Chowdhury also had a party called People's Democratic Conference of India. But Mamata appropriated them within the Trinamool Congress with the demand that they have to discard their separate party. Her strategy of giving 'imam bhata' and building terms with religious leaders is another way of the same strategy. As one respondent said, 'They would say what Mamata would ask them to say. Their syllabus is fixed for them by Mamata.'

3. There are certain pitfalls of identity politics. Mamata's imambhata (despite the fact that it is given from the waqf fund) and the over-trumpeting of such things by the Muslim brigade of Mamata have also antagonized a section of the Hindus and given the current right-wing wave in the country such measures can unwittingly play in the hands of the communal forces. It has also created rift within the Muslim community as there have been cases of infighting among the imams and muajjins who vie for the bhata/allowance.

4. Before the 2016 election, Mamata declared that she has completed 90 per cent of the works she promised to the Muslims. However, as the Preliminary Public Report on the Status of Muslims in West Bengal (2014) prepared by Social Network for Assistance to People and Guidance Guild shows, the situation of the Muslims has not changed much. Mamata's strategy has been to focus on the

religio-cultural and identitarian issues of the Muslim community. The Sachar Committee talked about mainstreaming the minorities, but such measures are only segregating them.

DALIT–MUSLIM ALLIANCE

There have also been attempts at forging a Dalit–Muslim alliance in West Bengal. Nazrul Islam, former IPS officer and a social worker who built schools and colleges in Domkol, Murshidabad and is quite vocal about the marginalization of the Muslims, Dalits and Adivasis in West Bengal, established a party called 'The Mulnibasi Party of India' in 2014. In his *Mulnibasi Istehar* (Manifesto of the Muslinasis), he identifies the Mulnibasis (autochthonous) as those who lived in India for millennia and did not come from outside. Thus, the STs, SCs, OBCs, Shudra and untouchable converts to Islam are the 'Mulnibasis'. However, he himself got less than 1,000 votes in the election. On 14 November 2016, a seminar on 'Sankhyalaghu–Dalit Khomotayon' (Empowerment of Minorities and Dalits) was organized at Malda district. It was organized by the A. K. M. Hasanujjaman Foundation, and leaders from BAMCEF and National Mulnibasi Sangh took part in the seminar. The main speaker was Nurujjaman, the Trinamool Congress MLA from Pursura, who is also the son of A. K. M. Hasanujjaman, the Muslim League MLA who participated in Ajay Mukherjee's government. In his address, Nurujjaman talked about the future plans of continuing with such seminars in the districts of Murshidabad and Dinajpur, the two other Muslim-intensified districts in West Bengal.

However, there are certain problems of such initiatives, too, that need to be mentioned. At times such attempts seem to be motivated by the aim of drawing the attention of the ruling party and securing one or two seats in election from it. This seems to be the case with Rezzak Molla's BNP as he switched to Trinamool Congress and left behind the idea of building a Dalit–Muslim alliance. Attempts such as Nazrul Islam's *The Mulnibasi Party* suffer from a lack of mass support. He built a party without a social movement. His is the case of an intellectual exercise without the preparatory groundworks. The idea of 'Mulnibasi' might be culturally closer to the Adivasis and the OBCs, but the Muslim Dalits might still hesitate, because of their religious identity, to be associated with the idea. Whether the initiative of the AKM Hasanujjaman Foundation is a genuine attempt at an alternative or just an attempt at co-opting the concept of Mulnibasi by the Trinamool Congress is yet to be seen. However, the leaders of BAMCEF and National Mulnibasi Sangh told that they are working at the socio-cultural level and are trying to make the Mulnibasis aware of their identity, their marginalization and ways of fighting back. When asked whether the Muslims feel associated with the concept, they said they are trying to make them aware. And one member, who is a Muslim, told me in private, 'BAMCEF and organizations like it are the only hope of the Muslims because if you mobilize as a Muslim, you will be called communal'. A Dalit–Muslim alliance thus seems to be the way ahead. But for that a long and arduous groundwork is necessary. And until such a scenario becomes practical, the Muslim community has to think about appropriate ways of resisting their minoritization. They need to look beyond identitarian issues and focus on issues of education, gender and caste hierarchies within the community, proportional representation, inclusion of the Dalit Muslims in the SC list and a general churning for socio-cultural upliftment. As Noorani writes:

> Empowerment of Muslims will not be achieved through communal mobilisation, but as part of a process in which Muslims participate actively in national politics, engage themselves enthusiastically on national issues, and bringing to the fore Muslim grievances as aspects of the injustices that scar Indian society.

> A keen sense of realism must inform this effort, besides considerable patience. No political party would risk its popularity by being seen as a 'champion' of the Muslims...A new climate would be generated in which the secular parties would find it easier to exert themselves to secure redress of Muslims' grievances. (Noorani 2004: 18)

In a democracy, the rights of the minorities and the issues of differentiated citizenship can create heated controversies. However, as Asghar Ali Engineer said, such differentiated citizenship and issues of difference enrich a democracy rather than obstruct it (Engineer in Jal and Ali 2016). The minority groups, such as a religious minority like Muslims, should also come up with alternative thinking and strategy. They need to think how they can, without sacrificing their identity, address the urgent issues of political, economic and other deprivation. When asked why the Muslims seem to rally behind Mamata instead of building their own political organization, one respondent said, 'Joto din na sabalok hoi totodin sat Mayer under ei thakte hobe' (Until they become adult, they have to deal with the stepmother). Thus, the way forward seems to be a multi-pronged or multi-layered strategy by the Muslim community. Apart from those religious leaders, there should be an emphasis on creating alternative civil societal foras where the Muslims can voice their discontent and their legitimate democratic demands. The academics and intellectuals also need to set discourses and give ideological guidance to the movement. There is a caste Hindu *bhadralok* (Brahmin–Baidya–Kayastha) hegemony in Bengal. The intellectuals need to offer counter-hegemonic discourses to it. And in this the Muslims need to think about coming together with other subaltern groups such as Dalits, Adivasis and other linguistic minorities for a radically intersectional political constellation.

REFERENCES

Ahmed, Hilal. 2014. *Muslim Political Discourse in Postcolonial India: Monuments, Memory, Contestation.* New Delhi: Routledge.

Ali, Zaheer. 2016. 'Problems of Indian Muslims: Real and Peripheral (an Overview)'. In *What Ails Indian Muslims,* edited by Muzaban Jal and Zaheer Ali. Delhi: Aakar.

Devji, Faisal. 2016. 'Is a Dalit–Muslim Alliance Possible'. *The Hindu,* 31 August.

Dutta, Milan. 2016. 'Muslimra Jokhon Rajneetir Votebank' (When the Muslims Are the Votebank of Politics). *Ananda Bazar Patrika,* 21 April.

Gorringe, Hugo, Roger Jeffrey, and Suryakant Waghmore, eds. 2016. *From the Margins to the Mainstream: Institutionalising Minorities in South Asia.* New Delhi: SAGE Publications.

Gudavarthy, Ajay, ed. 2012. *Re-framing Democracy and Agency in India: Interrogating Political Society.* New Delhi: Anthem Press.

Islam, Nazrul. 2014. *Mulnibasi Istehar (Manifesto of the Mulnibasis).* Kolkata: Kolkata Prakashan.

Jal, Muzaban, and Zaheer Ali. 2016. *What Ails Indian Muslims*. Delhi: Aakar.

Jeffrey, Robin, and Ronojoy Sen, eds. 2015. *Being Muslim in South Asia: Diversity and Daily Life*. New Delhi: Oxford University Press.

Noorani, A. G., ed. 2004. *The Muslims of India: A Documentary Record*. New Delhi: Oxford University Press.

Pandey, Gyanendra. 1999. 'Can a Muslim Be an Indian?' *Comparative Studies in Society and History* 41 (4): 608–629.

Chapter 7

Rethinking Minority Politics in India*

Shadab Arab

INTRODUCTION

India is a secular country consisting of diverse religions, castes, classes and cultures. Political parties in India have been greatly influenced by cultural diversity, social ethnicity, caste and religious pluralism and clashing ideological perspectives (Kumar and Lone 2013). With democracy deeply entrenched in the political system of India, deprived sections of the society are finding avenues to manage public affairs through the electoral process. When and where this accommodation has not kept pace with the pressures from different social groups for leadership positions in a party and government, new parties have emerged claiming to represent the aspirations of the weaker sections and backward classes (Suri 2005).

The chapter majorly focuses on Muslims and the peripheral form of politics practised by them alongside brief narratives on Dalits in the context of the Indian political system. It argues that the issues grappling

---

* A Preliminary Report on the Condition of Muslims in West Bengal (2014) prepared by SNAP and the Guidance Guild.

both the communities have been similar since independence under successive governments. However, following the exemplary political mandate secured by the right-wing BJP in the general elections of 2014, India witnessed an unprecedented overt surge in attacks on Muslims as well as Dalits. These concerted attacks on the minorities are initiated in the name of protecting the cow and its progeny by the *gau rakshaks* (cow protection front)—a revered animal in Hinduism; mass campaigns engaged in forced conversions of minorities to Hinduism that is referred to as *ghar wapsi* (homecoming—underlying the domination of Hinduism over every other religion); and love jihad or romeo jihad, which according to Hindu groups is a decoy by Muslim men to ensnare Hindu women and convert them to Islam (Human Rights Watch Report 2018). Through this triad and the cow vigilante groups, in particular, having affiliations with radical Hindu nationalist group that promotes an exclusionary form of Hindu nationalism, has deliberately attacked the Muslims and the lower-caste Hindus (Human Rights Watch Report 2018). According to India Spend's content analysis of the English media, Muslims comprised 51 per cent of Indians attacked in 63 incidents of violence centred on bovine issues over a period of eight years (2010 to 2017), while the percentage of Dalits stood at 8 per cent. It is imperative to note here that 86 per cent of 28 Indians killed in 63 incidents were Muslims. As a way to negotiate these increased attacks, this chapter reasons that Muslims and Dalits should forge a political alliance, instead of acting as a separate political entity, to combat the immediate challenge of greater entrenchment and institutionalization of Hindu nationalism and anti-minority sentiment. It stresses that Muslims, in particular, must attempt to overcome their limited representation in the country's political sphere and reach out to Dalits to forge a natural alliance—the reason simply being that they are not equipped amply to challenge the threat on their own. Such a positioning will also help the Muslims overcome the dominant rhetoric of forging an unholy alliance between religion and representation in Indian politics and instead follow the conventional secular politics by forming a natural alliance with the Dalits.

Before discussing the construction of the chapter, it would be prudent to highlight the context in which the word 'minority' is used here. Although the Indian Constitution has used the word 'minority' in Articles 29, 30, 350A and 350B, it has refrained from defining it. Thus, the chapter uses the following definition, 'minority is a group of people who because of their cultural characteristics are singled out from the others for differential and unequal treatment and who, therefore, regard themselves as objects of collective discrimination' (Wirth 1945) and identifies Dalits and Muslims as minorities. The chapter is divided into two main parts—the first part primarily discusses the comparable socio-economic situation of Dalits and Muslims, and the second part discusses the scope and opportunity of an alliance between the two.

PRESENT STATUS OF MUSLIMS AND DALITS

Muslims remain socially ostracized, economically deprived and politically underrepresented (Sachar Committee Report 2006). It has been more than a decade since the Prime Minister's High-level Committee on Social, Economic and Educational Status of Muslim Community in India, popularly called the Sachar Committee, published its reports, highlighting the deep and extensive deprivations Muslims in India face in the range of sectors—education, employment, public services and the like. It has been as many years since the central government announced a programme of interventions to ameliorate the condition of minorities, with Muslims making up the overwhelming majority. Latest data on development outcomes (Census 2011; National Sample Survey Organization 2011) do not show any significant improvements in the conditions of Muslims. It is, however, also true that data collection and systematic tracking and analysis of the change in those outcomes for Muslims have been inexact. Equally, given the limited scholarly attention on Muslim deprivation and development, we are not sure yet, in a sufficiently nuanced way, what works and what does not for Muslims, nationally as well as in regional settings. This is further evident by the finding of the 2012 report, 'Inclusive Development Paradigm in India', which states that 'neither the national nor any major state government have made efforts to evaluate the pro-poor and pro-minority policies; although they have made a number of policy statements and formulated targeted programs'. This is a significant gap in understanding, given that Muslims comprise 14.23 per cent of India's population

(Census 2011), and are counted, along with scheduled castes (SCs) and scheduled tribes (STs), among those making up the largest section of the marginalized in India.

The Sachar Committee found a clear and significant inverse association between the proportion of the Muslim population and the availability of educational infrastructure in most localities. It reported that the efforts of the Reserve Bank of India to extend banking and credit facilities under the Prime Minister's 15-point programme of 1983 have mainly benefited other minorities. They are grossly underrepresented relative to their populations across all government institutions, including the highest levels of government services.

Similarly, a special rapporteur report of 2016 from the United Nations that focused on caste-based discrimination in India highlighted that despite several constitutional provisions, SCs as a group has remained on the edge because of 'constant exclusion and dehumanization'. Ancient India's trend of subjugating the Dalits to the worst form of social and communal apartheid from rape to murder and casual violence continues in the present. The National Human Rights Commission's report on Prevention and Atrocities against Scheduled Castes (2011) states that every week 13 Dalits are murdered, five Dalits' homes or possessions are burnt and six Dalits are kidnapped or abducted. Further, 37 per cent of Dalits live below poverty in India, 45 per cent do not know how to read and write and a dismal 48.4 per cent of villages deny Dalits access to water sources because of segregation. Dalit children have to sit separately while eating in 37.8 per cent of government schools and more than half (54 per cent) of their children are undernourished. It went on to stress that even the reports prepared by the ministry of social justice and empowerment and placed before Parliament contain merely factual information received from states about registration and disposal of cases, without any meaningful analysis of the performance of the states which could form the basis for making corrective interventions. The above statistics demonstrate the inefficacy of the various Acts and laws enacted for the upliftment of Dalits, as the crimes committed against Dalits remain indirectly proportional to the conviction rates.

Poverty

According to the Sachar Committee Report, poverty among Muslims in 2004–2005 stood at 31 per cent, whereas for the SCs/STs at 35 per cent, which is actually a very slight difference. This was more pronounced in urban areas, where nearly half of all Muslims (44 per cent) counted among the poorest, compared to the national average of 29 per cent. The Sachar Committee Report found Muslims in Uttar Pradesh, Bihar, Assam and West Bengal, constituting the poorest sections of the population, along with SCs and STs. These are also the states where most Muslims live. The situation was similar in rural areas where the percentage of Muslims living below the poverty line was 33 per cent, whereas the national percentage lies at 28 per cent.

Panagariya and More (2013) reinstated the poverty ratio among Muslims at a dismal 33.9 per cent in urban centres and 36.2 per cent in rural areas, as against the national ratio of 20.9 and 33.8 per cent, respectively. The significantly high urban poverty among Muslims is reported again by the India Human Development Report 2011, using 2007–2008 National Sample Survey data, at 23 per cent, compared to 13 per cent for Hindus as a whole.

Other indicators of poverty show similar trends. The relative deprivation of Muslims, along with SCs and STs, was evident in their ownership of assets as well—the Access Index of Asset Ownership (defined as the share of assets owned by the community divided by the community's share of population) across social groups was the lowest for SCs, while across religious communities it was the lowest among Muslims (in 2002–2003). And the monthly per capita expenditure, based on National Sample Survey 2009–2010, shows Muslims and SCs/STs are among the poorest (Fazal 2013).

Food Security and Health

Malnutrition is an indicator of chronic hunger, which is critically linked to people's health status. As per the findings of the 2011 India Human Development Report, the percentage of adult Muslim women's malnutrition status was 35.2 per cent. It also pointed out that while female malnutrition has been reducing over time among other religions, it is increasing for Muslim women. It is not a surprise to know that SCs were found to be at a disadvantage where malnutrition among women stood at 41 per cent as against the national average of 36 per cent. The report continued to highlight that the incidence of women suffering from anaemia between 1998–1999 (49.6 per cent) and 2005–2006 (54.7 per cent) was observed to be the highest for Muslim women with about 6 per cent, while for the SCs, it increased by 2.3 per cent from 56 per cent in 1998–1999 to 58.3 per cent in 2005–2006.

Education

According to Census 2011, data on educational status by religious groups showed that 47.2 per cent of Muslims are illiterate, higher than the national rate and for any single religious community. As per the 2014–2015 All-India Survey on Higher Education Report, the gross enrolment rate for Muslims (13.8 per cent) in higher education trailed the SC figure of 18.5 per cent and the national figure of 23.6 per cent. It further stated a poignant figure, where Muslims accounted for a paltry 4.4 per cent of students enrolled in higher education, inversely proportional to their national population (14.23 per cent). SCs, with 13.4 per cent of the share of enrolment as against their national population of 16.6 per cent, fared better in this indicator. The report cautioned that 'if the trend is not reversed, there is almost a certain possibility that Muslims will fall far behind even the SCs and STs. Additionally, the dropout rate among Muslims (17.6 per cent) and SCs (15.4 per cent) is higher than the national average of 13.2 per cent (Gouda and Sekher 2014).

Employment

Among major religious groups, the India Human Development Report 2011 found the worker population ratio (WPR, another important determinant of socio-economic welfare) was the lowest for Muslims (536) among all the religions, representing the workforce per 1,000 population. The report went on to explain that the lower WPR among Muslim was essentially due to their lower participation in economic activities. However, WPR was much higher for the SCs when compared to all the segments of the population. WPR for SCs stood at 61.4 per cent in rural areas and 51.8 per cent in urban areas, as against 59.5 per cent in rural areas and 47.2 per cent in urban areas. This high statistic is explained as 'hardly surprising' on account of the SCs' poverty and elaborates that 'it is essential for them to work in order to survive'.

In the light of the above socio-economic indicators, it would not be wrong to suppose that Dalits and Muslims are grappled with issues that are similar in many if not in all ways. One might argue that there are developmental schemes—introduced only after six decades of independence—specifically targeting the Muslims. However, this is more of a cosmetic and marginal measure rather than a case of a sincere attempt at levelling the playfield. For strengthening the argument, one need not look beyond how the imperative recommendations of the Sachar Committee and the Ranganath Commission have not translated into positive discrimination in the form of policies and schemes by the government. In the case of Dalits, there is no doubt that the government has devised a comprehensive package of wide-ranging constitutional provisions, policies and schemes since the independence. Despite these efforts, it is inexplicable as to why in a globalized 21st-century India, caste oppression still exists and mitigation of socio-economic indicators has been marginal. Keeping Mendelsohn and Vicziany's (1998) study as my basis, I argue that this is because the government and the bureaucracy are riddled with prejudice and have been deliberately lethargic in implementing the exclusive programmes. In fact, the study appropriates that even if there is a concerted effort from the state apparatus towards an exhaustive implementation of the dedicated programmes, it will be marginally successful in transforming the plight of the Dalits. This is because these programmes are designed and entrenched in secondary and ulterior factors rather than targeting the primary areas responsible for the deprivation of Dalits. This facet is even more pronounced when the general programmes dedicated to the populace have a greater positive impact on Dalits (albeit at a lower level than the general populace) rather than dedicated programmes.

MUSLIM POLITICS

The years preceding partition and independence, partition itself, and the very fact of agitation for a separate Muslim state, had widely created the acceptance of Muslims as 'outsiders' as an axiomatic truth. Partition and independence marked a moment of uncertainty in the political and social life of the people of the subcontinent. There was re-designation of local castes and communities: those who had long adhered somewhat loosely to the label of Muslim, Hindu or Sikh were now categorically named as one or the other. (Pandey 2006)

Thus, a particular conception of the Indian nation emerged, in which the Muslims had an unenviable place, the Dalits and other oppressed castes and classes were invisible or only symbolically present as the backward part of the nation, to be lifted up by those who ruled in the general interest 'for the advancement of the nation as a whole, and other religious minorities and marginal nationalists had to work in collaboration with and in subordination to that other invisible category, the mainstream, Hindu majority' (Pandey 2006).

In a post-colonial India, 45 million Muslims formed a sizeable minority in a country where socio-religious composition had Hindus in a majority. In this context, it is significant to point that Indian Muslims who did not support the idea of partition were inclined towards strengthening Nehru's vision of a secular India (Noorani 2002). Noorani explains that between 1947 and 1951, through three major conferences and conventions in Lucknow and Delhi, the Muslim polity collectively came to the understanding that their constitutional interests would be better safeguarded by following conventional secular politics of Congress rather than attempting to protect themselves through a political agency that interplays religion with politics. The strategy of repudiating their political activities by not building an independent political agency reflecting political separatism and instead aligning forces with Nehru worked until his demise in 1964. However, as resonated in the writings of Balraj Puri (1993) and Mushirul Hassan (1988), after Nehru, the Congress indulged Muslims with mere tokenism by utilizing the Muslim citizenry as a metric system for electoral profits without actually assuaging a positive change in their social, economic and political spheres, an element that holds true even today. Further, as Asghar Ali Engineer highlights, in 1983, this is the predicament of the community coalesced with periodic communal riots across India, especially in towns where 'Muslims had attained a measure of economic stability through the practice of traditional artisanal and entrepreneurial skills', rendering them economically bereaved (Hassan 1988). To compound their problems further, there were instances of state machinery's obtuse and overt involvement in authorizing discriminatory and fatal actions against Muslims, as is visible in the case of Provincial Armed Constabulary's massacre of Muslims in Hasheempura in May 1987. Further, V. N. Rai in his study (Rai 2008) points out police administration's and the ruling dispensation's partisan conduct against the minorities in the communal violence of Bhiwandi (1970), Aligarh (1978), Jamshedpur (1979), Moradabad (1980), Meerut (1982), Delhi (1984), Mumbai (1992) and Gujarat (2002). Considering the above evidence in consolidation with the conventional socio-economic statistics presented, it would not be wrong to propound that the state machinery, through formal and informal organizations, in more than one ways has fostered and institutionalized an environment of discrimination against the minorities. To embellish this, one need not look beyond the Prison Statistics of India report which highlights that prison is one place where the proportional representation of Muslims is higher than their population percentage. Their proportion in the prison population was 20.13 per cent vis-à-vis their total population of 14.23 per cent (National Crime Records Bureau 2011; Census 2011). Further, social exclusion and dispossession of minorities have been recognized unanimously by all the committees and commissions established by successive governments. It reiterates the fact highlighted by Mendelsohn and Vicziany (1998) that even secular government in power are at the core communal, slaying the long-standing chronic facade of appeasement politics.

The rate of representation of Muslims in the Parliament was never proportionate to their population. If one is to do a trend analysis, the rate has only dwindled and today stands at a historic low of 71.42 per cent, with only 26 Muslim MPs in the current Lok Sabha. It should also be noted here that nearly half of the Muslim members of the Lok Sabha (11 of the 26 MPs) come from only two states – Uttar Pradesh and West Bengal (Verniers 2019). The situation speaks volumes as Muslims have tried all the three possible political alternatives available to them to negotiate their political representation, as propounded by Theodore Wright more than four decades ago in 1966. The three suggestions, based on the Western political have been: (a) formation of an independent political party that seeks to maintain an equilibrium through adequate political representation, (b) aligning forces with political parties that uphold the principles of secularism, equality and justice as enshrined in the Constitution of India and (c) working with pressure groups that would ensure the election of candidates with secular credentials believing in inclusive development.

The formation of an independent political party sounds a good strategy on the paper. However, it has been proven in the past that deploying it has not yielded the desired result. The most important reason, as a research by Omar Khalidi (1993) suggests and a trend analysis of the voting pattern of Muslims reveals, is that Muslims being a dispersed community do not vote en bloc against the popular contrarian understanding. Second, the strategy of supporting a secular political party has not paid huge dividends as has been demonstrated in this section. However, it is interesting to note that despite the partial treatment meted out, for much of the independent India, the Congress has been the chief beneficiary of the Muslim citizenry's suffrage for the lack of a credible alternative. It was also a strategy deployed essentially to keep at bay the right-wing nationalist party seeking towards the conceptualization of a Hindu nation that envisages obliteration of the minorities. In fact, data from the India National Election Study (2014) convincingly establish the fact that Muslims vote for parties that are committed to upholding the principles of secularism and inclusive development. Finally, the last strategy that was last used in the late 1960s when pressure forum, the Muslim Consultative Committee entered into an agreement to support candidates who were best poised to win an election in return of ensuring the socio-economic welfare of the community. Immediately after the election, the candidates disowned the community. The strategy has remained dormant since because clearly there is no likelihood of its success as the Indian political parties do not give their candidates the independent space to manoeuvre or engage in negotiations with their constituents.

After having exhausted all the possible alternatives available, I will discuss in the forthcoming section as to what strategy could possibly be employed to reinforce their presence in the Indian political system.

DALIT POLITICS

The evolution of Dalit politics can be neatly categorized into four phases: the Ambedkar phase, which formed the bedrock for the remainder of the three phases. These three phases will be traced through the rise and the fall of the Republican Party of India followed by the momentum gained by the Dalit Panthers and lastly the intensification of Dalit mobilization by the central Dalit figure of modern India, Mayawati, after she took over the reins of the Bahujan Samaj Party (BSP) from her political mentor, Kanshi Ram. With the help of available scholarship on the four phases of Dalit politics, I have documented how Dalits have exerted to carve an independent political space by confronting the mainstream and dominant political forces consisting mainly of the Hindu elites. These independent Dalit political parties were a result of disillusionment with the larger political forces, mainly the Congress, just as in the case of Muslims. The vibrant Dalit politics was centred on the assertion of their identity which met with a fair amount of success, unlike the Muslim politics which remained confined. However, on more than one occasion, the fledgling Dalit politics was impaired with internal discord that led to a loss of political momentum gained over the mainstream political parties. This, coupled with the fact that the assertive Dalit politics is largely considered an aberration, has ensured that the political space forged by the Dalit politics has not metamorphosed into substantive political articulation.

The scholarship on low-caste politics in general and Dalit politics in particular traces its advent in the middle decades of the 19th century, initiated by Jotirao Govindrao Phule (O'Hanlon 1985; Jaffrelot 2003). However, it was the unparalleled and erudite leadership of Dr Bhimrao Ambedkar that propelled the exigent emancipation of Dalits to the centre stage. In 1927, Dr Ambedkar provided pivot to the Dalit movement with the public burning of Manusmriti, a conservative Hindu code that enunciates the dominion of the upper-caste Hindus and the just position of the low-caste Hindus at the base of the caste hierarchy. This event laid the foundation stone for Dr Ambedkar to cultivate a Dalit identity that is independent of Hinduism. Ambedkar envisioned that mere activism will not help Dalits. Therefore, he resorted to providing them with a political arm by establishing the Independent Labour Party (ILP, representing mainly the SCs, peasants and labourers of different castes but belonging to the same class) in 1937 and its replacement, the Scheduled Caste Federation (SCF, with the objective of encompassing SCs at a pan-India level), in 1942, although with meagre success. In independent India, he joined forces with the Congress and played an instrumental role in drafting the Constitution of India in general and decreeing reservation for low-caste populace and abolishment of caste discrimination in particular. In his final days in 1956, he continued his tirade against anti-Hindu ideology by leading the mass conversion of Dalits (especially Mahars) from Hinduism to Buddhism, a religion with 'emancipation', as its main attribute. Taking cues from the failed ILP and SCF, his third attempt was to establish an organization, Republican Party of India (RPI), that focused on encompassing all dispossessed groups to ensure an equitable political claim on the state. The ideation was an extension of the structure of the ILP; this time it was only to represent the interests of SCs, STs and other backward classes (OBCs).

RPI as a formal political party came into being only in October 1957 after Ambedkar's demise. With the consolidation of the socially deprived groups, the pragmatic move was expected to bring in a tectonic shift by gaining ubiquitous political clout. However, a year into its political sojourn, the mercurial growth of RPI was constricted with the stress of factionalism (personal differences rather than ideological), no defined leadership, shift in the party's strategy with focus now on socio-economic issues, its limited appeal base (it was considered a 'Mahar only' party) and Congress's astute strategy of poaching and/ or endorsement of prominent Dalit leaders of the RPI and its factions were factors that arrested its ascendancy.

The political opportunism and submissive leadership of the RPI along with continued socio-economic and political oppression of the Dalits led to the emergence of Dalit Panthers in the slums of Mumbai in 1972. Led by the educated Dalit youth, it deliberately associated itself with the Black Panther movement in the United States, which invigorated the Afro-American freedom struggle. The movement was a departure from the RPI's reverence of commemorative politics around Ambedkar translating into static results instead of affirmative action for Dalits. It instead resurrected Ambedkar's anti-Brahmin and anti-Congress (as the party consisted of upper-caste leaders) stance and his doctrine, 'educate, agitate, organize', galvanized the movement. The movement exposed the Congress's overtures to Dalits as merely a subterfuge to keep them under the fold of Brahmin hegemony and Hindu feudalism. It also attacked RPI's apathetic attitude towards the Dalit cause and the practice of 'trade-off' politics. All these factors resulted in the movement gaining traction, especially in urban centres. When it was expected to become a potent political force at the national level for Dalits, it was plagued with personality clashes that led to internal splits. Thus, endemic nationalism and a one-dimensional sectarianism brought an abrupt end to an otherwise assuring movement.

After the Dalit Panther movement fizzled out, there was a political void in the Dalit leadership that was filled by Kanshi Ram in 1984, by establishing the BSP. As the name of the party suggests, it was never meant to be an exclusive Dalit party, but a conflation of the SCs, STs and OBCs. However, its adeptness to capture the subaltern's support remained largely restricted to the Dalits. When Kanshi Ram and her protégé, Mayawati, were unsuccessful in their bid to bring the 'subaltern into the cauldron', the BSP achieved Ambedkar's objective of tilting the scales in its favour by gaining political power through conditional alliances with different parties at different stages with which it did not even share a common ideological ground. The justification for such a political compromise was that Kanshi Ram, as a follower of Ambedkar, was merely adopting his indisputable solution of gaining political power to bring into effect fundamental changes for Dalits. As a matter of fact, Kanshi Ram meliorated Ambedkar's view with his own—political power in the *end*, even if the *means* employed to attain it compromises the core ideology.

Notwithstanding the unconventional politics practised, the party was successful in creating and to some extent sustaining a national presence.

It instilled a robust Dalit identity and consciousness among the Dalits. Further, unlike the previous Dalit parties, the unseemly phenomenon of poaching or absorbing of Dalit leaders (with a huge following and a solid social base) by dominant political parties was absent. An aura of empowerment for Dalits was created around Mayawati when a Dalit woman spent four separate terms as the chief minister of Uttar Pradesh bringing in radical changes that politically empowered Dalits. It would not be wrong to conclude with Jagannathan's words that, 'in Mayawati, the Dalits finally discovered their true power of agency after Ambedkar—their right to represent themselves and safeguard their interests' (Jagannathan 2012).

HISTORY OF THE DALIT–MUSLIM ALLIANCE

The Dalit and Muslim coalition is not a new trend in the Indian politics. In the year 1980, Indian gangster and smuggler Haji Mastan and Dalit leader Jogendra Kawade tried bringing Muslims and Dalit on one platform with the formation of the Dalit–Muslim Suraksha Mahasangh to protect the constitutional rights of Muslims and Dalits through adequate political representation. However, their attempts at forging such an alliance did not work out. In the later years and even during the present times, the idea of a Dalit–Muslim coalition always existed in the margin of mainstream politics. However, it was never able to secure a political mandate which in turn would bring about a positive change in the socio-economic conditions of both the Muslims and Dalits. Further, 'any attempts to form the same have been thwarted time and again by both communal and secular outfits'. Maulana Nasir Maudani from Kerala, who was trying to forge a Muslim–Dalit unity in the nineties, was put behind bars for years on flimsy charges of terrorism. Similarly, Asaduddin Owaisi, who is known for articulating the constitutional rights of the community and their daily concerns, has been asked time and again why he only talks about Muslims. He is often reduced to a religious fanatic and a fundamentalist by the secular outfits. Journalists like Barkha Dutt have written columns on how dangerous the rise of Owaisi is for secular India (Ashraf 2016).

The Bahujan Mukti Party (BMP), a political party formulated in 2012 by the Backward and Minority Communities Employees

Federation, is up against the Brahminical system as it defies the age-old notion that Aryans are indigenous Indians. They propagate that SCs, STs, OBCs, nomadic tribes, denotified nomadic tribes and religious minorities are the native Indian descendants and call themselves *Mulniwasi*, meaning original Indians.

The party contested 419 seats in the Lok Sabha elections of 2014, Muslim candidates representing 100 of them—a first in the Indian political system. Unable to secure a single seat, the party succeeded in uniting the Dalits and Muslims in a common vision of political representation.

In the same year, a retired police officer, Shamsher Pathan, launched the Avami Vikas Party with Baban Kamble, a Dalit activist and editor of *Samrat*, a leading Dalit newspaper. Their main objective was to strengthen the Dalit–Muslim unity so that both the oppressed communities could better fight for their rights. The party contested the state and general elections but is yet to taste any success (Ali 2013).

In spite of the numerous attempts at forging an alliance, it is difficult to comprehend as to why the coalition has not yet turned into an impactful partnership (Devji 2016). However, the much-touted Dalit–Muslim association seems to be paying dividends with the emergence of All-India Majlis-e-Ittehadul Muslimeen (AIMIM) in Maharashtra. The interest in the coalition rekindled again when AIMIM gave an impressive performance in the state assembly elections in October 2014 in Maharashtra. A year later, it went on to emulate the success in the Aurangabad Municipal elections and won 26 seats of the 54 seats contested. The winners included four Dalits and, as a matter of fact, several of its Dalit candidates lost by thin margins. The scenario was similar in the 2014 state elections of Maharashtra. AIMIM's first tremor was felt in 2012 when 12 of its candidates won in elections to the Nanded Municipal Corporation. Having witnessed the results of this coalition with Dalits, BSP supremo Mayawati urged the Muslims of Uttar Pradesh to support the BSP in the state elections in 2017 (Ashraf 2016).

To surmise, Muslims never had an independent leadership. As a result, their leadership has largely rested with the Congress, the Left and other regional parties. Time and again, these hegemonic political forces have represented Muslims as a religious category rather than a sociological group, where the matters of Islam take precedence over everything else (Ashraf 2016).

In the case of Dalits, their politics has constantly revolved around the critique of Hindu religion and the elite dominant political parties, such as the Congress and the BJP, conversion to an emancipatory religion of Buddhism. The Dalit politics of identity and a caste consciousness is deeply ingrained at the grassroots level. Despite this success, it never managed to realize its full potential because of the challenge of co-option by the political parties and internal rivalries.

However, there is a critical difference between Dalits and Muslims. Dalits have been armed with constitutional provisions such as reservation and the Scheduled Castes and Scheduled Tribes Prevention of Atrocity Act, a vibrant Dalit leadership and an Ambedkarite pride (that is not reticent in the face of caste-based oppression) have ensured that they assert for their socio-economic and political rights. This basic difference is further elucidated in the following section.

DALITS' AND MUSLIMS' DIFFERENT PRIORITIES
Muslims' Wrong Priorities

Since the election of the Bharatiya Janata Party to power in 2014, Muslims have constantly found themselves at the receiving end of majority politics and communal violence arising out of it. Campaigns such as love jihad, *Ghar Wapsi* and cow vigilantism are specifically targeted at the Muslims and Dalits to terrorize and suppress them. Minorities residing in states with low socio-economic status particularly fall prey to mechanisms of hate-crimes for lack of sound redressal machinery and position of influence in the country. The cruel lynching of Mohammed Akhlaq in 2015 on the mere suspicion of beef-eating stands evidence to the theory of Senechal (1996) that violence is not targeted at the real source of deviant behaviour but vulnerable targets. Such violence is an act of scapegoating, directing and venting frustrations on innocent victims or alleged offenders to send a message to the community as a whole (Senechal 1996).

In 2016, eight alleged Students Islamic Movement of India (SIMI) terrorists were gunned down by the Madhya Pradesh state police in an encounter. When the liberal section of the society questioned the authenticity of the encounter and termed it extra-judicial killings, the Muslim leadership, All-India Muslim Personal Law Board (AIMPLB), did not engage in condemning the atrocity. Instead, the mass mobilization was focused on the issue of abolition of instant triple *talaq* and the Uniform Civil Code bogey raised by the union government. This shows that the Muslim community has prioritized matters of religion over relevant problems of justice and equality. Hence, political parties have also tried to appease Muslims by granting religious privileges rather than social and political rights. A case in point is the Hajj subsidy being given to the Muslims.

Rationally speaking, such virulent incidents had the potency of stirring up widespread Muslim outrage and condemnation as it explicitly attacked the basic fundamental rights of the Indian Muslims. When an insidious attempt of undermining constitutional rights of a minority community becomes a routine and which does not evoke a requisite resistance, then there are bound to be more Akhlaqs, more youths languishing in prisons for a decade or so before a fair trial, educational institutions refusing admissions, cosmopolitan societies refusing a home based on your religion.

In contrast, whenever there has been an issue of infringement or interference into Muslim Personal Laws with the present discourse or revered Muslim personalities were denigrated, the Muslim community has mobilized in order to protest and condemn the same. In the present context, AIMPLB gearing up to mobilize the Muslims to safeguard the Islamic jurisprudence of the contentious 'triple talaq (divorce)' was experienced during the Shah Bano case and banning of the controversial Taslima Nasreen's and Salman Rushdie's books. As a matter of fact, different regional Muslim organizations at different times have gone into an overdrive and viscerally declared financial rewards to anyone who would assassinate them. In fact, the concept of religiosity and piety is so deeply entrenched that sometimes it even manifested violence. This was evident when a protest by Muslim community in Malda in 2016 turned violent over Akhil Bharatiya Hindu Mahasabha's leader Kamlesh Tiwari's spiteful observance of Prophet Mohammad as homosexual. The 'peaceful protest turning into a violent event' was not a solitary occurrence. In 2012, a Sunni Muslim seminary mobilized Muslims to protest against the ethnic cleansing of Rohingya Muslims in Myanmar which turned violent. This exhibition of violence can be explained as flash occurrences that neither help the Muslims achieve the objective of an egalitarian society nor establish an efficacious Muslim stand. It establishes to the state and the wider civil society a sense of Muslim identity and consciousness that is rooted in the strengthening of religiosity of the Muslims instead of strengthening of socio-political and economic empowerment of the Muslims. Also, such solitary occurrences of violence do more damage to the already negative image of Muslims by slotting them as perpetual offenders and delinquents.

It has been observed that Muslim seminaries like Islamic Research Foundation and Darul Uloom Deoband spend a large proportion of their budget on the growth of religion, inculcating piousness through the religious congregation, religious real estate and religious personalities. They do so because it somehow fulfils their religious obligations and they get a sense of community, a sense of collective security and wellbeing. But what is also important to consider is how they have acted as a community in a critical situation. The Muslim community and the leadership have recurrently failed to render solidarity in times of crisis. Political security, protection against unlawful hate crimes, economic stability and social uplift should be the projects collectively undertaken by the leadership and the masses. My observation here is that Muslims are one generation behind all other major religions and castes.

Dalit's Priorities Spot On

In July 2016, when Dalits were physically abused by the members of cow protection outfits in Gujarat over skinning dead cows, despite knowing that skinning cattle carcasses is their traditional occupation, the Dalits put up a united stand and reacted strongly. They stopped attending the bovine carrion and strategized to leave truckload of carcasses in the municipal offices for the elite Hindus to handle. The incident eventually graduated to a mass protest where thousands of Dalits were out on the streets of Gujarat in various towns, villages and cities protesting the atrocities against Dalits and specifically the

Una incident. Transport services were badly affected in the Saurashtra region of Gujarat, fearing vandalization of buses. Schools and colleges remained shut in Saurashtra. After the anti-reservation movement in the mid–1980s, this was perhaps the first time when Gujarat witnessed a Dalit mobilization of such a magnitude. Also, Dalit mobilization has always been a constant phenomenon in independent India, though it could not become a national movement translating into positive development of its constituents. It also dispelled the notion of meticulously built Hindutva allegory, which has successfully portrayed Dalits as the foot soldiers of Hindu society, and not as the persecuted lot stuck at the nethermost rung of the inhuman social order perpetuated over centuries. Also, unlike the Muslim community, Dalits have always had stalwarts in Dr B. R. Ambedkar, Kanshi Ram and Mayawati, who participated in the Indian political system by formulating their own independent political agency and ideology in order to fight against the injustices being met out to them.

THE WAY FORWARD

The Dalit leadership wields a limited influence. But such is the impact of influence that it yields results in favour of the Dalits. The illustration here is that whenever physical violence and atrocities are unleashed on Dalits—as happened in Una—they mobilize and present a solid united front, which is indicative of their assertion and reaction to injustice. This is the critical difference between Dalits and Muslims. However, what was unique about the Una uprising was the coming together of the Dalits and Muslims. That the Dalit–Muslim mobilization across Gujarat was largely spontaneous without any political party mobilizing the masses could be inferred as a statement of intent to the ruling dispensation. Such was the impact of the slogans 'Dalit–Muslim Bhai Bhai' and 'Jai Bhim, Jai MIM' that it forced the ruling dispensation to strategically condemn only the atrocities of *gau rakshaks* or cow vigilantes against the Dalits. There was deliberately no mention of the atrocities committed against Muslims by the *gau rakshaks* so that the Dalits do not move away from the umbrella of Hinduism (Chaturvedi 2016). The BJP is strongly attempting at wooing Dalit leaders by inducting Ram Vilas Paswan, the convenor of Lok Janshakti Party in Bihar, first and Ramdas Athawle, the President of Republic Party of

India, later in the union cabinet. When assembly elections took place in Uttar Pradesh in the first quarter of 2017, even Congress attempted to harness Dr B. R. Ambedkar's ideology to amass Dalit votes.

We can assume that there is a severe lack of a national Muslim and Dalit leadership. The existing religious Muslim leadership remains confined to protecting Islamic jurisprudence. The phenomenal rise of AIMIM in states with a high population of Muslims has rekindled a hope. This, along with the rise of regional parties such as the Peace Party of India in Uttar Pradesh, the All-India United Democratic Front in Assam, Manithaneya Makkal Katchi in Tamil Nadu, has made crucial inroads. This does not add up to great political clout but goes to show that there is a deep realization among the Muslim community that most political parties have taken them for granted and merely practised symbolic politics.

The existing political set-up is itself steeped in corruption and fratricidal wars. As a result, what we have is the classic case of 'Mexican standoff', where the state prioritizes its electoral interests by neutralizing emerging voices and not focusing on a substantial social and economic engagement of the dispossessed groups. Similarly, the disadvantaged group of Muslims and Dalits are unable to effect an egalitarian society that they strive for while acting as an independent entity. Thus, to expect that this government will change course, correct its errors and bring in an equitable development would be a folly. A bigger folly would be to expect a replacement government will be able to correct the situation of the oppressed communities.

If both the Muslims and the Dalits are to surmount their adversity, a coalition of caste-based and religion-based parties at both the centre and states is the way ahead for them. It is highly unlikely that both the communities will ever be able to bargain for a higher representation in the mainstream political parties. Therefore, the leadership will have to come from within both the communities. Just the way it happened in Una.

REFERENCES

Ali, M. 2013. 'Post-Sachar Reservation Politics'. *Economic & Political Weekly* 48 (39): 13–15.

Ashraf, A. 2016. 'For Dalit–Muslim Unity, Mayawati Must Focus on Caste, Not Religion'. Scroll.in, 18 October. Available at: https://scroll.in/article/819260/for-dalit-muslim-unity-mayawati-must-focus-on-caste-not-religion (accessed on 6 August 2019).

Centre for the Study of Developing Societies. 2015. *India National Election Study 2014.* New Delhi: CSDS.

Chaturvedi, S. 2016. 'Modi on Gau Rakshaks: How to Woo Dalits and Alienate Muslims'. Daily O, 11 August. Available at: https://www.dailyo.in/politics/narendra-modi-gau-rakshaks-dalits-gujarat-up-cow-politics/story/1/12308.html (accessed on 6 August 2019).

Department of Higher Education, Ministry of Human Resource Development. 2016. 'All India Survey on Higher Education (2014–15)'. Available at: http://aishe.nic.in/aishe/viewDocument.action?documentId=206 (accessed on 17 September 2019).

Devji, F. 2016. 'Is a Dalit–Muslim Alliance Possible?' *The Hindu*, 31 August.

Engineer, A. A. 1983. 'Socio-economic Basis of Communalism'. *Mainstream* 21 (45): 15–18.

Fazal, T. 2013. 'Millenium Development Goals and Muslims of India'. Oxfam India Working Paper Series OIWPS – XIII. New Delhi: Oxfam India.

Gouda, S., and T. V. Sekher. 2014. 'Factors Leading to School Dropouts in India: An Analysis of National Family Health Survey-3 Data'. *IOSR Journal of Research and Method in Education* 4 (6): 75–83.

Government of India. 2011. *Census of India.* New Delhi: Registrar General and Census Commissioner of India, Ministry of Home Affairs.

Hassan, M. 1988. 'Indian Muslims since Independence: In Search of Integration and Identity'. *Third World Quarterly* 10 (2): 818–842.

Human Rights Watch. 2018. *World Report 2018 Events of 2017.* Available at: https://www.hrw.org/sites/default/files/world_report_download/201801world_report_web.pdf (accessed on 17 September 2019).

Jaffrelot, C., ed. 2003. 'The Renewal of Dalit Politics: The BSP Party of the Bahujans'. In *India's Silent Revolution: The Rise of the Lower Castes in North India*, 387–409. London: Hurst & Co.

Jagannathan, R. 2012. 'Why Indian Muslim Politics Is about to Change Forever'. *Firstpost*, 19 April.

Khalidi, O. 1993. 'Muslims in Indian Political Process: Group Goals and Alternative Strategies'. *Economic & Political Weekly* 28 (1–2): 43–54.

Kumar, Sudesh, and Mudasir Ahmad Lone. 2013. 'Coalition Politics in India: Conceptual Analysis, Emergence, Course of Action and Aftermath for Society'. *ACME International Journal of Multidisciplinary Research* 1 (3): 55–63.

Mendelsohn, O., and M. Vicziany. 1998. *The Untouchables: Subordination, Poverty and the State in Modern India*, 289. New York, NY: Cambridge University Press.

National Crime Records Bureau. 2011. *Prison Statistics India 2011.* New Delhi: National Crime Records Bureau, Government of India.

National Human Rights Commission Report. 2011. *Annual report submitted to the Central Government of India, 2010–2011.*

National Sample Survey Organization, Government of India. 2011. *Key Indicators of Employment and Unemployment in India, 2009–10*. Ministry of Statistics and Programme Implementation Report KI (66/10). Available at: http://mospi. nic.in/sites/default/files/publication_reports/Key_Indicators_Emp_%26_ Unemp_66th_round.pdf (accessed on 18 September 2019).

Noorani, A. G. 2002. 'The Partition of India'. *Frontline* 18 (26).

O'Hanlon, R. 1985. *Caste, Conflict and Ideology: Mahatma Jotirao Phule and Low Caste Protest in Nineteenth-Century Western India*. Cambridge: Cambridge University Press.

Pandey, G. 2006. 'Marked and Unmarked Citizens'. In *Routine Violence: Nations, Fragments, Histories*, 132. Stanford, NJ: Stanford University Press.

Panagariya, A., and V. More. 2013. 'Poverty by Social, Religious and Economic Groups in India and its Largest States, 1993–94 to 2011–12'. Working Paper No. 2013–02, School of International and Public Affairs (SIPA) and Institute for Social and Economic Research and Policy (ISERP), Columbia University, New York.

Planning Commission. 2011. 'India Human Development Report 2011: Towards Social Inclusion'. Institute of Applied Manpower Research. Government of India. Oxford: Oxford Unievrsity Press.

Planning Commission of India. 2011. *Annual Report Submitted to the Government of India*, New Delhi.

Puri, B. 1993. 'Indian Muslims since Partition'. *Economic & Political Weekly* 28 (40): 2141–2149.

Rai, V. N. 2008. *Combating Conflict: Perception of Police Neutrality during Hindu–Muslim Riots in India*. New Delhi: Manas Publications.

Sachar Committee Report. 2006. 'Social, Economic and Educational Status of the Muslim Community of India'. Prime Minister's High-Level Committee Cabinet Secretariat Government of India, New Delhi.

Senechal, R. 1996. 'Collective Violence as Social Control'. *Sociological Forum* 11 (1): 97–128.

Suri, K. C. 2005. *Parties under Pressure: Political Parties in India since Independence*. Project on State of Democracy in South Asia. New Delhi: Lokniti. Programme on Comparative Democracy. Centre for the Study of Developing Societies.

Theodore, P. W. 1966. 'The Muslim League in South India since Independence: A Study in Minority Group Political Strategies'. *American Political Science Review* 60: 579–599.

Verniers, G. 2019. 'Verdict 2019 in charts and maps: Nearly half of India's Muslim MPs come from only two states'. Scroll.in, 2 June. Available at: https://scroll. in/article/925440/verdict-2019-in-charts-and-maps-nearly-half-of-indias-muslim-mps-come-from-only-two-states (accessed on 17 September 2019).

Wirth, L. 1945. 'The Problem of Minority Groups'. In *The Science of Man in the World Crisis*, edited by R. Linton, 347–372. New York, NY: Columbia University Press.

Chapter 8

The Forgotten of the Conflict in Indian Jammu and Kashmir

On the Exile of the Pandit Minority

Nathalene Reynolds

Was it a consequence of Pakistan's propaganda that never ceased to emphasize that most of the population of the former princely state of Jammu and Kashmir was Muslim? Or was it the expression of dominant Muslim and Hindu collective mentalities that, despite an apparent attachment to communal harmony, were, nonetheless, marked by antagonistic political and socio-religious values? At the start of 1990, the Pandit community of the Kashmir Valley felt itself forced into a hasty exile. A specifically Muslim nationalism was asserted in Kashmir, which had hegemonic ambitions, since it sought to express itself in the name of the whole of Jammu and Kashmir.

Had the Valley—influenced by the armed struggle initiated by the Jammu and Kashmir Liberation Front—already given up on secularism? Or was it, at least at that time, moving away from the principle, as it was already the backdrop for the expression of a phenomenon that was impacting on many political movements in the rest of India, that of 'secular sectarianism' (Gudavarthy 2014)?

The chapter begins by re-examining the disputed circumstances which gave rise to a movement in the Kashmir Valley that rejected India's presence. It will then focus on the exodus of the Pandit community and the fate of those from the group that fell victim to militancy. Few have addressed the important question as to the 'restoration' to the exiled of their status as 'full citizens' in Jammu and Kashmir of which they have been de facto deprived. The chapter will also provide an opportunity to explore the friction that has existed between the Kashmiri Pandit and Muslim communities since, at the very least, the Partition. In view of the movement that has arisen following the death of the Hizbul Mujahideen leader Burhan Wani, and the challenging relations between India and Pakistan, the moment may not lend itself to the task of genuine dialogue between Kashmiri Pandits and Muslims.

In this chapter, it should be emphasized that my aim is not to deny the long and difficult struggle that Kashmiri Muslims continue to lead. As a researcher, it is not our task to advocate either for them or for the Pandit community. Having written widely on that struggle, I will examine the interpretation of the conflict made by a Pandit minority community that has been somehow neglected by both their fellow Kashmiris and the political powers in New Delhi. Many readers may react negatively towards the arguments I make, given that the Kashmiri Pandits are close to the only political grouping that has offered them support, namely, the Hindu nationalists, whose position on other issues has provoked sharp criticism within India and elsewhere. I will simply try to look at an aspect of the Kashmir conflict that has been given little attention by foreign researchers. I also encourage readers to consult my other writings on the Kashmir conflict, which look, amongst other things, at the severe, if not to say unacceptable, response of India.

INTRODUCTION •
The Kashmir Valley at the Crossroads?

Foreign researchers in the subcontinent who have focused on events in the Kashmir Valley since the 1980s have often seemed to have a soft spot for the struggle for what the Muslim-majority population has termed 'azaadi'. The meaning of this Urdu word remains open to interpretation, since it can mean both 'independence' and 'freedom'. There was a little naivety in the use of 'azaadi' by Kashmiri Muslims as a kind of magic wand, a wave of which was to rid the area of its various political and socio-economic ills, and this may be what draws the sympathy of those not from the subcontinent. Or is it rather the endurance shown by the Muslim population that is a cause for admiration, the persistence in fighting an unequal battle against India's not inconsiderable forces when pragmatic 'submission' would seem the most rational course of action?

In any case, Kashmiri Muslims, seeking to assert their identity within a federation that, of course, included various other religious minorities, struggled to agree as to the definition of 'azaadi'. Did inhabitants of the Valley (members of the majority community) look to become masters of their destiny, reckoning on the economic assets that their 'nation' could exploit? Aware that the combatants were ill-prepared for any fight, the Pakistani 'friend' grasped this unexpected opportunity and declared that the whole of the Indian state of Jammu and Kashmir had never ceased—since events at the end of 1947—to wish to be joined with the 'country of the pure' (*Pak-i-stan*).

The Indian Union, meanwhile, accused the Islamic Republic of Pakistan of conducting a 'proxy war' on its territory, engaging in a 'state terrorism' that India struggled in vain to have condemned internationally. Pakistan retorted by denouncing human rights violations in Jammu and Kashmir; it declared that it merely gave its diplomatic and moral support to the Kashmiri 'cause'. As for the Kashmiri separatist leaders, right from the beginnings of the armed movement, they found themselves having to perform a tricky balancing act: Their credibility and therefore political survival depended on their opposition to an India that rejected any concessions. In addition, they owed loyalty to Pakistan and the political and military line[1] defined by its powerful intelligence service, the Inter-Services Intelligence (ISI), which had no

---

[1] In the subcontinent, polarizing alternatives such as 'militancy' and 'terrorism' tend to be used to refer to armed movements.

scruples about dishing out 'punishment' (death[2]) for any expression of rapprochement with India. Ironically, and without much moral agonizing, they came to request police protection from the state of Jammu and Kashmir, which granted this. The same state was already choosing to imprison or place them under house arrest from time to time, on occasion for long periods, a practice which continues to this day. India, meanwhile, carried on offering these strange opponents medical treatment in the renowned hospitals of its capital. However, there is no longer unconditional respect for these leaders, for their mode of life or for the decisions they take or give their backing to. One may also wonder whether this factor (increasing widespread elsewhere in the world) will not lead Muslims, Hindus and Sikhs in the Kashmir Valley to take a more impartial view (or at least more 'humane' one, dropping partisan considerations) of the events that have recently marked their history.

---

[2] Abdul Ghani Lone's assassination on 21 May 2002, the anniversary of another sad death, that of Mirwaiz Mohammed Farooq in 1990, may have been an example of this. It was widely assumed that the Mirwaiz had been one of the first at that period to envisage negotiations with India and that this may have triggered his murder. The killing of Lone was a message to moderates who might be tempted to compromise with the Centre, and probably constituted a response to the secret discussions that one faction of the All-Parties Hurriyat Conference (APHC) was having or planned to have with the National Conference that was back in power in Srinagar.

It should also be emphasized here that Mirwaiz Omar Farooq recently dared a remark that would hitherto have been unimaginable in the Valley. He was reacting to a comment made by a leader of the hard-line wing of the APHC, Syed Ali Shah Geelani, who had said that a separatist group was trying to conduct secret negotiations with emissaries of Narendra Modi. Farooq asked 'who does he want to die this time?' (Fayyaz 2004); he thus tacitly accused Geelani for the murder of his father in 1990 and of promoting an atmosphere conducive, in the words of one journalist, Ahmed Ali Fayyaz, 'to political assassinations in Kashmir'.

The All-Parties Hurriyat Conference was founded on 9 March 1993. This umbrella group that brought together the great majority of Kashmiri separatist groups split into two on 7 September 2003, the first moderate and the other more radical.

Outline of This Chapter

It seems useful to begin with a brief look at a document dating back to 1945 of the government of Maharaja Hari Singh. The text enables us to see the geographical composition of the princely state of Jammu and Kashmir and its various communities. We will then touch upon the status of Muslims in the Valley.

Thereafter, we will examine the origins of what the majority of observers call the insurrection, militancy or the rebellion, which broke out in the late 1980s.[3] For once, we will approach this period from the perspective of the Pandits who fell victim to militancy.[4] The Valley, it is clear, had become the scene of public assertions of 'incompatible identities' (Widmalm 1997: 1005). Paradoxically, its Muslim component, at least initially, did not reject its support for a secularism that several currents of Kashmiri political thought already by the start of the 1990s no longer hesitated to challenge; doubtlessly they detected an Indian value that was by then unacceptable to them. The Valley was certainly unhappy at the absence of free and fair elections, decrying the tacit alliance between the legal Kashmiri political class and successive Union governments following the imprisonment of Sheikh Mohammed Abdullah in August 1953. Indeed, much of the country saw the expression of various forms of 'secular sectarianism' (Gudavarthy 2014). Muslim-majority Kashmir moved towards asserting a Muslim nationalism with hegemonic ambitions, a phenomenon to which we will return later. As for the Pandit community in the Valley, its fear was increasing in leaps and bounds, as *lihaaz* (the principle of peaceful coexistence; in practice, the adoption of a low profile by Pandits) seemed more and more threatened (Pandita 2013: 502).

The armed struggle started at the end of the 1980s breathed new life into different tellings of old episodes of the princely state's history. The somewhat modified versions of more recent events that Kashmiri Muslims tend to propagate from year to year seek, if not to ignore,

---

[3] This article will look only at Kashmir itself.

[4] Readers unhappy with this approach may look at this author's other published works, that examine in detail the suffering of Kashmiri Muslims as a result of the conflict.

then at least to excuse some of the most regrettable acts that tarnish the image of the movement. This is especially the case with regard to the exodus of the Pandits at the start of the 1990s. Kashmiris of the Muslim faith continue, for the most part, to refuse to acknowledge the immense injustice that befell their Pandit fellow citizens.

We seek here to provide a space in which to look at how the Pandit community sees the conflict. As mentioned in the abstract, recording their views implies neither support nor opposition on the part of the author. One must note that the position of the Kashmiri Pandits as a whole is not unmarked by a mixture of anger and frustration: The community judged itself forced to abandon its social position and property, and above all, like the Kashmiri Muslim community, feels an immense attachment to the land in which it was born and raised. One may also detect in the extracts we record in this work the impact on the analyses made by Kashmiri Pandits, of geopolitics and a kind of Islamophobia that has spread around much of the world in the aftermath of the attacks of 11 September 2001 and the start of the 'war on terror'.

JAMMU AND KASHMIR, A 'SOVEREIGN AND INDEPENDENT' PRINCELY STATE

Sheikh Ashiq Ahmad, President of the Kashmir Chamber of Commerce and Industry of Srinagar, remarked during a conversation in September 2015 that the institution had been founded in 1935, at a time when Jammu and Kashmir had been a 'sovereign and independent state'. He was implicitly paying homage to the man who ruled what was at that time a princely state, Maharaja Hari Singh. He was oblivious to the antagonism that opposed the small Dogra minority to the rest of the Hindu community, and above all to the majority of his subjects in the principality, of the Muslim faith.[5] According to Sheikh Ahmed,

---

[5] It should be recalled here that the princely state, which spread across 220,000 square kilometres and included peaks of more than 6,000 metres above sea level, was made up of five parts—Jammu, Kashmir, Baltistan, Ladakh and Gilgit. In the first of these, Muslims were estimated on the eve of independence as making up 53 per cent of the population. The districts of Poonch, with the exception of the town of Poonch itself, and Mirpur were almost entirely Muslim. The Valley was

the territory also enjoyed a unity that Indian Jammu and Kashmir, but also Pakistani Azad Jammu and Kashmir and Gilgit–Baltistan, have singularly failed to instill.[6]

A Princely State with Varied Provinces

Was Ashiq Ahmad not simply restating one of the new theories that have recently appeared in Jammu and Kashmir?[7] Ironically, this is approved by many of the Pandits who were forced into exile at the start of the 1990s. They applaud the recognition, implicit in their eyes, of the enlightened role played by the Dogra dynasty that long stood accused of exercising an anti-Muslim despotic rule linked to Hinduism. They emphasize that the Maharaja tended to appoint members from his own community (the Dogras) to public office, even if they were less well-qualified than the Pandits. It is the case that the Dogra dynasty ruled over a rather artificial grouping of territories; doubtless the support of its own community was indispensable.

Documents from the *India Office Records and Private Papers* collections held in the British Library in London bear witness to the

---

93 per cent Muslim. In the northern part of the state, Gilgit and Baltistan, the population was almost exclusively Muslim, while Ladakh was populated with Buddhists and Shia Muslims, the district of Kargil being home to most of the latter.

[6] The part of Kashmir administered by India, which Pakistan called Indian-Occupied Kashmir, covered two-thirds of Hari Singh's state (Jammu, the Kashmir Valley and Ladakh). Article 370 of the Indian Constitution guaranteed the autonomy of what would become the state of Jammu and Kashmir. The part administered by Pakistan (termed Pakistan-Occupied Kashmir by India) was, as early as 1949, split into two: Azad Jammu and Kashmir and the Northern Areas, which comprised Gilgit and Baltistan (the region was officially renamed Gilgit-Baltistan as of August 2009). Lastly, since the brief Sino–Indian border war of October 1962, the region of Aksai Chin, with an area of 37,244 square kilometres, uninhabited since at an altitude of 4,300 metres, has been controlled by China.

[7] The inside pages of daily newspapers in Jammu and Kashmir, as elsewhere in India, are dedicated to debate, and play a significant role in spreading alternative interpretations of history. Numerous readers take up the ideas presented therein enthusiastically, generally without quoting their source, and seek to give the impression that they are themselves the originator of these novel theses.

lengths to which the maharajas of Jammu and Kashmir went to promote the unity of a principality comprising diverse regions,[8] the outcome of hazard, conquest and alliances.[9] Moreover, the Maharaja's government published White Papers that underlined the quality of its administration, in terms of both education and health care. One of these documents, dating from 1945, made clear the intention to demonstrate—on the eve of the departure of the British colonials—that Jammu and Kashmir was more than capable of looking after itself as an independent unit. The text contrasted the princely state to others under the British Raj:

> The total area of Jammu and Kashmir State is 84,471 square miles... is the largest State in India. It is larger than Hyderabad, about as large as Mysore, Bikaner, Gwalior and Baroda put together, and two-third the size of the whole of the Bombay Presidency. (IOR/V/27/272/40, 1945: 1)

---

[8] By way of example, one may cite the following document: IOR/V/10/1264 Indian States (1914).

[9] It is worth mentioning an interesting paradox: Supporters of a unified Jammu and Kashmir do not hold back in castigating the British colonial power (in fact, at the time, the East India Company) for having, under the terms of the Treaty of Amritsar of 16 March 1846, sold the Kashmir Valley for the sum of 750,000 pounds sterling. This step was in fact what brought about the princely state of Jammu and Kashmir.

By way of illustration that readings of history vary from one side to the other, the princely state recalled that:

> Jammu, Kashmir, Poonch, Ladakh, Baltistan and Gilgit had all along been under numerous dynastic rules before the advent of the Dogras. The Jammu and Kashmir State as it exists today is, therefore, the creation of Maharaja Gulab Singh. Mr. K.M. Pannikar says in his book: Gulab Singh: Founder of Kashmir (London: Martin Hopkinson, 1930: "In a century barren of historical achievement in India, Gulab Singh stands out as a solitary figure of political eminence .... He is the only ruler in India's long history who could be said to have extended the geographical boundaries of India .... No previous Indian ruler, not even Samadra Gupta or Akbar, had ever dreamt of invading Tibet: and though Zorawar, who ventured too far, paid the penalty for his adventure, the Maharaja's forces routed the Tibetan army and extended the border of India to the other side of the Himalayas". (IOR/V/27/272/40, 1945: 21)

The White Paper stressed the geostrategic position of Jammu and Kashmir:

> On the north it is bounded by Chinese and Russia Turkistan, on the east by Chinese Tibet, on the south by the Punjab and on the west by the North-Western Frontier Province. The territories of three powers, viz., Britain, China and Russia, and of the independent kingdom of Afghanistan meet on the northern borders of the state.
>
> Physical features—In addition to a small strip of land along the borders of Jammu, which is a continuation of the great plain of the Punjab and a bleak tract adjoining the Karakorum Mountains, the territories of His Highness the Maharaja Bahadur of Jammu and Kashmir include valleys formed by the Chenab and the Jhelum and the middle reaches of the Indus. (IOR/V/27/272/40, 1945: 1)

The paper also underlined the rivers that watered the princely state, especially the Ravi, the Chenab and the Jhelum, that guaranteed prosperity, notably through agricultural produce. It described in detail the various regions of which the principality was composed, concluding by restating its geographical diversity and its exceptional strategic location.[10]

---

[10] For example, part of this long document read: 'Geographical divisions–The generally accepted geographical divisions of the territories are as follows:

1. The sub-montane and semi-mountainous Tract consisting of the plain contiguous to the Punjab and broken kandi country skirting the Himalaya ranges. The rivers Ravi, Chenab and Jhelum and several perennial streams flow through the southern plain area, which borders upon several Punjab districts. Rice, wheat, maize and other crops are grown in this area. ....
2. The Outer Hills, consisting of the comparatively low hills to the south of the mountain ranges. This division comprises the whole area covered by the ranges of low hills to the south of the Pir Panjal mountains, which divide the two provinces of Jammu and Kashmir, one from the other. The altitude of the greater part of this belt varies from 2,000 to 4,000 feet, though the hills in Bhadarwah reach heights of over 5,000 feet. ... The higher elevations are covered with pine and deodar forests. The cultivation is greatly helped by the proximity of the Pir Panjal mountains, whose tremendous altitude causes the

Princely Rule That Was Despotic or Enlightened?

There remains the question of the Maharaja's administration. The Congress party was keen to depict—without nuance—the maharajas, rajas and nizams reigning over the 565 princely states that were part of British India as despots with no concern for the well-being of the populations over which they ruled. It is true that much of the subcontinent was in thrall to what was often termed feudalism. Pro-independence Congress leaders, for their part, had one immediate concern: they wanted to ensure rapid 're-integration' (the word then in use) of these territories spread across what would become independent India.

---

moisture-bearing winds to deposit most of their aqueous vapours in this part of the country. Rice and wheat are grown in some parts, while maize is the staple food.

3. The Jhelum Valley, consisting of the valleys that drain into the Jhelum and the Kishanganga rivers. The mountains enclosing this tract have an average altitude of 12,000 feet. Many of the peaks exceed 14,000 feet,.... The Jhelum Valley situated at over 5,000 feet above the sea level, and the beautiful lateral valleys of the Sindh and the Liddar (the three together forming the Kashmir Valley) and the hilly tract of Muzaffarabad are included in the division. The Kashmir valley is fertile and yields abundant harvests of rice. Fruits of various kinds are produced. Wheat and maize are grown. In Muzaffarabad district, agriculture is precarious and the cultivated area is small.

4. The Tibetan and Semi-Tibetan Tract, consisting of the middle reaches of the Indus. The river has its source in Lake Manasarovar in Tibet and traverses the whole of the division running from south-east up to the bend round Nanga Parbat, where it assumes a south-westerly course. The mountains in the north stretch up to the Pamirs and reach great heights; one of the peaks, Mt. Godwin Austin, 28,250 feet above the sea level, is the second highest peak in the world. ... The cultivable area in the Ladakh district is very small and the rainfall deficient, and agriculture is carried on by artificial irrigation. Grim (a kind of wheat) is the chief crop and is grown even at a height of 15,000 feet. The small tract of Gilgit enjoys good climate and cultivation and produces wheat and other crops and fruits....

The first two of these divisions form the province of Jammu, the third is Kashmir proper, while the fourth comprises the district of Gilgit and the frontier illaqas of Skardu, Ladakh and Kargil. ...' (IOR/V/27/272/40: 1–3)

Historians by and large agree as to the pitiful situation that Kashmiris found themselves in the princely state. Prakash Chandra (1985: 39), for example, notes that:

> The absolute backwardness of the Muslims was the product of the communal policy of the Maharaja to keep them out of power and patronage. Even the Kashmiri Pandits were victims of Dogra racism and casteism in the initial period because more than 60 per cent of gazetted posts went to Dogras, especially Rajputs, despite their (the Dogras') inferior educational qualifications.

> The Maharaja regarded the Kashmiris as a race of slaves. He did not provide them with equal opportunities in trade, industry, education, jobs, agriculture and above all for their upliftment as a community of culture. In fact, he discouraged the evolution of a regionalized community of culture in Kashmir. The Muslims of the state, thus, became the worst sufferers from the triple dictum of racism, communalism and casteism. This was inherent in the legal philosophy of juridical structure under the Maharaja.

Moreover, the Dogra dynasty, supported by the Punjabis, used religious and ethnic ties to bolster its support.[11]

This is not the place to examine the poor status of Muslims in Jammu and Kashmir in general and the Valley, our main focus of attention, in particular. The events of 1931 serve to illustrate the resentment felt by the Valley's majority community; the demands contained in the memorandum dated 19 October 1931 underlined as much the *Hindu Law of Disinheritance or Conversion* as the issue of raising Muslim representation in the ranks of public servants in proportion to their number within the population of the princely state (Glancy Commission 1931). It is beyond doubt that the discrimination Muslims suffered in the princely state was shocking and unacceptable,[12] but one

---

[11] This is but a very simplified presentation of the situation of the state. The reader seeking to learn more may consult two articles by Navlakha (1991) and Chandra (1985).

[12] Cf. the excellent article by Copland (1981).

of the tasks of the historian is to examine events by the standards of the period, avoiding an anachronistic imposition of fundamental rights or ideals of equality.

The princely state certainly seems to have sought to perpetuate dynastic—and Hindu—rule, scarcely showing concern for the well-being of its subjects. At the time, poverty and illiteracy were rampant across the whole of the subcontinent. It seems relevant here to look more into the spread of literacy in the principality. This issue continues to nourish the view amongst Kashmiri Muslims that the Pandits of the Valley, as co-religionists of the Maharaja, maintained better relations with the government and thus enjoyed privileges including access to education. It no doubt explains, at least in part, the antagonism that continues between the two communities, even as the National Conference was presiding over Jammu and Kashmir and put an end to the subordinate position of the Muslim community. However, the latter seems to have considered that the Pandits retained privilege, benefitting from the patronage of New Delhi rather than that of the Maharaja. This was ironic given that the provinces of Jammu and Ladakh already complained bitterly that Kashmiri Muslim community appropriated the lion's share of the state budget.

The White Paper quoted above, *A Handbook of Jammu and Kashmir State*, drawing on the 1941 census data, provides data (Table 8.1) as to

Table 8.1 *Literacy levels of various Communities in the State*

Community	Persons[a]	Literates	Percentage
Muslims	2,615,491	110,692	4
Hindus	708,954	106,877	15
Sikhs	55,815	17,765	32
Buddhists	37,153	1,920	5

Source: IOR/V/ 27/272/40 (1945: 11).
Note: [a] Above 5 years of age.

Table 8.2 *Literacy per 1,000 from 1921 to 1941*

	1921	1931	1941
State	26	41	70
Jammu Province	27	49	74
Kashmir Province	26	35	70
Frontier District (excluding Gilgit Agency)	19	25	31

Source: IOR/V/ 27/272/40 (1945: 11).

the levels of literacy of the various communities (IOR/V/27/272/40, 1945: 11).[13]

Table 8.2 shows the progress of literacy from 1921 to 1941.

Unfortunately, we do not have figures by province and by community. Interpreting the tables reproduced here, we can see that only 4 per cent of the Muslim population that made up '77.11 per cent of the total population' (IOR/V/27/272/40, 1945) was literate. Nonetheless, it is still difficult to conclude that the Maharaja's administration promoted access to education for a Pandit community that was, by tradition, a holder of knowledge. Moreover, it seems that it was the small Sikh minority that had become the most literate (perhaps a result of Jammu being a part of the Sikh Empire prior the rule of the Dogra). We might also question the reliability of the source on which this analysis is based; even at the time, the 1941 census data were controversial.

---

[13] The total population of the sate according to the census of 1941 was 4,021,616. The distribution according to religion: Muslims: 3,101,247; Hindus: 8,09,165; Sikhs: 65,903; Buddhists: 40,696; Others: 4,605 (IOR/V/27/272/40, 1945: 11).

A NEW ERA IN THE VALLEY:
SECULARISM, KASHMIRI NATIONALISM OR WAHHABISM?[14]

The Rejection of a Secularism Indian in Essence?

In the aftermath of the accession of the princely state of Jammu and Kashmir to the Indian Union (26 October 1947), New Delhi boasted of its attachment to secularism, for which Jammu and Kashmir, a Muslim-majority state that, moreover, bordered Pakistan, became the example *par excellence*. Sheikh Mohammed Abdullah, leader of the National Conference and, according to New Delhi's argument, representative of the wishes of the people of the territory, had opted, following the invasion by tribal groups from Pakistan in the third week of October 1947, to join the Indian Union. Congress leaders, in particular Jawaharlal Nehru, had nurtured close links with the National Conference, which in 1941 had re-joined the All-India States' Peoples' Conference. This was an organization that brought together political parties of the princely states which were in favour of progressive reforms or joining a future independent Indian state. It was through Nehru's influence as the organization's president that Abdullah had become its vice-president in 1946. The future Indian prime minister, from then on, hoped for either a full accession or at least the development of privileged links which would ensure Indian hegemony. His trump card was doubtless the stated policy of both the Indian Congress Party, as leader of the independence movement, and the National Conference to put an end to all forms of feudalism. India, contrary to the expectation of the Muslim League, held another trump card, this one geographical. Through the award of the Boundary Commission, it received three (Batala, Gurdaspur and Pathankot) of the four *tehsils* (sub-districts) of the Gurdaspur district of Punjab. Batala and Gurdaspur—like Shakargarh that would go to Pakistan—had a slight Muslim majority. They provided New Delhi with much easier

---

[14] This is the term that some Pandits exiled in Jammu choose when they feel free to express themselves.

access to Jammu and Kashmir, feeding conspiracy theories in Pakistan of an Indo-British plot.[15]

Such episodes acquired fresh significance following the Rajiv Gandhi–Farooq Abdullah Agreement of 2 November 1986. This was rather an electoral pact that would allow the latter to return to power provided he agreed to form a coalition government, with 60 per cent of the seats in the assembly going to the National Conference and the remaining 40 per cent to the Congress. The term 'Agreement' was clumsy, since it recalled that which had paved the way for Sheikh Abdullah to recover power in 1975, thereby disavowing his long years spent in opposition. In any case, the Valley judged that the Congress party had been responsible for its subjection, since, far from respecting the autonomy promised on 26 October 1947,[16] it had pushed the state of Jammu and Kashmir into forced integration. Kashmiris were, therefore, unable to tolerate Congress' effort to exercise hegemony over their political life. Moreover, the agreement was in effect a cartel that shut out free opposition in the state; the two new allies, anxious to ensure victory, were even worried about the opposition that the weak Muslim United Front might provide (Widmalm 1997: 1017, 1019). The election results were, therefore, once again, rigged.

---

[15] It fell to Sir Cyril Radcliffe, president of the Boundary Commissions of Bengal and Punjab, to resolve, in conformity with the power vested in him by the India Independence Act, disputed border issues. He had no particular knowledge of the subcontinent, travelling there for the first time after being nominated to the post. This, at least, is the generally perceived version of events. The question is more complicated than that. A similar line had been envisaged when Lord Wavell had been Viceroy. In a document dated February 7th 1946, Wavell stated that: 'In the Punjab the only Moslem majority district that would not go into Pakistan under this demarcation is Gurdaspur (51 per cent Moslem). Gurdaspur must go with Amritsar for geographical reasons and Amritsar being sacred city of Sikhs must stay out of Pakistan. But for this case for [of] importance of Amritsar, demarcation in the Punjab could have been on divisional boundaries. Fact that much of Lahore district is irrigated from upper Bari Doab canal with headworks in Gurdaspur district is awkward but there is no solution that avoids all such difficulties' (Mansergh 1977: 912).

[16] India is of the view that the accession treaty was signed on 26 October 1947; Pakistan argues that it took place the following day, when Indian troops had already been airlifted to Srinagar.

Following the assembly elections of 1986, the Valley no longer hid a mixture of resignation and contempt for Indian democracy, the principles of which India boasted about without, at least in Jammu and Kashmir, respecting the practices. It also rejected the Kashmiri political class. The latter never shied away from parroting for Kashmiri exceptionist messages in successive electoral campaigns, but once re-elected quickly forgot the promises it had made, and reverted to the main objective, that of personal enrichment. This was how many Kashmiris came to the decision to write off 40 years of association with India.

Of yesterday's hero, Sheikh Abdullah, who had marked the first period of Kashmir's modern history, only his 'treachery' (symbolized by the signature of the Accord with Indira Gandhi) was remembered, and then that of his son, whose ascension his father was considered to have brazenly promoted.[17] The armed opposition no longer adhered to the argument of the Sheikh that, in view of the unenviable fate of Azad Jammu and Kashmir, belonging to India was a 'necessary evil'. It aimed to remove all legitimacy from the struggle that the Sheikh had led, thus reducing to nothing the Kashmiris' legalist political tradition and leaving them little choice thereafter but to give their unconditional support to the armed struggle.

The consequences of the erasure of the Abdullah legacy were far-reaching: The younger generation, born well after the tribal invasion of 1947, had to choose its points of reference and thus a fresh political programme with neither the time nor the objective historical elements that such a task necessitated. It was faced with a political stage that was irrevocably divided between a National Conference too close to New

---

[17] Jagmohan (1991: 204), who was twice governor of Jammu and Kashmir (26 April 1984–11 July 1989, and 19 January 1990–26 May 1990), talks of a booklet known as the *Lal Kitab* (Red Book), which was clandestinely circulated that listed the misappropriation of funds in which Sheikh Abdullah and his family were implicated. The author emphasizes that the booklet—whatever were the political motivations of those behind it—presented accusations of such precision that only the stature of the Sheikh prevented "the people" from believing them. In any case, Abdullah, even weakened by illness, could not be unaware of the scale of corruption afflicting Jammu and Kashmir, in the form, for example, of improper allocation of land for hotel construction or of concessions to industrialists.

Delhi and a militant movement which lacked the means to act without its Pakistani 'friends'—whose help was conditional and instrumentalized Islam whenever convenient in order to mask their true aims.

The Issue of Kashmiri Secularism

There is still the question of how genuine Sheikh Abdullah's commitment to secularism (and, by extension, that of the Kashmir Valley more generally) was. In a written interview given on 13 March 2011 to this author, Professor Kashi Nath Pandita, former Director of the Centre of Central Asian Studies of the University of Kashmir, laid emphasis on one factor that

> contributed to the rise of Sheikh Muhammad Abdullah as the outstanding leader of Kashmir in early 1920s. One was the silent but forceful movement carried out almost underground by youthful Kashmiri Pandit students in Lahore in alignment with prominent Kashmiri Hindus and Muslims long settled in Punjab. (Pandita 2011)

Pandita stressed the unique environment of the period: Marxist–Leninist ideology was seducing a significant section of the Indian intelligentsia. At the same time as getting rid of the colonial presence, this line of thought also wished to bring an end to the poverty and backwardness that accompanied it. The problem of the power of the princes—deemed illegitimate—was also talked about. Which were the ideological anchors of the young Sheikh Abdullah as he returned as a fresh graduate from Aligarh Muslim University to an area where the majority had scarcely any access to education? Abdullah founded the National Conference in 1938–1939 since he

> found that in Muslim Conference the Mirpur leadership adopted domineering role and relegated Kashmir leadership and Kashmiri segment to backburner. In particular, the Sheikh believed that:
>
> (a) Kashmiris formed the major demographic segment within a geographical entity.
> (b) Hindus of Kashmir and Jammu regions were as much oppressed and deprived as the Muslims

(c) A Muslim-centric organization like Muslim Conference could not
be the right instrument for the deliverance of Kashmiri nation, and

(d) only a secular organization could succeed in ousting monarchy and
replacing it with popular rule. (Pandita 2011)

Pandita suggests, however, that the Sheikh was simply being pragmatic.
It was only in 1942 that he met Nehru and was made familiar with secularism. Abdullah thought that 'close relations with Nehru immensely
supported his leadership of Kashmiri nation. He could cleverly sell his
no two-nation theory commitment to Nehru and convince him of his
secular credentials' (Pandita 2011).

Furthermore, 'If the movement was limited to Kashmir only, it
would be profiled as communal movement in which Muslim population was pitted against a Hindu Dogra ruler' (Pandita 2011).

Lastly, Pandita, who himself fled Kashmir when the first murders
of Pandits occurred, comments that: 'in comparing Kashmiri Hindu
mindset with Punjabi Muslim mindset, the Sheikh preferred a docile,
servile underdog Pandit to aggressive, headstrong and acquisitive
Punjabi Muslim mindset. He had personal knowledge and experience
of both' (Pandita 2011).

K. N. Pandita concludes that 'in Sheikh's political geometry, secular
mask was the best option to carry forward his agenda' (Pandita 2011).

The Expression through Arms of a Kashmiri Nationalism with Hegemonic Ambitions

The 'azaadi' movement that began at the end of the 1980s sought
to re-unify the former provinces of 'Greater Kashmir', that is to say,
the former princely state of Jammu and Kashmir. This project, thus,
included the provinces of Jammu and Ladakh.[18] Paradoxically, it paid
little attention to the aspirations of the populations (mainly Hindus,
Sikhs in the former, Buddhists and Shia Muslims in the latter).

---

[18] No reference was made to the fate of the territories under Pakistan
administration—or occupation. Doubtless, the militants were eager to avoid upsetting their Pakistani 'ally'.

Moreover, was 'azaadi' not an essentially Kashmiri movement that did not even court Muslims from Jammu (with the exception of the Kashmiri-origin part of the population of Doda[19]) or from Ladakh? In such circumstances, what space was reserved for minorities, especially those who were particularly few in number? The small Sikh community (1.89 per cent;[20] Government of India 2001) may often, in relative terms, have been spared, but it was marked permanently by a few episodes. The Chattisinghpora massacre, in Anantnag district, saw 36 Sikhs slaughtered (20 March 2000). Yet, in Kashmir, the Sikhs (at least an extreme section of the community) had an aura of prestige, a result of the 'glorious failure' of the 'Khalistan' (Sikh homeland) movement. After its armed militants holed up in the Golden Temple in Amritsar, the army carried out Operation Blue Star on 6 June 1984. The case of the Kashmiri Pandits was different, as we will see in the next section.

A PANDIT COMMUNITY JUDGED LOYAL TO THE 'INDIAN ENEMY'?

It should be recalled that a process of rewriting of history, or at least a reinterpretation of events that have left their mark on the subcontinent following the departure of the colonizers, become especially clear after the rise of militancy in Kashmir, and continues to this day. Kashmiri separatist leaders sought to promote the Pakistani line of argument. Roles were, thus, reversed. We will give a single example here: In October 1947, the Indian Union had not flown troops in to 'relieve' Jammu and Kashmir, but had invaded. As for the tribes living under Pakistan's jurisdiction, they had tried to bring their support to Muslims suffering under the yoke of Dogra rule. Did the parties to the conflict that broke out at the end of the 1980s not try to counter the account

---

[19] The Muslims of Doda were quick to express their reserves with regard to militancy (cf. especially Blank 1999). It is true that the Indian security forces were more prepared to fight this phenomenon when it spread to Jammu in the second half of the 1990s. Indeed, the character of militancy had changed compared with its beginnings in the Valley at the end of the 1980s. In addition, the Muslim population of Jammu and Kashmir was, privately at least, fed up with being held hostage by both the Indian security forces and the various groups operating in the area.

[20] According to the most recent census figure, they represented 0.98 per cent of the Valley's population (Government of India 2011).

that the Nehru administration had given of the tribal invasion, that is, that it had attacked all Kashmiris, regardless of their religion?[21] In this way, independent India turned the accession of Jammu and Kashmir into a symbol of the secularism it intended to promote. It lauded the intercommunal harmony of which the National Conference claimed to be the guarantor and which the tribal invasion had in a sense unwittingly reinforced.

Reality, especially from a social perspective, was rather less straightforward. In the March 2011 interview already mentioned, Kashi Nath Pandita emphasized that:

> From the times of the Mughals, upper class of Kashmiri Pandits had managed to have a toehold in the administration. This class owned considerable land holdings and was concentrated in the city of Srinagar. It was socially and culturally well-knit and maintained its status by showering munificence on poor and deprived Muslim neighbours who were thankful even for the pittance they received for various services rendered. They were quick to pick up Farsi, the official language of the ruling Mughal Governors of Kashmir. It reinforced their position as government functionary. Thus secularism in Kashmir earned social legitimacy. (Pandita 2011)

Was it this privileged position that made the Pandit community the target of enmity, as others (Muslim, for the most part) envied the social position they occupied? Gilbert Etienne (1996: 27–28), meanwhile, remarks that:

> In 1989, of the civil servants serving in senior central government posts or senior management in state enterprises, 83.66% were Hindus, as

---

[21] K. N. Pandita indicated to the author in a conversation on 14 September 2011 that the tribals coming from Pakistan had massacred 3,000 Sikhs around Baramulla, managing to identify them thanks to local guides from the Muslim community who volunteered readily for this 'task'. More generally, he is of the view that the tribals had not, as the Nehru government asserted, targeted all Kashmiris indiscriminately, but mainly the Sikh and Hindu communities (Pandita undated). Such is also the analysis of Rahul Pandita, who retraces this sad episode in his book *Our Moon had Blood Cloths: The Exodus of the Kashmiri Pandits* (Pandita 2013). Space precludes a detailed look at this here.

against 6.89% Muslims and 8.35% Sikhs .... At the junior levels, 79.27% were Hindu. Even if the proportion of Kashmiris was doubtless much higher amongst those employed by the State of Jammu and Kashmir, these figures are cause for concern. In 1959, it had been decided between Srinagar and Delhi that 50% of the central cadre civil servants posted in the state would be drawn from the state civil service. In 1989, only 25% of the members of the Indian Administrative Service posted in J&K were Kashmiris (we are unaware of the proportion of these who were Pandits). In the state banks, Kashmiri Muslims represented only 1.5% of the senior staff.[22]

However, it was only a minority of the Pandit community that enjoyed a privileged social position. Thus:

the conditions in rural Kashmir were different. The Pandit minority was very thinly dispersed in villages and smaller towns. They were not close to the corridors of power nor had they a toehold in the administration of the State. As such they were not in any position to be munificent to the majority of Muslims in their neighbourhood. Conversely, they were dependent on their Muslim neighbours for assistance in their agrarian activities. Thus appeared the class of 'kashtkaran', the actual tillers of land. And they were all from the majority community. Crop sharing became the basis of contract between an owner and the tenant. Both understood the imperative of mutual understanding and support. In this way developed another facet of Kashmir secularism. (Pandita 2011)

After the armed movement picked up, Pandits were deemed Indian collaborators, all the more so since few even voted for the National Conference. Rahul Pandita, for his part, underlines the apolitical character of his community. Returning to the concept of 'lihaaz' and how it influenced social life most of the time, he writes that:

this lihaaz, this peaceful coexistence, would be threatened every now and then. It was as if these minority Pandits were to be blamed for everything that went wrong. It could be anything as our experience would tell us. (Pandita 2013: 502)

---

[22] Translation from French by the author.

Killings, the Sign of a Reign of Terror?

One might date the start of the ideological confrontation between India and Kashmir to September 1989. Pandits become the symbol (and unfortunately also the target) of an India that Pakistan had long qualified as Hindu. Indeed, many consider that the assassination on 14 September of Tikka Lal Taploo, a 58-year-old Pandit, High Court lawyer and vice-president of the Jammu and Kashmir chapter of the Bharatiya Janata Party (BJP, Indian People's Party) targeted the Hindu community as a whole. It is difficult to make out the case that the Jammu and Kashmir Liberation Front (JKLF) was only attacking the anti-Muslim positions of that party. Underlining the point that the attack took place in broad daylight and the killers made good their escape without difficulty, Governor Jagmohan asserts that it marked the start of a concerted campaign against the Pandits of Kashmir. It is worth quoting the words of the man whom some consider to be responsible for the exodus of that community from the Valley. Jagmohan (1991: 322) draws attention to the fear which began to prey on the Pandit community which asks itself what would be the fate of its members living in isolated villages, if they were not even safe in the middle of Srinagar.

On 4 November, the death of Maqbool Butt[23] was 'avenged' by the killing, once more in broad daylight and once more a Pandit, of the retired judge, Neel Kanth Ganjoo, who had pronounced the death sentence. Again, some regarded this as a 'communalist' act. However, the JKLF would not have drawn back from similar 'reprisals' had the judge been Muslim: It meant to demonstrate its power to reply, and its intention to 'punish' the key supports of the Indian state. Nevertheless, the Hindu community of Kashmir was alarmed by the growth of the

---

[23] After the kidnapping and killing on 3 February 1984 of Ravinder Mhatre, Deputy High Commissioner of India in the United Kingdom, New Delhi decided to go ahead with the hanging in Delhi's Tihar Jail of JKLF leader Maqbool Butt on 11 February 11, after the execution had appeared to have been stayed.

activities of the Liberation Front.[24] Even if it claimed to be guided by 'kashmiriyat',[25] the JKLF version appeared to be a purely Muslim one.

Some 100,000 members of the Pandit community, which at the time numbered about 140,000 persons, emigrated from the Valley to Jammu Province, the city of Delhi and other parts of India from January 1990 onwards (Bose 1997: 71). Such are the facts presented—in some-what partisan fashion—by Sumantra Bose, who avoids using the term 'exodus', indicating the population movement lasted until the month of March 1990. He states that:

> The ostensible catalyst was the killing of several dozen persons belong-ing to this group by 'militants' between September 1989 and March 1990. (Bose 1997: 71)

The political scientist criticizes certain journalists and Pandits, suggest-ing that in claiming that many Pandits had been killed, their property burned and their womenfolk raped, they were trying to demonstrate that such 'terrorist violence' amounted to 'Pan-Islamic fundamental-ism in Asia' (Bose 1997: 71). Sumantra Bose underlines the serious-ness of these allegations that, if proved, would bear witness to a brutal upheaval—initiated by a 'mass upsurge of extreme intolerance, cruelty and hatred', as well as challenging the 'centuries-long harmonious coex-istence of the Valley's Pandit community and Muslim majority, sus-tained by the majority's eclectic, mystical Sufi tradition'. The Kashmiri insurrection would be 'nothing but a communal terrorist campaign' that

---

[24] According to the 1981 census, 124,078 Hindus (the majority being Pandits) lived in Kashmir. There was no census in 1991 because of the conflict, but Sumantra Bose (1997: 100) estimates that, given a natural growth rate of 2 per cent, the Pandit community would have then numbered around 140,000.

[25] Gul Mohammed Wani (1995: 3–4) notes that the Kashmir movement was based on an identity linked to a 'historic unity' and 'isolation' which was a corollary of its particular geographical circumstances: a fertile plain, surrounded by a range of mountains, 'a valley large enough to form a kingdom for itself and capable of supporting a highly developed civilization'. 'But the passes also became routes of foreign domination and subjugation, leaving a deep impress on folk memory. This in turn promoted a sense of Kashmiriyat: of a distinct, common politico-cultural identity, which continues to dominate the people's vision of their future.'

had 'systematically targeted the lives, property and places of worship of a tiny and vulnerable community' (Bose 1997: 71).

> A people who wantonly violate the basic rights of their own minorities cannot possibly have a moral right to demand self-determination for themselves, leave alone claim any 'democratic' credentials for their struggle. (Bose 1997: 71)

CONCLUSION: THE KASHMIRI PANDITS CONFRONTED BY THE PROBLEM OF RETURNING 'HOME'

The question as to the legitimacy of the struggle for 'azaadi' remains open, provoking fierce debate both amongst the various parties to the conflict and observers in the subcontinent. The arguments presented here will presumably attract sharp criticism, especially since in the space available it is difficult to avoid oversimplification. In reflecting on the exile of the Pandits, Kashmiri Muslims are quick to give credence to the theory that Jagmohan orchestrated the exodus, with a view to sheltering Hindus and enabling an assault on militancy. Above all, people are more and more ready to criticize the Pandits for the opportunities that their exile has offered them. They are accused, unlike the Muslims of the Valley, of being eligible for university reservation quotas in the rest of India. Ironically, it is their social success that makes them (again) the object of jealousy, even as most Kashmiri Muslims continue to reject India's presence in the Valley. In any case, their respective positions remain poles apart; Muslim and Pandit community blame each other for the failure of a secular model and accuse each other of not having favoured it. K. N. Pandita (2011) rails at the 'agenda for communal and parochial administrative policy and culture' that Sheikh Abdullah put in place upon his return to power in 1975. He believes:

> Secularism in Kashmir is a myth. Pro-Islamism is the interpretation of NC's [National Conference] secularism. If you are pro-Islamist you are secular otherwise you are a Jan Sanghi meaning rabid Hindu communalist. Up to the outbreak of insurgency in 1990, Kashmir leaders used to gloat over their slogan of Kashmir secularism. They quoted Bud Shah and others in support of their secularist interpretation and often made

it synonymous with Kashmiriyat. But when Kashmir insurgency was over taken by the Wahhabis, the word secularism vanished in thin air. Fanatic Muslim mullahs told their audience that it was blasphemy to talk of secularism in Kashmir. It was also blasphemy to talk of nationalism. All that Kashmiri Muslims should talk about is ummah as directed by the Quran. So today we have Wahhabism over-shadowing all aspects of life and civil society in Kashmir.

There remains the question of a possible return, probably mainly of older members of the community (since the younger have for the most part settled elsewhere in India). The discourse of separatist leaders such as Yasin Malik makes one think. The JKLF leader first stuck to the line that was widespread in the Valley, namely, that the Pandits were welcome back. When the minister of home affairs, Rajnath Singh, had asked the state of Jammu and Kashmir to identify land on which to establish 'composite townships' for Kashmiri Pandits who had been displaced in 1989 due to the insurgency, Yasin had declared:

> The land belongs to them. But if you want that they should not live together, then you are creating walls of hatred. In Palestine, the Jews and Muslims are killing each other. We want them to live the way the other Kashmiri Pandit brothers and sisters are living. (Singh 2015)

Thus, the Pandits who wanted to return 'home' would have to accept terms that are at the very least rather odd: going back to the 'mother-land' without reconciling themselves with the painful past, even this meant nothing more than a reference to the issue of their security.

Syed Ali Shah Geelani, for his part, did not mince his words:

> In the garb of the return of Kashmiri Pandits, a State within a State is being created. It is a ploy to make Kashmir the next Palestine and rob people of their land ....
>
> I have told the Home Minister that they can't stay separately. If it happens, then everyone will stay together. It is a symbol of our diversity. There is no plan, no decision... but it is being floated that a separate homeland will be created. That is not possible. (Singh 2015)

There remains the issue of 'Kashmiri land' belonging to all those born there, each enjoying equal rights. The Valley, in spite of a willingness to take a somewhat different route to the Indian nation as a whole, is not immune to its influence. Ajay Gudavarthy, in a significantly titled article—Sectarianism of the 'Secular Brigade'—published in *The Hindu* wrote:

> Secular sectarianism of feminists, Dalit, the Left and religious minorities has, over a period, ghettoised communities and advanced a sectarian political imagination leading to a political end that they are now finding difficult to negotiate.
>
> ...they all seem to have contributed to a shrinking political imagination that has in turn contributed handsomely to the rise of right-wing politics.
>
> Citizenship, as a political practice, is instantiated in the right to speak for others, and not in speaking for one's own self alone .... The way forward... seems to be opening up internal dialogue within communities as also across themselves. (Gudavarthy 2014)

REFERENCES

Blank, Jonah. 1999. 'Kashmir: Fundamentalism Takes Root'. *Foreign Affairs* 78 (6): 36–53. Available at: www.jstor.org/stable/20049531 (accessed on 17 April 2014).

Bose, Sumantra. 1997. *The Challenge in Kashmir. Democracy, Self-Determination and a Just Peace*. New Delhi: SAGE Publications.

Chandra, Prakash. 1985. 'The National Question in Kashmir'. *The Social Scientist* 13 (6): 35–56. Available at: www.jstor.org/stable/3520318 (accessed on 14 May 2014).

Copland, Ian. 1981. 'Islam and Political Mobilization in Kashmir, 1931–34'. *Pacific Affairs* 54 (2): 228–259. Available at: www.jstor.org/stable/2757363 (accessed on 14 May 2014).

Etienne, Gilbert. 1996. 'Le conflit du Cachemire' (The conflict of Kashmir). *Relations Internationales* 88 (Winter): 21–33.

Fayyaz, Ahmed Ali. 2004. 'Separatist Camp Agitated over Geelani Remark'. *The Hindu*, 21 April. Available at: www.thehindu.com/news/national/separatist-camp-agitated-over-geelani-remark/article 5931672.ece (accessed on 14 May 2014).

Glancy Commission. 1931. *Kashmir Riots, Middleton Inquiry Report*. Glancy Commission Report V/26/272/8 (Orders on the Recommendations of Glancy Commission).

Government of India. 2001. Census 2001 Data Online, Government of India. New Delhi: India Portal. Available at: https://india.gov.in/census-2001-data-online (accessed on 6 August 2019).

———. 2011. *C-1 Population by Religious Community*. New Delhi: Government of India. Available at: www.censusindia.gov.in/2011census/C-01.html (accessed on 6 August 2019).

Gudavarthy, Ajay. 2014. 'Sectarianism of the Secular Brigade'. *The Hindu*, 20 November. Available at: www.thehindu.com/profile/author/ajay-gudavarthy (accessed on 1 November 2016).

India Office Records and Private Papers. London: British Library.

IOR/V/10/1264 Indian States. 1914. *Administration Reports. Jammu and Kashmir 1912–1913 to 1916–1917*. Report on the administration of the Jammu and Kashmir State for the Sambat year 1968 (1911–1912), by Diwan Bahadur Diwar Amar Nath, C.I.E, Chief Minister to His Highness the Maharaja Sahib Bahadur, Jammu and Kashmir State. Jammu: Printed under the supervision of Diwan Alim Chand, G.C., Superintendent Sri R.P. Press.

Jagmohan. 1991. *My Frozen Turbulence in Kashmir*. New Delhi: Allied Publishers.

Jammu and Kashmir Government. 1945. *Handbook of Jammu and Kashmir State*, 2nd ed, V/27/272/40A. Jammu: Ranbir Government Press.

Mansergh, Nicholas, ed. 1976. 'Document 406, 1946. Field Marshal Vixcount Wavell to Lord Pethick-Lawrence, Telegram L/P&G/8/525: f 103, 7 February 1946, Bangalore'. In *The Transfer of Power 1942–7. Volume VI: The post-war phase: new moves by the Labour Government 1 August 1945–22 March 1946* 912–913. London: Her Majesty's Stationery Office, London, Constitutional Relationship between India and Britain.

Navlakha, Gautam. 1991. 'Bharat's Kashmir War'. *Economic & Political Weekly* 26 (51): 2951–2955. Available at: www.jstor.org/stable/41625458 (accessed on 17 April 2014).

Pandita, Kashi Nath. n.d. *Kashmir: Pakistani Tribal Attack 1947*. Jammu: Sanjeevani Sharda Kendra.

Pandita, Kashi Nath. 2011. 'Secularism of National Conference and Promoting Kashmir Nationalism'. Written interview with this author, Jammu, 13 March.

Pandita, Rahul. 2013. *Our Moon Has Blood Clots: The Exodus of the Kashmiri Pandits* (ebook). Noida: Random House Publishers India.

Singh, Neha. 2015. 'Srinagar: Separatists Protest Against "Composite Townships" for Kashmiri Pandits; Yasin Mallik Arrested'. *International Business Times* (Indian ed.), 10 April. Available at: www.ibtimes.co.in/srinagar-separatists-protest-against-composite-townships-kashmiri-pandits-yasin-mallik-628793 (accessed on 5 November 2016).

Wani, Gull Mohd., ed. 1995. *Kashmir: Need for Sub-Continental Political Initiative*. New Delhi: Ashish Publishing House.

Widmalm, Sten. 1997. 'The Rise and Fall of Democracy in Jammu and Kashmir'. *Asian Survey* 37 (11): 1005–1030. Available at: www.jstor.org/stable/2645738 (accessed on 17 April 2014).

PART III

Left and Its Fragments

Chapter 9

Governance as Practice and Politics as Intersectionality
Socializing Governance, Localizing Theories

Anindya Sekhar Purakayastha, Manas Dutta and Tirthankar Ghosh

There is no 'we' without a 'they'.

—Slogan of Podemos

We have the vote but not the voice.

—Indignados slogan

Just as governmentalization of locality was unaccompanied by a localization of government, the left in West Bengal pressed its government into crevices of the social without socializing the government.

—Bhattacharyya (2016: 18)

Is the Indian Left or any form of liberal leftist political imaginary across the globe suffering from ideological myopia that ill-equips them to accommodate new radical reformulations and adjustments? In spite of repeated setbacks, do they fail to realize that changing political contexts necessitate rethinking of political epistemes and organizational applications? The present chapter probes into such queries in the light of the discussion on 'secular sectarianism' in the existing political paradigms that critiques all forms of rigid ideological orthodoxies or sectarian closures premised on class, caste, religious or other categorical identities. In this context, we shall focus on Left sectarianism which we believe has led to ideological stagnancy and gradual decline of the Left. Drawing on the findings of recent works in this domain, such as *The Phoenix Moment: Challenges Confronting the Indian Left* (Bidwai 2015) and *No Free Left: The Futures of Indian Communism* (Prashad 2015), we would see how ideological sectarianism has been instrumental for the diminishing presence of the Left in the Indian democratic arena. Borrowing analytical findings from these and from other related recent critical works, we would try to build our argument for alternative forms of Left populism as enunciated by Chantal Mouffe in her recent writings. Communism, Marx argued, is often defeated and often on the wrong track, but only by struggle and self-critique can it 'draw strength from earth and rise again…' (Prashad 2015), and in the subsequent sections, we would read into the possibilities of such 'self-critique' that can possibly strengthen the Left.

Notwithstanding the supposed redundancy of the Left across the globe, some may argue that in the worldwide ascent of conservative right-wing forces that see the triumph of Donald Trump and the Brexit aspirations, progressive Left politics, far from becoming redundant, may emerge as all the more relevant today. However, for the Left to be relevant, a comprehensive auto-critique of its ideological closures is required, and to do that it needs to allow its fundamental flaws to be analysed for possible reconstruction. This chapter toys with the idea of such overhauling exercise of the introspection and acknowledgement of mistakes in order to understand what went wrong with the Left and how can they learn from serious flaws of ideological orthodoxies. Recent literature in this direction, such as *Podemos: In the Name of the People* (Errejon and Mouffe 2016), *Returns of Marxism: Marxist Theory in a Time of Crisis* (Farris 2016) and *Government as Practice: Democratic Left in a Transforming India* (Bhattacharyya 2016) have already argued in that direction and borrowing their findings, we would unpack the fallacies of theoretic rigidity and applicational mistakes in Left political practices with specific focus on India. The year 2016 marked the thirtieth year of the publication of Ernesto Laclau and Chantal Mouffe's path breaking *Hegemony and Socialist Strategy: Towards a Radical Democratic Politics* (2001) that prescribed a reformulation of Left or traditional Marxist paradigms so that new political optics can emerge, which are more conducive to contemporary democratic necessities. Initially, the book generated a lot of controversies, as most Marxian scholars dubbed it as anti-Marxist, but for many the book enabled them to rescue Marxian political philosophy from regimented and unimaginative applications. Today, when social democratic parties across the world are going through serious credibility crisis and when right-wing forces are calling the shots, it is high time to re-read Laclau and Mouffe in the backdrop of recent events of Left political defeat and the triumph of the Far Right. Following Chantal Mouffe, we would submit that the Left in the world, and in India to be precise, have suffered so badly because they did not adapt themselves epistemologically to the changing needs and realities. For the Left to be politically more productive, a substantial paradigm shift is necessary, and Mouffe and Laclau's theory of 'antagonism' and 'Left populism' can contribute in a significant way towards a Left renaissance that can pose a counter-hegemony to the menacing rise of the Far Right. The present chapter, therefore, argues for a radical and reformulated version of Left politics, which is parliamentarian in nature but at the same time transcends the familiar tropes of representative democratic politics. We also take on board the crisis of democracy in the post-saffronization, post-Brexit and post-Trump times only to find new ways of imagining radical Left populism that can, we argue, deepen forces of democracy in India and in other parts of the world. In doing this, we would refer to existing versions of such creative use of Left populism in Spain and in Greece, and then subsequently we would engage with the uncreative and lopsided misadventure of Left democratic politics in West Bengal, India, which led to the demise of the Left in the state's democratic fabric after three decades of electoral victory. In what follows we would first engage with the Mouffean critique of traditional Left ideologies that can pave the way for new non-sectarian possibilities.

MOUFFE AND THE CRITIQUE OF TRADITIONAL LEFT IDEOLOGIES

In her recent analysis on the growing political decline of the Left, Chantal Mouffe has reiterated what she and Laclau said 30 years back:

> Marxism also understands the idea of antagonism, but the problem is that it thinks that there is only one form of antagonism, class, which cannot be eliminated. We on the other hand maintain that there are several types of antagonism, and that there cannot be a society where the possibility of antagonism has been eradicated. There is a radical negativity, which can never be overcome, and society is thus always divided. (Errejon and Mouffe 2016: 52)

This exclusive emphasis on class as the sole revolutionary category makes the Left blind to other multiple zones of subjugations and marginalities, and the Left continued with this mode of ideological shortsightedness for long that led to its sectarian complacency. The Left, therefore, is terribly mistaken in its political orientation that prevents it in adapting to changing needs. The question that stares the Left now is: Why are the right-wing groups gaining more popular support across the world? Does such right-wing populism suggest that fascist ideologies are proving to be more attuned to people's needs? In other words, does it signify that the Left has completely failed to understand people's aspirations and their affective needs, helping in that way fascist forces to consolidate their positions? The Left traditionally has always sneered at the idea of populism as it has deemed it ideologically demeaning to cultivate ideological popularity the way the fascist forces do. However, changing conditions of life in which the right-wing parties are consistently thriving through a clever engineering of populist measures should spur the Left to think out of the box and redefine the popular in its own terms so that a counter-hegemony of the popular can be launched. Mouffe is absolutely right when she observes:

> It has to be acknowledged that right wing populists as is currently the case with Marine Le Pen in France, often have much better grasp of the nature of the political struggle than progressives. For instance, they understand the formation of collective identities, and recognize

that politics consists of in building an 'us'. Right wing populists also understand the role of common affects – what I call the passions – in the construction of an 'us', as well as the importance of symbols and the need to offer an alternative... but the problem is that parties on the left tend to believe that the only response is to appeal to reason. Trying to awaken passion is something that the fascist right does. (Errejon and Mouffe 2016: 66)

Such notions of popular affect are seldom talked of in leftist operative plans. The frenzy with which right-wing leaders like Trump and Farage capture the popular mood makes us clueless about how to thwart them with alternative counter-currents, and one reason for the right wing to dominate is the complete abandoning by the Left of popular passions in their political deliberations. Mouffe, therefore, is against jettisoning all forms of 'collective affects' that leave the entire space for popular passion for the Far Right to dominate and

another serious mistake is to relinquish to them [right wing] the battle for hegemony in the sphere of national identification. It is a mistake to hand over to the most reactionary forces the opportunity to put forward, uncontested, their own view of what the country stands for – their project for a strong country will in reality be built against the weak, against outsiders, against national minorities, or simply be based on chauvinism. (Errejon and Mouffe 2016: 68)

Instead of crying hoarse over the popular nationalist jingoism of the Far-Right forces, Mouffe, therefore, asks why the Left cannot think of posing with a form of 'democratic, progressive and popular patriotism' (Errejon and Mouffe 2016: 68). Mouffe tried to offer answers to these questions in the book *Podemos in the Name of the People* (Errejon and Mouffe 2016), which begins with a reference to the alarming popular discontent on the existing political order that finds two different political expressions; one is a growth of progressive movements, committed to challenging the economic disparities and consequent austerity measures, and the other is the sinister political articulation of the Far Right as a reflection of this mass discontent. This perfectly reflects the contemporary political condition across the globe.

New left-wing political formations such as the *Syriza* in Greece and the *Podemos* in Spain are reflections of collective angst and disaffection with the old political order. These are instances of progressive political imaginaries being undertaken in different parts of the world, but at the same time the opposite is also happening, as in the United States a business tycoon and a reality TV star Donald Trump has become the president of America through his toxic demagoguery, and we have similar examples in UK Independence Party headed by Nigel Farage and the National Front in France, Swedish Democrats and Danish People's Party and the Bharatiya Janata Party in India. What does the Left have to offer in this context of the worldwide triumph of the Far-Right forces? Is the Left, as the right-wing groups claim, completely decimated? Mouffe and others have attempted an answer on this, and this rise of the conservative and fascist forces constitutes the backdrop of the conversation in the book, *Podemos in the Name of the People* (2016), which is written in the form of a dialogue between Chantal Mouffe and Inigo Errejon who is the political secretary of Podemos. Both Mouffe and Errejon revisit the salience of the points raised in *Hegemony and Socialist Strategy* after 30 years of its publication, and it emerges as a timely intervention into the ongoing debate on the decline of the Left and its political sectarianism. In what follows we shall explicate further the current crises of the Left.

DISINTEGRATION OF SOCIAL DEMOCRACY AND LEFT ESSENTIALISM

According to Mouffe and Errejon, the present crisis in traditional social democracy lies at the heart of a political polarization whose void is being filled in by movements of both the Left and the right wing. Social democracy, it is said, relied on an alliance between the industrial working-class and the progressive middle-class people, but now under the coercive impact of global capital, this alliance has disintegrated. The dismantlement of the industrial sector in Spain through a gradual regression to peripheral economies such as tourism and services has seen the curtailment of the rights of individual governments on questions of national economy. Mouffe accuses the Left parties for their easy surrender to neoliberal hegemony that accepted without challenge the idea that there is no alternative to neoliberal globalization. This led to social democracy's dramatic shift to the Right, accepting the essential principles of its neoliberal opponents, such as privatization, deregulation, reduced taxation on the rich and so on. Such dilution of critique of global capital, according to Mouffe, led to the evolution of the British Labour Party under Tony Blair. This compromising defeat of the Left in the face of global capital speaks volume of their lack of imagination and their inability to adapt to shifting ideological conditions. The Left seems to surrender without any attempt to forge new alliances and new affinity formations to constitute a political assemblage that can throw a challenge to capital and conservatism. Chantal Mouffe and Ernesto Laclau foresaw this crisis, and answering on the genesis of the *Hegemony and Socialist Strategy*, Mouffe recently observed that what they were proposing as the 'socialist project' 30 years back was actually defined in such a way so that it can articulate various new struggles, such as feminism, Black rights movements and other forms of dissidences other than class. For Mouffe and Laclau the question was why 'was there a disconnect between those movements and the traditional Left?' And in analysing the reasons, they realized that 'the problem was of a theoretical nature: these new fights could not be interpreted in terms of class' (Errejon and Mouffe 2016: 16). We would argue that this ideological problem resulted in the sectarianism of the Left which dispirited it in aligning with other ideological formations who also suffer from other forms of subjugations.

What prevented the Left in understanding the different non-class–based new struggles is 'their essentialist conception of political identities, which saw them as preceding their discursive articulation. There are many forms of essentialism, and in the case of Marxism it was a class essentialism' (Errejon and Mouffe 2016: 16). In terms of solutions, Mouffe and Laclau proposed for a 'heretical and heterodox' version of Marxism to establish their project of new socialist strategy, and Mouffe's observation is highly significant in the context of any discussion on political sectarianism:

> Our main standpoint was that we had to reformulate the socialist project in terms of a radicalization of democracy. That enabled us to break simultaneously both with the Jacobin tradition and with economic determinism, because you cannot speak about the radicalization of democracy without recognizing that there are different forms of

subordination that might give rise to a variety of antagonisms, and that all these struggles cannot be viewed simply as the expression of capitalist exploitation. This is the thesis that is at the core of our political approach in *Hegemony and Socialist Strategy* – and it caused a wide debate in the Marxist left. (Errejon and Mouffe 2016: 20–21)

This brings us to the question of democracy and radicalization of the political imaginary within the democratic fabric, and we are alive to the growing global discontent against democracy because of the failures of social democratic models. The Left was expected to contribute in that radicalization of the social democratic drives, and following Jacques Ranciere and others who have discussed on alternative forms of demo-cratic imaginations, we are keen to see how the Left can learn from its past fallacies and can unlearn the dogmatism it has embraced ever since the inception of Left democratic politics. We would discuss, as a case study, the successes and failures of the democratic Left in West Bengal in India, where it ruled for more than three decades to understand if the theoretic sectarianism of the Left was ingrained in its political orientations since its beginning. In what follows we would, therefore, focus on the heretical and creative versions of the Left that relies more on intersectionality and localization or socialization of theories.

HERETICAL AND HETERODOX VERSIONS OF THE LEFT

Debates on new adaptations and revisions of traditional standpoints have been doing the round in leftist circles for long, and as we have discussed so far, the Left has to fashion a heretical and heterodox ver-sion of leftism, otherwise it would surely be 'left in the lurch'. We would see in the following sections how the Left has actually suffered in that way in West Bengal, India, after ruling the state for more than 30 years. The recent work *Returns of Marx: Marxist Theory in a Time of Crisis* (Bellofiore 2016) rightly observes:

A Marxism without Marx of *Capital* … because it is precisely the lesson of Marx that obliges us to rewrite constantly the critique of political economy: it sets the task of constant revision … because it takes up the problem from Marx, without needing to repeat his solutions faithfully always and everywhere, according to the letter. (p. 62)

Such rethinking would enable the revision of Marxian essentialism or Left orthodoxy, and some would argue that Marxism itself allows such potential possibility of revision.

> Marxism also consists of an attempt to break up and to fight these dog-matisms and the effects of dominance which flow from it. The twentieth century witnessed various different renovations of Marxism with an emancipator and anti-authoritarian purpose ... What does Marxism mean? Does it mean reference to Marx, bowing to his big head? Or, do we, indeed, understand Marxism as a 'system', a 'worldview' [Weltanschauung] but this time without the dogmatism of 'orthodox' Marxism (whereby what is considered as an expression of dogmatism, changes historically)? (Heinrich 2016: 66)

In this context, one may go back to Mouffe, who recalls that Gramsci himself talked about the 'Revolution against "Capital"', seeing in the Russian revolution an act of innovation and daring against the canons, including those of his own school of thought', and hence in relation to Gramsci, Mouffe would admit that their (Mouffe and Laclau's) use of Gramsci in *Hegemony and Socialist Strategy*:

> is slightly heterodox. For instance we retrieve his idea of 'war of posi-tion' about the struggle inside the institutions which Gramsci saw as the preparation for the war of manoeuvre at the time revolutionary rupture. But we left the war of one out. Not in the sense that there would not be any kind of rupture but because counter-hegemonic struggle is a pro-cess involving multiplicity of ruptures, to disarticulate the many nodal points around which the existing hegemony is structured. Another example: Gramsci says that the central core of a hegemony must always be fundamental class, and that is something else we dropped. Honestly I don't think that in doing so we were unfaithful to Gramsci. In fact I am convinced that if Gramsci had lived in our times, he would have reached a similar conception to ours. (Errejon and Mouffe 2016: 39–40)

When we talk of such creative and non-programmatic trajectories of democratic Left, then two recent exceptions come to our minds, and these two examples indicate how a new innovative and progressive, democratic Left politics can be envisaged in the current conjuncture. We have in our mind the *Syriza* in Greece and the *Podemos* in Spain, and one may imagine similar, though a context-based, renewal of democratic Left politics in India, and for that the Left in India needs to take stock of its own mistakes and obstinacies.

In Greece, Syriza, born out of a coalition of different Left movements around *Synaspismos*, the former Euro-communist party of the interior, succeeded in creating a new form of radical party whose objective was to challenge neoliberal hegemony through parliamentary politics. The aim was clearly not the demise of liberal democratic institutions but rather their transformation into vehicles for the expression of popular demands. In Spain, the meteoric rise of *Podemos* in 2014 was due to the capacity of a group of young intellectuals to take advantage of the terrain created by the *Indignados* to organize a party-movement. The group intended to break the stalemate of the consensual politics established through the transition to democracy but whose exhaustion was now evident. Their strategy was to create a popular collective will by constructing a frontier between the establishment elites (la Casta) and 'the people'. These innovations have sounded the death knell of Left sectarianism and have ushered in new popular hopes in a different version of popular Left.

We all would agree that Pablo Iglesias, Podemos secretary-general since 2014, symbolizes today a new chapter of popular hope in European political imaginary and in many European countries we now encounter what can be called 'a populist situation'. What are the takeaways here for us in South Asia or in India to be precise? One thing is sure, a vibrant democratic politics can no longer be conceived in terms of the traditional Left–Right axis, and here we need to think of creative alignment building or radical intersectionality. In this context, we would love to read out the observation of Dwaipayan Bhattacharyya (2016) from whose book, *Government as Practice: Democratic Left in a Transforming India,* we have borrowed part of our title. Bhattacharyya, we believe, is bang on target when he observes:

> The need, therefore, is to conceive class as a category bound to a communal mode of power, inextricable from its social and cultural dimension by any economic or historicist abstraction. This is particularly relevant in the global south where capital fails to undertake a complete subsumption of precapitalist social forms and to universalize itself as a

replica of industrially advanced economies. There is no escape for the Left, if it wants to be relevant, from a deep engagement with what can be called the society's inner domain. It has to stand in solidarity with struggle for recognition against all forms of exclusion, for minority rights of the religious, cultural, linguistic and sexual groups against all varieties of majoritarianism, … if the Left continues to fail in playing a role of use for a working class that is incessantly mobile and yet intuitively rooted through modern technologies of communication … it is only by politicizing the social, by destabilizing the status quo, by redrafting the contracts with its basic constituencies and by ideologically reinventing its understanding of the everyday in a rapidly transforming world that the Left can hope of inaugurating a dialogue between its pragmatic goals and pragmatic conducts, a new governance as practice. (Bhattacharyya 2016: 48–49)

Given that, how do we redraft a new chapter of democratic Left that can usher in some hope in today's transforming India? The fact remains that today we cannot generate democratic hopes through the traditional grammar of political operationality. The transformations of capitalism brought about by post-Fordism and the dominance of financial capital are at the origin of a multiplicity of new democratic demands. These demands can no longer be addressed by simply reactivating the Left–Right confrontation: They require the establishment of a different type of frontier. What is at stake is the connection of a variety of democratic demands with the potential to create a 'collective will' struggling for another hegemony. This also reminds us of Ajay Gudavarthy's important reading of post-civil society mobilizations and assemblages in his works such as *Politics of Post-civil Society: Contemporary History of Political Movements in India* (2013) and *Reframing Democracy and Agency in India: Interrogating Political Society* (2012). As civil society–based institutional and party-based overtures have failed miserably to consolidate our democratic everyday practices, Gudavarthy has rightfully focused on post-civil society political stake-holders and operators. For him:

Politics of post-civil society can be pursued only by the simultaneity of multiple actors in differential social locations … Its [post-civil society's] process of transformation are not merely against instrumentalized strategies and sectarian mobilization but positively in favour of transformative dialogue and action. Post-civil society is a political condition marked

by the inter-subjectivity of political movements, not around common
class composition as a given structure or with a singular focus on or
against the state …. (Gudavarthy 2013: 233)

Viewed from this angle, the democratic demands in our society cannot
all be expressed through a 'verticalist' party form that subordinates mass
movements and people needs. Let us bring in some theoretic parallaxes
here. Mouffe and Laclau have been of the opinion that, if required, it is
not always possible or desirable to force democratic demands expressed
through horizontal social movements into the hierarchical verticalist
mode. However, we need a new form of political organization that can
articulate both modes, where the unity of progressive people will be
constituted not, as in the case of right-wing populism, by the exclusion
of immigrants, but by the determination of an adversary represented
by neoliberal forces. This is what Mouffe and Laclau understand by
'left-wing populism'. We would argue that Dwaipayan Bhattacharyya's
notion of 'Government as practice' borders onto an in–depth discussion
on such possible left-wing popularity that deepened people's democracy in West Bengal since the 1970s. This model of governance as
practice subsequently got mired in the verticalist mode of electoralism
and party-centric command–service approaches. Such a massive focus
on electoral triumphalism from the Left and its complete erasure of its
originary ideological cause of people's democracy or popular support
through an addressal of popular affects led to the demise of the Left and
democratic socialism in West Bengal. Can the Mouffe Lacalau model
of Left populism be adopted by the Left and for that can it abandon
its orthodox and non–people-centric emphasis on mere dogma? A
renewed 'government as practice' can rebuild Left populism, but to
do that, the Left needs to go for a comprehensive introspection and
auto-critique of its own ideological aporias, and in the subsequent section we are going to discuss various fallacies as practised by the Left.

GOVERNMENT AS PRACTICE: SOCIALIZING GOVERNANCE AND LOCALIZING THEORY

Keeping in mind the argument of Left populism, political passion and
agonism, something that we discussed in the previous sections, an

intersectional and dialogic mode of political theorization and democratic practice can be conceptualized, and to establish the importance
of that mode, now we would examine the leftist model of 'governmentalization of locality without localization of government ...' as
practised in West Bengal (Bhattacharyya 2016: 29). We also would
engage with the converging and coalitional dynamics of 'constitutive
ambiguities of civil society' that allow new forms of post-civil society
politics in the democratic space (Gudavarthy 2013: 6). Such ambiguities
and intersectional sites of democracy in India explore the possibility
of embracing within the leftist ideological ambit hitherto unaccepted
ideological *Others*. The idea of 'people's democracy' cannot operate
within the regimented domain of democratic centralism which the Left
has followed in its governmental practices so far in India. We take the
34-year-old Left Front rule in West Bengal as our empirical base to
problematize the Left's continued misrecognition of social marginalization as a political register that requires serious political attention. For
the Left, 'class was the only caste' in West Bengal, and such political
mistakes necessitate new dialogic approaches of conversation across
ideological boundaries. Recent works such as *Democratic Governance
and the Politics of the Left in South Asia* (Dasgupta 2015) and *Marxism:
With and Beyond Marx* (Bagchi and Chatterjee 2014) point towards such
new ideological openings, where the Left engages with caste, religion
and gender issues as relevant political tropes, and such socialization of
ideology for better localized implementation deepens the amplitude
of the democratic space.

While analysing the success and failures of the left in West Bengal,
Dwaipayan Bhattacharyya argues that although the Left had a rich
legacy of mass struggle behind its ascending to power in West Bengal,
but it failed to pursue the continuity of social movements concerning the issues of primary education, health-care facilities, caste and
religious discriminations, agricultural and non-agricultural wages,
compensation due to displacement and regular supplies as well as
proper distribution of food through the public distribution system. In
this context, Bhattacharyya, while studying the Left's rise and fall in
West Bengal, has put forward his thesis of 'party-society' that constituted a 'well-orchestrated, locally embedded, and vertically connected
party-machinery' of the CPI(M) in West Bengal, and this notion of

party-society is in sharp contrast with Partha Chatterjee's thesis of 'political society'. Party-society has emanated from certain limitations that existed in the dynamics of political society in terms of its extent of domination in the socio-political spheres of rural West Bengal. It supposedly surpassed all socio-religious divisions and asserted itself as 'moral guardians in the public life of the society and the private lives of the families' (Bhattacharyya 2016: 215), where governmental institutions (e.g. panchayats) got integrally entangled with the organization and functioning of the Left political parties. Rural West Bengal, thus, became a site of 'a specific form of sociability—that of 'party-society' which appeared as a 'modular form of political society in West Bengal's countryside' (Bhattacharyya 2016: 215–216).

However, the CPI(M) in West Bengal believed only in the assertion of 'class' as the sole political identity or representation over everything else and thereby ignored the pragmatism of ethnicity and religious beliefs which are no less revolutionary in the formulation of subaltern solidarity in Indian politics. Bhattacharyya rightly observes:

> As no major political party upholds the demands of any particular identity group in West Bengal, the parties generally attempt to appeal to the entire population in a village locality, thus undermining the role of particular communities as social and political agents. So, while political society produces contingent communities, party-society tends to supersede settled community structures either by suppressing them, or rendering them irrelevant to the organizational domain of government and politics. (Bhattacharyya 2016: 216)

In the parliamentary elections of 2004, the Left parties in West Bengal received maximum Dalit (57 per cent), OBCs (55 per cent) and Muslim (45 per cent) votes in the state. Bhattacharyya is of the opinion that this sort of support from the OBCs was the result of recognition of the West government, which was among the last state governments to recognize the OBCs as an official category. However, the Left failed to do justice to this massive support and decided not to push ahead with the social agenda of Muslim and Dalit upliftment. The Left in West Bengal decided to remain complacent with the machinery of the party-society that brought it electoral win, abandoning in the process real concerns for other forms of governance as practice with which it begun its political chapter in West Bengal. The Left fell into the comfort of rule and power when restoration of electoral stability, instead of procuring grounds of massive popular protest and social mobilization, emerged unfortunately as the supreme agenda for the Left. Bhattacharyya (2016) believes that 'party-society, consequently, began to change into an instrument for balancing a congeries of interests, a device for negotiating and reconciling the irreconcilables' (p. 221). Party-society soon fell under certain dilemma on where it had to straddle between the ways of regaining the spirit of movement with the inevitable task of governing the population.

The prolonged detachment from social realities and satisfaction with the munificence of administrative power prompted a section of the party's leadership to acquire bureaucratic habits of conducting itself, and in that way various corrupt and accumulative tendencies thrived among the Left vanguard. The initial reformist linkage with the everyday lives of the masses and communities got lost and, gradually, the governmental institutions (such as the panchayat), which once helped the party to innovatively respond to popular demands, started to become dated and ineffective. It not only failed to handle new aspirations and demands of the population, but what is worse, for maintaining order and peace, the party began to exercise its control over them so much so that they became non-participatory and secretive, often acting in contravention to the welfare of the population (Bhattacharyya 2016: 221).

All these clearly show how the Left got used to the seductive comfort zones of assured electoral victory and decided not to focus on social restructuring or localization of theory. They abandoned the model of government as practice and adopted a monolithic party monopoly system that stopped caring for non-electoral ground-based reforms. In what follows we would elaborate more on that and would try to enquire the reason for this retreat from the paths of government as practice. We would try to historicize the reason for Left's aversion to intersectionality or localization of political theory and we wonder if the root cause of this aversion can be located at the very genesis point of the left in India. In the subsequent section, we would dwell on that.

THE LEFT IN INDIA AND THE ISSUE OF DEMOCRACY: A THEORETICAL INQUIRY

Critical opinion on the history of Left politics in India points to a mistaken ideological position at the very beginning of Indian Left, and Sobhanlal Datta Gupta, in his brilliant essay 'The Left in India and the Issue of Democracy: A Theoretical Inquiry' (Datta Gupta 2015), pointed out this ideological fallacy in the Left in the present-day context in India. Datta Gupta blames M. N. Roy, the founder figure of the Indian Left, for not considering the Left as a possible hegemonic force in India in the 1920s. Roy's understanding of the Left ideology, Datta Gupta claims, was primarily Eurocentric in nature. He believed that Indian society was based on class, whereas other crucial issues such as caste, community and most importantly religion were ignored while understanding the ground realities of Indian society (Datta Gupta 2015: 59). Roy ignored the fact that India is an agrarian country with a feudal structure, and Indian society is believed to be divided not just vertically along class lines but also horizontally along the lines of religion and caste and so on (Datta Gupta 2015: 62). Indian nationalism, according to Roy, was a spent force, which had, he alleged, joined hands with British imperialism, and hence Communists may stay clear of that. The ideas of Roy regarding Indian society were later echoed in the words of Jyoti Basu, the chief minister of West Bengal. Such misunderstandings of Indian society and political reality are yet to be corrected by Left leaders, and such flawed ideological sectarian legacies still continue amidst Left circles. The tragedy of the Communist movement in India and, especially West Bengal, for the last three decades or so witnessed certain possibilities, which could have introduced an alternative Left perspective to address the social issues. Would it be unfair to blame the founding fathers of the Indian Left for foreclosing the possibility of radical socio-political intersections and in that way did it predetermine/foreclose the destiny of the left in India? Early Left leaders in India simply ignored the cultural pluralities and social complexities such as caste and religion. As a result, the Left leadership over the years failed to carry out revolution at all-India level as it lacked the understanding of such social realities.

The Left in India or in West Bengal in the last three decades or so was convinced that the party is always right and it can never do any wrong, and this blinkered vision led to the fallacious presumption that the party represents the masses. The Left Front came to power in West Bengal in 1977 and initially it was full of promises, but its performance, especially in the field of governance, was not at all impressive. After all, people voted the Left to power not for short-term agitational politics but for long-term governance, which would be beneficial for the masses. The challenge before the Left Front government in West Bengal was how the people-centric governance can address the burning problems of administration that plagued the daily life of the common man. Now the question arises: Why did the Left parties in West Bengal fail to understand the voices of the masses and also the ideas of pluralism? Dwaipayan Bhattacharyya, who carried out a wonderful study of the operating mechanisms of the Left during its three-decade-long rule in West Bengal, has diagnosed the problem most correctly:

> The Left chose to reify a rendition of Marxism as the scientific truth that had a limited interface with its actual practice, its 'politics of small change'. Little attention was paid to absorb 'the concrete lived experiences' into the empty space of theory,' which could have been its unique contribution to Marxian praxis. As a result its 'small' political actors, dedicated and sincere foot soldiers working tirelessly at the grass-roots level, were condemned to remain as 'ordinary tales of the unrecognized'. Any possibility of the lowest and the most marginal rungs of the society to emerge as the top leaders of the left was jettisoned. We have seen how the mainstream left's social politics in West Bengal deliberately kept thin. Here it can be argued, that the inability (or refusal?) of the left to theorize its contradictory practices and move beyond 'economism' strengthened its middle class, upper caste and overtly male leadership. Since the late 1980s, as the left was rapidly spreading across the political fields of West Bengal on the wave of its successive electoral triumphs, its early moment of government, government as practice, ironically was slipping off its balance. (Bhattacharyya 2016: 38–39)

We can see here how close Bhattacharyya's analysis resembles the views of Mouffe and Laclau in their *Hegemony and Socialist Strategy,* and what Bhattacharyya calls 'government as practice' is not a far cry from Mouffe and Laclau's notion of Left populism. Government as practice, according to Bhattacharyya, works its way 'through the messy terrain of contradictions' and these contradictions of ground reality can actually be:

productive or constitutive in a government's engagement with diverse population groups. The West Bengal experiences show that a government can work its way through these contradictions as long as it productively connects the ground realities with policymaking at the top ... Government as practice, we show below, demands a full recognition of these contradictions, which make the process of governing unwieldy, demanding a dynamic use of tools for working daily through unknown, uncharted and unexpected contingencies. That is, a populist government cannot afford to be unilateral or unequivocal in its orientation, be as a rational-bureaucratic actor, a strategic patron, or an instrument for specific class interests. (Bhattacharyya 2016: 28–29)

If we return to Mouffe and Laclau's notion of Left populism with the West Bengal example in mind, then we realize that what Mouffe and Laclau pointed out in their analysis of Left ideological dogmatism in *Hegemony and Socialist Strategy* exactly replicates what Bhattacharyya has tried to figure out through his analysis of the blunders of the Left. Paraphrasing Laclau, Bhattacharyya said:

The language of governmental discourse—whether Left or Right—is always going to be imprecise and fluctuating not because of any cognitive failure, but because it tries to operate performatively within a social reality which is to a large extent heterogeneous and fluctuating ... we can recall some key contradictions from West Bengal's 'heterogeneous and fluctuating' social reality as constitutive of the government by the left. (Bhattacharyya 2016: 29)

In what follows we would see how the intellectual think tank of the Indian Left has started to think in terms of such contradictions and heterogeneity vis-à-vis the everyday grammar of democratic governmentality.

LEFT IN THE LURCH: DEMOCRACY, IDENTITY POLITICS AND CLASS POLITICS

In the preceding sections, we have discussed how the Left has suffered for its refusal to accept the widening gap between its ideological fixities and the empirical social reality and the tragedy is the Left intelligentsia in India continues to ignore these mistakes. Prabhat Patnaik (2015), while talking about 'Democracy, Identity Politics and Class Politics', talked about the distinctiveness and differences of identity politics and class politics within democracy. He favoured class politics as opposed to the notion of identity politics and, yet, he warned that class politics must be concerned with social oppression within the larger context of struggle against the spontaneity of the capitalist system. Patnaik elaborated by saying that while class politics must support and demand affirmative action in the form of reservation for a particular group (such as Dalit, minority) in educational institutions, it cannot remain confined only to this. It must simultaneously fight to ensure that the necessity for reservations itself droops away, through an overcoming of the scarcity of opportunities that capitalism entails.

In other words, as Patnaik argued, political agencies should not divide the pursuit of identity politics and class politics in society. He further argued that some agencies design themselves specifically to pursue class politics, while others design themselves to pursue identity politics to achieve their goals. According to him, the Left in India, West Bengal in particular, makes a serious attempt to remain committed at all times to the pursuit of class politics. Being committed to the class politics, the Left sometimes also preferred identity politics on occasions to make decisions over a distinct issue. Nonetheless, it never favoured the synchronization of both the issues in understanding the larger spectrum of society.

Indeed, the real democratic process at any time is characterized by a tussle between these two contending elements: the pursuit of identity politics, on the one hand, and the pursuit of class politics, on the other. Patnaik argued that the institutionalization of a neoliberal economic regime with all its charisma (free flow of globalized finance) reduces the scope for class politics and provides a substantial impetus to identity politics. He also argued that the era of globalization becomes the era of persistent pursuit of identity politics. Here, the idea of *government as practice* again emerges as significant as it implies the act of balancing for a non-sectarian mode of intersection of plurality of approaches for the sake of people's democracy. However, any such practice requires a comprehensive overhauling of existing ideological positions of the Left parties, and in what follows we would examine the lack of democratic dialogue and introspective auto-critique in the Indian Left.

Ravi Kumar (2015), in his strongly argued views as articulated in his essay 'Remaining Democracy: Radicalizing Dialogue and Dissent as an Organizational Practice within the Indian Left', argues for the issue of democracy within the Left—be it extreme or moderate/anti-parliamentary or pro-parliamentary. There has to be democracy within the organizational forum and open popular democratic spheres of the Left. While analysing the inescapable necessity of renewing democratic voices within the party organization, Kumar questioned the prevailing argument regarding the notion of democratic centralization in the Left parties. Democracy has always been an emotive issue for the Left (in India as well as abroad), which very often confronts the idea about the extent and form the party should conform to while practising democracy. For Kumar, Indian democracy is twofold: democracy as a political system and democracy as the everyday structure of life. Since the last few years, there have been attempts to provide corrective suggestions to the democratic Left to be 'more' democratic by localizing their theory and by a greater socialization of Left ideology so that the Left can play a bigger democratic and popular role. Kumar suggests that in the name of democratic centralism 'Pluralities of voices cannot be restricted and ability and openness to experiment cannot be termed problematic at such a political juncture' (Kumar 2015: 96). He prescribes for the introduction of 'dialogue' and 'dissent' within and outside the party organizations because such dialogues 'continue to provide inputs to the organizations about the changes required in strategies of struggle'. Getting swayed by the presupposition of vanguardism the party leaders had become 'the pundits and the cadres appear as Dalits' (Kumar 2015: 98). This prolonged absence of debates in the party allowed the party colossus to be so arrogant and complacent that it went on ignoring

> ...the neglect of the social sectors, with the state lagging behind in various social indicators and implementation of welfare schemes. This was particularly true of the socially deprived sections like the Muslim

minorities, adivasis, Dalits and women, who had totally gone off the government's radar. (Bose 2015: 110)

Prasenjit Bose, who represented the party's economic wing, was expelled from the party for his deviation and open revolt over such blinkered party lines, yet this culture of dialogic absence continues in the Indian Left.

There exists a dilemma in Left politics about what kind of relationships would exist between the party and the masses—a model that would be sanctioned by the party leaders. The method which had been implemented by the CPI(M) had lacked the element of a dialogic communication with the common people and regarding the collapse of the Left Front government in West Bengal, Kumar has raised a few valid questions which deserve to be mentioned here: Where and why did the disconnect between the masses and organizations happen? Why did not the organization realize that the masses were not with them? Kumar argues that what happened in Nandigram or Singur (considered by many to be the visible route for the electoral defeat of the Left) in West Bengal did not happen merely because other anti-organizations became more active but it also happened because traditional Left revolutionary politics was ill-prepared to engage with the masses for quite some time on the question of class struggle and issues central to labour–capital conflict. The absence of this engagement happened because of the Left's electoral complacency and public disconnect (Kumar 2015: 93). More dialogues with the popular affect and popular anxieties and needs would make the Left more relevant politically, and we would conclude on this note of alliance formation, intersection and dialogue.

CONCLUSION: CHALLENGES AND THE PHOENIX MOMENT

The preceding analysis foreshadows the tough challenges before the liberal democratic Left and to arrive at the distant possibility of a phoenix moment of rebirth the Left has to answer why it has:

> never adequately theorized caste or religion, despite their signal importance in India. Nor has it given the issue of gender the salience it deserves

in India's patriarchal and viciously male-supremacist society. And [why] it has failed to incorporate the question of ecology and destruction of nature centrally into its critique of capitalism. (Bidwai 2015: 20)

All attempts to question the liberal Left must enquire why the liberal Left is too blasé to ask popular issues and whether the main reason for the failure of much of the Left is the failure 'to take a stand on some very real issues'. People like Mr Trump and Mr Wilders succeeded because they seem to take a stand on issues that worry ordinary people in their countries. Their answers might be all wrong, but at least they face up to the questions (Khair 2016). From such practices of dialogue, dissent and auto-critiques can perhaps emerge the new Left which is required in the present political conjuncture. That new democratic Left can renew its 'governance as practice' by correcting its fallacies and blunders and in that way can deepen democratic practices in India. The Left government in West Bengal—for almost its entire period—received sustainable support from the socially marginalized population groups, the scheduled castes and the scheduled tribes, but the Left preferred not to treat social marginalization as a problem requiring urgent attention; it either handled it as a function of poverty and inequality, resolvable through economic development and distribution, or proposed that class as a collective subsumed every other form of exclusion, segregation or indignity. Even when the Left broke the stranglehold of the landlords in rural regions and opened up a more inclusive and deliberative public sphere, it allowed the existing social hierarchies to persist, leaving it largely unproblematized. Bhattacharyya observes:

> This hierarchy between the upper castes and the Dalits across higher and lower governmental bodies turned the latter into mere foot soldiers of the Left, who were martyred, incarcerated and alienated from their homes and families helping the upper caste leaders to flourish and to establish their complete control. (Bhattacharyya 2016)

The 'strategy of electoral clientelism' resorted by the Left resulted in democratic vacuity, which was usurped by the right wing. It is high

time the Left re-energize the agonistic political sphere through a conflictual mode of Left populism which practices a people-centric form
of democratic governance.

REFERENCES

Bagchi, Amiya Kumar, and Amita Chatterjee. 2014. *Marxism with and Beyond Marx*.
New Delhi: Routledge.
Bellofiore, Riccardo. 2016. 'Chrysalis and Butterfly, Ghost and Vampire: Marx's
Capital as the "Gothic" Critical Political Economy of Zombie Capitalism'. In
Returns of Marxism: Marxist Theory in a Time of Crisis, edited by Sara R. Farris.
Amsterdam: Haymarket Books.
Bhattacharyya, Dwaipayan. 2016. *Government as Practice: Democratic Left in a
Transforming India*. Delhi: Cambridge University Press.
Bidwai, Praful. 2015. *The Phoenix Moment: Challenges Confronting the Indian Left*.
Noida: Harper Collins.
Bose, Prasenjit. 2015. 'The Indian Left at a Time of Crisis'. In *Democratic Governance
and the Politics of the Left in South Asia*, edited by Subhoranjan Dasgupta. New
Delhi: Akar Publication.
Dasgupta, Subhoranjan. 2015. *Democratic Governance and the Politics of the Left in
South Asia*. New Delhi: Akar Publication.
Datta Gupta, Sobhanlal. 2015. 'The Left in India and the Issue of Democracy: A
Theoretical Inquiry'. In *Democratic Governance and Politics of the Left in South
Asia*, edited by Subhoranjan Dasgupta. New Delhi: Akar Publication.
Errejon, Inigo, and Chantal Mouffe. 2016. *Podemos in the Name of the People*.
London: Lawrence and Wishart.
Farris, Sara R. 2016. *Returns of Marxism: Marxist Theory in a Time of Crisis*.
Amsterdam: Haymarket Books.
Gudavarthy, Ajay. 2012. *Re-framing Democracy and Agency in India: Interrogating
Political Society*. London: Anthem Press.
———. 2013. *Politics of Post-Civil Society: Contemporary History of Political Movements
in India*. New Delhi: SAGE Publications.
Heinrich, Michael. 2016. 'A Short History of Marx's Economic Critique'. In
Returns of Marxism: Marxist Theory in a Time of Crisis, edited by Sara R. Farris.
Amsterdam: Haymarket Books.
Khair, Tabish. 2016. 'Questioning the Liberal Left'. *The Hindu*, 14 September.
Kumar, Ravi. 2015. 'Remaining Democracy: Radicalizing dialogue and Dissent
as an Organizational Practice within the Indian Left'. In *Democratic Governance
and the Politics of the Left in South Asia*, edited by Subhoranjan Dasgupta. New
Delhi: Akar Publication.

Laclau, Ernesto, and Chantal Mouffe. 2001. *Hegemony and Socialist Strategy: Towards a Radical Democratic Politics*. London: Verso.

Patnaik, Prabhat. 2015. 'Democracy, Identity Politics and Class Politics'. In *Democratic Governance and Politics of the Left in South Asia,* edited by Subhoranjan Dasgupta. New Delhi: Akar Publication.

Prashad, Vijay. 2015. *No Free Left: Futures of Indian Communism*. New Delhi: Leftword Books.

Chapter 10

What Is Left for the Left in West Bengal

The New Left and the *World of the Third*

Dhritiman Chakraborty

Why on earth did the left in West Bengal depart from its 'government as practice' and decide to put a programmatic thrust for rapid industrialization disregarding decades of its pragmatic politics?

—Dwaipayan Bhattacharyya (2016: 184)

Both the Left-wing and the Right-wing, thus, remain complicit in the fore-grounding of third world-ism, and the fore-closure of world of the third.

—Chakrabarti et al. (2015: xxii)

INTRODUCTION

This chapter deals with this preponderant question: What is left for Left politics in the province of West Bengal, its traditional bastion where it remained in power for over three decades before the historic defeat in the 2011 assembly election. In subsequent times, this once-considered invincible political regime, its robust electoral machinery that years after years yielded victory for the Communist Party of India (Marxist)-led Left coalition in the state, completely crumbled and eventually got wiped out, so much so that it is no longer the principal opposition party in the state. With the rise of right-wing Hindutva politics, the caste, ethnic and religious identities playing crucial role in whipping up the popular sentiments, a new churning is under way in the politics of West Bengal. In fact, many are already predicting a 'post-communist' transformations (Chandra et al. 2016) in the polity. While many of these transformations are quite irreversible in nature, this chapter aims to further prod whether the Left politics has any resonance in the midst of these new tidings in the political arena. Can we imagine a new contour of Left in the state that can cater to varying demands of social justice and representation? Is it the time for Left to reframe its core ideological stand, and do away with the historical materialist line of thinking that allegedly made them removed from praxis? A revival of Left in the state is not just significant from the perspective of West Bengal, it has rather larger national implications, especially when we are desperately searching for an alternative to the dominant two coalition systems—the United Progressive Alliance and the National Democratic Alliance—spearheaded by Congress (I) and the Bharatiya Janata Party, respectively, at the centre. As Ashok Mitra (2011), a noted economist with distinct Left leaning, has aptly put, 'Enduring Left dominance in West Bengal was the hypothesis around which radical dreams began to be woven in the nooks and corners of the country.' A defeat in West Bengal is, therefore, a serious dent in that radical imaginary, just as the revival of Left would restore radical edges to the otherwise bland political spectrum.

The 2011 debacle for Left in West Bengal was made possible, as many have argued (Mitra 2011; Nielsen 2010; Patnaik 2011), due to the two successive anti-land acquisition peasant movements, first at Singur and then in a much more intense and robust manner at Nandigram in West Bengal, which helped consolidate the anti-incumbency sentiment which was slowly gaining grounds since the early 1990s, and then congealed into a robust anti-Left force under the leadership of Mamata Banerjee, who is now the chief minister of

West Bengal. Therefore, both these movements are extremely crucial to first understand 'what the left front did wrong in West Bengal' (Mitra 2011), as well as to imagine its possible revival in the future. In pursuing this primary research question, the chapter brings in some of the seminal analyses that have looked into various aspects of this defeat, and in the process argues that the reconstruction of Left cannot materialize by a general recourse to 'government as practice' (Bhattacharyya 2016), but through a definite template of that 'practice' that is reflective of the coercive and exploitative dimensions of neoliberal economy, the aggressive informalization of labour and a capitalocentric optic that has successfully rendered all other modes of economic practices completely invisible, therefore absent. In fact, the spontaneous logic that is often attached to these notions of 'practice' is also suspect. It is within the same hegemonic field in which the forces of domination are operative these creative and everyday practices are carried out. This is why we need to more penetrate the framework of practice and parse out its different dynamics that are rarely transformative, and most of the times politically compromised. What Dwaipayana Bhattacharyya (2016) has described as 'government as practice' basically derives its strength from a broader spectrum that he, by taking cue from Michel Foucault, calls 'government in general'. This praxial mode of governance works through different oppositional forces that together constitute a continuum where most of the given binaries such as just/unjust, liberalism/clientelism, reformist/conservative and so on are cohabiting in a single temporal frame. He is, thus, hinging upon a notion of political subjectivity that emerges from these myriad practices, these constant negotiations and confrontations in everyday life. Barring the first decade of the Left Front rule when many socially reformist policies were announced, the Left regime in West Bengal has, over the years, become oblivious of this vast terrain of politics. He is, therefore, convinced that:

> There is no escaping for the Left, if it wants to be relevant, from a deep engagement with what can be called the society's 'inner domain'. It has to stand in solidarity with struggles for recognition against all forms of exclusion, for minority rights of religious, cultural, linguistic and sexual groups against all varieties of majoritarianism ... if the left continues to

> fail in playing a role of the vanguard in these everyday issues of popular politics, it will be of little use … it is only by politicizing the social and … by ideologically reinventing its understanding of the 'everyday' in a rapidly transforming world that the left can hope to inaugurate a new dialogue between its programmatic goals and pragmatic conducts, a new government as practice. (Bhattacharyya 2016: 48–49)

Therefore, the only hope that Left has is to socialize its praxis and, conversely, politicize the hierarchic social. It has to be open to what, taking cue from Ajay Gudavarthy, we can call 'refolutionary' modes of political articulation—'a combination of reforms and a revolution, beyond the tyranny of the binary opposition' (2013: 230). While all these paradigms leave the political subjectivity question largely contingent on momentous eruptions to emerge in the future, we need, however, to question what are the possible underlying dynamics of any such imaginary of eruption, what are the frictional points of these eruptions, and last but not the least, can we adequately elaborate on these frictional points without a necessary recourse to the material conditions of production and distribution that constantly mediate the political acts in one way or the other. While it cannot be denied that the Left has to reorient its politico-economic matrix to lend voices to the multitude of dissent, it is, however, not clear in what sense the politics of Left would remain distinct from any caste-based, identity-focused movements that frequently invoke the same language of social justice and progress. If Left has to reorder its strategies and remain more grounded to multiple registers of discrimination, it has to first decide its priorities, and define its possible 'vanguard' role to represent these plethora of social issues that are, at times, contradictory and even self-conflicting. More importantly, this whole terrain of 'government as practice', the numerous social forces that interact and refract through the prism of practice, do not just exist in void. The practices do not imply a dematerialized space where what counts as politics are only those manifold acts of negotiations that hardly pose any challenge to the reigning power structure and the status quo. In our celebration of praxis and the everyday modalities of life, we should not lose sight to intricate networks of power that determine which practices are acceptable, and therefore permissible, in a hegemonic space of democracy.

What is 'possible' is hence distinguished from 'impossible', just as what is permissible and what is the breach of that permissible limit is also discursively structured. Therefore, the challenge lies in tearing into this consensus and finding what is hidden and foreclosed as a possibility in this prefigured territory of politics. Without a grasp over this constant mediation by the social and economic forces, the interplay of identity issues that are materially invested at multiple axial points of production, any conceptualization of Left would remain incomplete. If we take out all promises of radical reform from a political imaginary and look for only momentary eruptions, the intermittent flare-ups of anger, why do we need this appellation 'Left' as a suffix to identify a political action? We should not overuse the category of Left to the extent that it becomes empty and abstract, without anything in specific to contribute.

An analysis, such as this, can only unravel new ways of rethinking Left politics that remain both rooted to class issues and disposed to contingent social factors that have rendered politics immensely contentious in our contemporary times. Even though Dwaipayan Bhattacharyya offers the most sophisticated and incisive analysis till date on the Left's sudden disappearance from the politics of West Bengal, it needs further engagement on how this focus upon the social can remain equally alert to issues of development-induced displacement, its dehumanizing effects on labour and the livelihood issues, and the constant decimation of all other forms of economic practices that are not fully co-opted into the capitalist chain of production. The emerging Left in an 'emerging' world (Ghosh 2012) has no other choice than to expand its ideological horizon and look for alliances across intersectional and inter-subjective issues (Banerjee 2012), it has to ceaselessly explore what is more rhetorically expressed as bidding TATA (there are thousand alternatives) to TINA (there is no alternative) syndrome, famously endorsed by Margaret Thatcher in the 1980s.

What has been found in the Singur movement is that there has been a sizeable presence of agricultural labourers, non-recorded *bargadars* (sharecroppers) and contract workers who depended on the agricultural produce for subsistence. In fact, they were the mainstay of this movement that begun after the West Bengal government forcefully acquired 997 acres of fertile lands in the midst of a full crop season and gave it to the TATA Motors Corporation to build their iconic small-car factory in 2006. Since 2006, when the movement first started, this section of the population withstood all kinds of pressures, suppression and allurements. Eventually, in the face of an impasse where no negotiation looked possible, the entire battleground shifted to one arduous and time-consuming courtroom proceedings. It took little over a decade for the final verdict to come in August 2016, which instructed the government to return the lands to the respective farmers. But the verdict was disappointing for a large section of this farming community that had no lands and mostly worked as sharecropper and landed labourers. The verdict did not clearly state what would happen to those unrecorded bargadars, labourers who were dispossessed of livelihood, and the number of agricultural workers who were involved in secondary works like the business chains that were responsible for transporting the vegetables and other produces to markets. In the face of this disenchantment, anger and frustration, they have sporadically tried to organize people for a new movement, but given the way the entire anti-land acquisition bloc has reorganized itself in the wake of this verdict with a new party at the helm of power and the waning hold of Left in village politics, the future undeniably looks bleak.

How can we take this population on board while talking of Left politics anew? If Left parties have to learn and undertake a course correction, they have to engage with this section of the deprived peasantry, their caste and other cultural affiliations (as most of them are from low caste-class background), the impending threat of dissociation from their only means of labour, their collective being-in-the-world, their language–logic–experience–ethos that is excluded from the capitalocentric worldviews. This space of the outside which is inextricably intricated in the circuit of global capital has the potential to offer counter-hegemonic subjectivities. Left has to think of this space to construct a new language of class politics without getting reduced to a programmatic rhetoric of proletarian revolution. The Singur movement has so far been discussed as a question of dignity (Sau 2008), of how development–dissident politics has worked (Banerjee 2006), intervention of biopower and governmentality (Roy 2014), misgovernance and ideological detractions (Basu 2013; Jal 2012; Patnaik 2011) and ambiguities in the politics of democracy in India (Nielsen 2016). This chapter brings in the class question without the class essentialism to finally analyse what is stated right at the top, what is left of Left in West Bengal.

GOVERNMENT AS PRACTICE AND THE POLITICS OF LEFT: DO WE NEED ANY UTOPIA?

In 2016, the book *Government as Practice, Democratic Left in a Transforming India* by Dwaipayan Bhattacharyya, which is mentioned in the introduction of this essay, was published. This book is a product of his almost two decades of research into the politics of Left in West Bengal, its electoral manoeuvrings that shied away from the ideological high grounds. He zeroes in on the word 'practice' and then places it against the notion of 'transforming India', and how through an interaction among these two variables, 'practice' and 'transforming realities', the politics of democratic Left can be revived in India. This is perhaps the first comprehensive study of its kind which has tried to account for how and why the Left parties faced an ignominious defeat in West Bengal in 2011, and how the entire Left movement hastened into a tailspin since then. There are some dominant strands of his argument which mainly focus on how the Left parties consolidated themselves, how their priorities changed from radical reformist concerns to moderate acts of 'politics of middleness' (Bhattacharyya 1999) to finally a conservative ideological mould that led to the last disastrous phase of rapid industrialization, forceful acquisition of land and the resultant massive resistance in West Bengal. This book is, in a nutshell, a concise analysis of what really happened to the Left politics, their retraction from 'government as practice', innovative policies such as 'agrarian reforms and decentralization programs' to 'routine and repetitive course in which governance turned into more of a technical conduct' (Bhattacharyya 2016: 42). Therefore, the final defeat is seen as an outcome of this gradualist decline, from a dynamic and inventive force to one of programmatic and power-centric establishment that led to 'massive entropy eating into the very foundation of its regime' (Bhattacharyya 2016: 42). He then details on the central problematic of 'practice', its whole discursive theoretical lineage in the works of Antonio Gramsci, Michel Foucault and Karl Polyani. His central point is that the functioning of governance needs to be seen as a 'continuum', a 'process that evolves with practice and defies any functional, structural or ideological bipolarity between 'positive' or 'negative' (Bhattacharyya 2016: 28) qualities. Hence, he proposes a new concept of governance as 'government in general', an 'embedded' practice of countless negotiation, persuasion, interaction and reconciliation. Governance is itself a messy terrain which cannot be adequately rendered by resorting to discursive and definitive categorical imperatives connected to the 'empty space of theory' (34). Therefore, he argues for a governance in the post-transitional milieu where the Left has to 'negotiate with the forces of capital' to jack up its politics of class 'as a category bound to a communal mode of power, inextricable from its social and cultural dimension' (48). It is evident that he is hinting at a more praxis-oriented, socially responsive politics, bringing about a bottom-up approach which envisages politics as unfolding within the terrain of governmentality, 'the only real space of political struggle and contestation' (Foucault 2009: 144). Therefore, according to this hypothesis, what is left for Left in West Bengal is to basically acquire a new imagination, 'to inaugurate a new dialogue between its programmatic goals and pragmatic conducts, a new *government as practice*' (Bhattacharyya 2016: 49, italics is original).

This thesis is part of a long tradition of structural analysis of Left's regime in West Bengal (Davis 1983; Ruud 2003) that upheld the sheer hiatus between Left's radical rhetoric and its practice of governance, its sole focus on electoral equations that drove them away from these lofty ideals. However, with Bhattacharyya's book, a decisive change is discernible towards more flexible and fluid understanding of structure that drew more upon the larger tradition of placing politics in the quotidian and routine activities of everyday life. Following the student movements in France in 1968, the new autonomous social movements in different parts of the globe including Italy and Mexico, the increasing influence of Thatcherism and Reaganism, the dissolution of the Soviet Russia towards the end of the Cold War in 1991 and the aggressive rise of neoliberal market economy across the global south, politics of resistance was poised for new imaginaries, new assemblages of radical utopia expressed in critical registers such as 'multitude', 'radical democracy', 'Left populism', 'new socialist strategy' and last but not the least, 'politics of immanence'. There has been a decisive shift towards exploring new cartographies of immanent subjectivity, of stressing on molecular changes in the socius in place of the usual emphasis on systemic and transformative politics, large-scale radical breakthroughs. This is what Abu-Lughod says about this emerging aspect of resistance politics:

> ... unlike the grand studies of peasant insurgency and revolution of the 1960s and early 1970s, what one finds now is a concern with unlikely forms of resistance, subversions rather than large-scale collective insur-rections, small or local resistances not tried to overthrow of systems or even to ideologies of emancipation. (as quoted in Roy 2014: 251)

Notwithstanding differences in opinion, almost similar standpoints can be found in numerous other works in recent times, by Partha Chatterjee (2012), Richard J. F. Day (2005), John Holloway (2002), K. O'Brien (1996), Uday Chandra (2015) and so on. The following quote from Chandra further clarifies the point:

> [W]e wish to direct readers to the Latin root of resistance *re+sistere*, literally enduring or withstanding, to re-orient the older emphasis on opposition or negation towards a logic of negotiation. (2015: 565)

One can also recall formulations such as 'calculative rationality' (Scott 1985), 'lawfare' (Comaroff and Comaroff 2009), 'everyday forms of resistance' (Roy 2014) and 'contentious politics' (Tilly and Tarrow 2007) in the context of this tremendous shift in the optic, from politics of transcendence to a concept of immanence, negotiation and pragmatic calculations. It is self-evident that 'negotiation' and 'everyday' emerged as the two most dominant conceptual markers that sort of refurbished the whole repertoire of political vocabulary in the last 50 years. Partha Chatterjee's deliberation on 'political society' as a rendition of 'un-heroic everyday politics', the 'new in the quotidian' (2012: 310) is perhaps one of the most contentious formulations in recent times that, by and large, shares the same thrust for defining the newness in contemporary politics. He unequivocally puts his position as follows:

> The question that appears to have receded from view is one that used to be asked in the twentieth century: is it possible to think of modern poli-tics outside the norm-deviation and norm-exception paradigms? That question does not seem to be thinkable today except in a non-realist

theoretical mode. Since I am able to deal with politics only when *it is real,* whether in the past, present, or future … not attempt to answer that utopian question. (Chatterjee 2011: 25–26; emphasis is mine)

There is no gainsaying in the fact that the older modes of insurgent subaltern subjects that the Subaltern Studies Collective in its initial volumes dealt with, or the proletarian class subjects devoted to the cause of socialism and communism is no longer considered as the only singularly desirable political act in our context. With the change in political economy, the infiltration of hegemonic corporate capital that made the capitalist and non-capitalist production systems compete in a single commodity space, politics of resistance is bound to be layered and often interrelated.

But, what the Left leaderships can do in a scenario like this? Should it just try combine these spaces that are sometimes contradictory in nature and reformulate its class question to accommodate identity issues, or should it play an anchoring role and try tease out the materialist issues that are nevertheless operative in new domains of coercion and marginalization. In discussing the concept of communism in the *Economic and Philosophical Manuscripts, 1844,* Marx constantly reminds us that the construction of a communist society is not accomplished via a programmatic route whereby the laws of private property and the demands for individual freedoms are abolished. Rather, the formation of communistic society requires 'a very severe and protracted process' (Giddens 1998: 17), through which the man will get to realize his social and species identity. This realization is reached through a tripartite process of abolition, preservation and reconstruction. This clearly shows Marx's early engagement in the Hegelian dialectics and transcendence. Importantly, these early works of Marx represent ample evidence on how he tried to position the critique without referring to any grand utopian idea. This 'return of the man as social', 'the positive abolition of private property' and a creative overcoming of alienation in social, cultural and economic spheres also require some semblance of what we call practice. To undertake this shift from negation to negotiation, from rejection to positive abolition, one needs to creatively think of practices of different types and nature. If politics has become coterminous with practice, we need to adjudicate between which practices are transcending the limits of biopolitics, its discursive structuration of life, and which practices are resorting to acts of conformism and uncritical submission to power. Even though the *Manuscripts* is an early contemplation on this fledgling idea of communist society, it is evident that Marx approached the issue of utopia as a necessary process for socializing and restoring man to his authentic 'species' identity. Utopia is not a foreclosure on possibilities; rather it leads us to explore the productive amplitude in man, the creative emancipation of man from his restrained and alienated existence in the capitalist order of society. Any imaginary of futural Left in India has to, in some measure, relate to this thin and flexible idea of utopia, its generative and inventive potentials to increase the capacity of man.

TWO THESES ON THE FUTURE OF LEFT'S POLITICS IN BENGAL

There are mainly three seminal positions along which this question of what is left for Left has so far been debated in India. Starting with why Left failed, what could explain all the glaring loopholes that severed the prospect of the party and the much alleged self-contradicting, pro-industry role it adopted in Singur and Nandigram that dealt a serious blow to the party's organization at the bottom figured prominently in these deliberations in the pages of *Economic & Political Weekly*, immediately in the aftermath of the 2011 assembly election in West Bengal. Sumanta Banerjee (2012), Prabhat Patnaik (2011), Hiren Gohain (2011), Dipankar Bhattacharya (2011), Arup Baisya (2011), Murzban Jal (2012), Achin Vanaik (2012) and Pranab Kanti Basu (however, I am referring to one Bengali piece here, 2013) took part in this extremely engaging conversation with differing standpoints on some salient questions such as how to revalidate the Left's basic agenda of anti-capitalist politics, of pursuing a politics of transcendence within the ambit of parliamentary democracy, and realigning with all the progressive forces committed to the socialist causes. What emerged out of this engrossing critical dialogue can be summed up in two interrelated points. If some have argued about detractions from the basic ideological premise to explain the entropy in the party, others are much more vitriolic in attacking how ideological considerations were completely shunned, how the sole thrust for power left corrosive effects on the supporters at the ground level. However, these positions are not quite contradictory to each other; rather they explore the future potential of Left in the Indian context. Prabhat Patnaik first tried to explain the evental uprisings in Singur and Nandigram as an outcome of, what he calls, 'a process of empiricisation', by which he means how CPI(M) as the major party in the Left coalition distanced itself from its core electoral constituencies of farmers and workers, and in the process lost the delicate balance it maintained between electoral imperatives and the ideological commitment to the 'politics of transcending capitalism'. As long as Left succeeded in creatively working through different modalities of governance, it won the popular mandate in successive elections. However, the situation changed immensely after 2011. In his words, 'I shall call this process which has caused the decline, a process of "empiricisation", by which I mean the pursuit of a political praxis that is uninformed by the project of transcending capitalism' (Patnaik 2011: 12). For Patnaik, empiricization mainly stands for 'mundane and pedestrian' politics which has hardly any anti-imperial emancipatory agenda. He refers to B. T. Ranadive and then argues how politics of small change shall fail to generate any normative politics. He strongly makes the point that how some comrades were taken into the misconception that industrialization shall lead to proletarization, which would then free them from regressive old community ties. Contrarily, this whole idea proved to be a complete fallacy, and the party subsequently became estranged from its 'basic classes'. He, therefore, recommends that the CPI(M) has to work on resuscitating this class support. Even though he does see a possibility of CPI(M) correcting its stance, he cautions that in case it fails, some other Left forces shall replace it.

The second position is forwarded in the joint opposition to this stand of Patnaik by Gohain, Bhattacharya and Baisya among others. Their main argument is that Patnaik is belittling the intensity of the event which rather exposed how CPI(M) turned into a ruling-class party, abandoned all its previous inclinations for democratically transforming the society, and gradually sucked into the discreet charm of parliamentary politics. Gohain decries CPI(M)'s position in Singur and Nandigram as:

Practical assimilation to the attitudes of ruling-classes was seen at its worst in suppression of popular protests at Singur and Nandigram. There 'party interest' definitely has overcome the interest of basic classes. Can one call it mere 'empiricisation' and leave it at that? (Gohain 2011: 80)

Moreover, Bhattacharya fleshes out a more scathing attack on CPI(M) by stating:

The CPI(M) had moved away from this communist policy quite early on in the course of its protracted parliamentary journey. Against the backdrop of the inspiring victory of the CPI(M) and its Left Front partners in 1977, the slogan that had captured the imagination of Left ranks was none other than *'bam front sarkar sangramer hatiyar'* (Left Front government is a weapon of struggle). But it did not take the CPI(M) long to realise that such a slogan would not be tenable with the imperatives of a stable government. Thus the slogan was soon effectively withdrawn and replaced by *'bamfront sarkar unnayaner hatiyar'* (Left Front government is an instrument of 'development', experienced by the people mostly as bulldozer of development). In the wake of Singur, Nandigram and Lalgarh, a good majority of people in West Bengal saw it degenerate further as *'utpiraner hatiyar'* (instrument of repression). (Bhattacharya 2011: 73)

He charts in detail the whole trajectory of how CPI (M) 'abandoned the communist attitude to the question of power in a bourgeois state to opt for a social-democratic framework of relief and reform through power-sharing' (Bhattacharya 2011: 73). This turn in approach and the subsequent alliance with the neoliberal bourgeois forces destabilized the whole mechanism of the party, and the party increasingly found itself on the wrong side of history. This second critique is much more unsympathetic as it does not hold the detraction from ideology as the only reason for its massive defeat. Rather, the complete desertion of class politics and the increasing proclivities to side with bourgeois tendencies sap Left out of its revolutionary energies. Any possibility of Left's survival depends on how it can recast its revolutionary and transformative goal under the present regime of global capital.

The third position, held by Bhattacharyya (2016) and already discussed at length, entails an elaboration of the logic of practice and everyday politics. This is substantially different from the above two. Actually, his understanding of 'practice' is in negation to some of these positions which he considers as 'ideological critique'. He, in fact, introduces two other arguments by Atul Kohli, who defined West Bengal in the 1990s as the best ruled state in India, and Pranab Bardhan et al., who talked of clientele and patronage politics in West Bengal that sustained CPI(M) in power for an extraordinary period of time. The defeat of Left, according to Bardhan et al., is not because of an ideological and functional slippage; rather it was more owed to its dwindling capacity of evenly distributing the scarce resources. Bhattacharyya (2016) defines these respective positions as 'functional' and 'structural' critique which he then contends are suffering from a basic binaristic presupposition, that there is a sharp division between good and bad qualities coupled with an inherent assumption that as the Left parties shifted to the wrong side of the binary, it could not hold the momentum towards its victory. Instead of this dualistic frame of things, what Bhattacharyya (2016) proposes in his book is the notion of 'practice' which is basically an assortment of these opposing positions, of straddling both 'empirics'/'ideology', 'good governance'/'bad governance' and 'transcendence'/'immanence'. Bhattacharyya then concludes this discussion by suggesting three things that the Left parties have to learn to enunciate a new trajectory:

a. understand the logic of postcolonial capital
b. form knowledge about the dynamic of popular politics
c. recognize how these two dynamic can be reconciled 'in a rapidly changing society' (p.207).

Now, these three positions, as discussed above, are basically focused upon two theses: (a) Left needs an ideological course correction and a robust stand on neoliberalism and postcolonial capitalism in India. (b) Left needs to reconnect with the social and cultural issues to repair its lost contact with the complex social formations of hierarchy. The latter position is, undoubtedly, much more resonant with the current situation and pushes Left to envisage a whole new discourse of popular politics. This is so far the most cutting-edge intervention that dared to think of a contour of new Left in India. Notwithstanding this tremendous ingenuity in thinking, there, however, remain some relevant doubts. Even though it is true that something out of the box is required to shake up the ossified ideological assumptions that CPI(M) regurgitated all these years, it does little to highlight whether a simple adoption of praxial paradigm can ensure that the Left can stall the recurrence of any such mistakes it committed in Singur and Nandigram in the future. Questions can also be raised on whether the Singur movement took place due to an absence of a dynamic link between the 'embedded' and 'elevated' structures of power, or does it reflect a deeper malaise, the Left's inability to produce a critique of this neoliberal economic drive to accumulate and plunder the natural resources in the name of development. Even if we agree on the necessity for a practice-oriented paradigm of governance, we do not know whether, on the sheer merit of it, a government will be able to resist the onslaught of this predatory growth. As almost all parties in India are now contemplating on how to channelize popular dissidence to score electoral points, we need to be specific on how Left can both straddle this dual compulsion of establishing ground-level connections and, at the same time, play a vanguard role to give shape to popular issues of disaffection and disenfranchisement.

On the other hand, any stringent reassertion of ideological purity would not just jeopardize the prospect of any resurgence; it might simply reduce Left to a nonentity in the national arena. When India is seeing a number of social movements erupting on regular intervals in different parts of the country, Left politics rather needs to pump a new synergy to these million mutinies to, use the words of Praful Bidwai (2015), radicalize 'the continuing popular struggles and deepening democracy' to imagine a 'New Left' (p.235). What Patnaik and others are arguing smacks of a neo-conservative approach without any clue to how Left can negotiate with the sectarian demands, the emerging forms of capitalist model of development and the current phase of populist politics in India. Singur and Nandigram cannot be entirely scrutinized on ideological grounds, on an out-and-out anti-industry critique, nor can we lend full-throated support to what Bhattacharyya says here, 'Was it a mistake for the parliamentarian left to invite the likes of the Tatas and the Salim group to West Bengal? *I do not think so...*' (emphasis is mine) (p.206). Whether to invite an industrial group or not cannot be the point of discussion for Left politics. Moreover, the fact that this question has acquired such currency in the public psyche is itself a pointer to how the capitalist hegemony is at work, how questions are shaped in a discursive manner to deny any space to alternative thinking. Therefore, what weighs on us is to curve out a new space working through these apparent oppositional positions, of neither siding with the terms of once again reclaiming ideological fixities, nor completely buying into the performative, praxis-dependent positions that sometimes blur the difference between politics of Left and the politics in general. Could there be an alternative position that can better connect the thinking-real (abstraction) with the concrete-real (praxis) to formulate a new horizon of politics? Can we have an imaginary of Left political that can further politicize and qualify the basic premise of Bhattacharyya's thesis, 'government as practice' (2016)? Can we have a paradigm of practice that is not restricted and thus fore-grounded as the only viable materiality of politics within the discursive domain of neoliberal governance? One should always appoint a critical gaze on analysing 'Everyday' and acts of 'negotiation' to understand how far they are implicated in the workings of global capital, the continued thrust on accumulation and class exploitation, and the range of legitimizing phrases and idioms, such as 'inclusive development', 'per capita income', 'GDP growth', 'fiscal stabilization', 'policy efficiency as against policy paralysis' and so on, which are unscrupulously used and popularized to hegemonize a singular template of life and living.

Taking these points in mind, the next part of the chapter discusses the case of the Singur movement, teasing out some nuggets in the story that remain underrepresented in most of the accounts of this movement, and how, by focusing on them, a new matrix of Left politics can be glimpsed.

THE SINGUR MOVEMENT AND THE *WORLD OF THE THIRD*

In May 2006, the Left Front government got a landslide victory and returned to power uninterruptedly for the seventh time in a row.

Buddhadeb Bhattacharjee became the chief minister, and after assuming power, he immediately embarked on his avowed task to rapidly industrialize the state. In fact, the Left parties went to the election with this singular agenda of turning the fate of West Bengal's cash-strapped economy, the dismal state of revenue collection, and its sorry state of industry. Consequently, corporate companies such as Jindal, TATA and Salim group from Indonesia were invited to invest in West Bengal. As the proposals came in numbers, praises showered on him from all corners, including the CEOs of the top industrialist houses in the country, Buddhadeb Bhattacharjee emerged as the new talisman, one who is endowed with this historic task of bringing back the golden days of Bengal. He proudly declared:

> The world is changing. We are also changing. If you follow our party literature you will see our attitude towards investment and foreign capital. Most of our party leaders in the State and Central Committee understand the changes taking place in the world. (*Telegraph* 2008).

After years of being caught in stagnation, the 'Brand Buddha' became the new swan song of development in the state. Riding on this mood of triumphalism, the Singur saga started to unravel. During the months of June–July, the government decided to acquire nearly thousand acres of land for the project that would include a giant car factory, other ancillary factories and construction spaces for logistic requirements. The rest of the episode is widely known and vividly rendered in Banerjee (2006), Sarkar (2007), Roy (2014), Bhattacharyya (2016), Nielsen (2015) and Das (2013). Hence, we do not need to repeat it here, except to just tear out some basic points of contention. If for Banerjee (2006) and Sarkar (2007), the major issue is the way acquisition has been handled, the high handedness of the state apparatus involved in the process, for Roy (2014) and Das (2013), the concern shifts to the political character of this entire acquisition process, how a range of negotiations, contestations, compromises were worked out under the veneer of rational and rigorous functioning of bureaucracy. Bhattacharyya (2016) argues the case of Singur as a proof of this classic case of the disjuncture between Left and the larger social. He cites the slogan of *Krishi amader Bhtti, Shilpo amader bobhishot* (Agriculture has been our foundation, industry is our future), which was widely used by the then Left Front government, as a derivative of a particular Leninist model of progress.

There are, therefore, four ways in which the Singur incident has been described: (a) government's oppression, the forceful acquisition of lands, (b) the political character of land acquisition, (c) estrangement from the grounded realities owing to an ideological frigidity and (d) the sheer change in the class character of the Left parties. What, however, is missed in these studies is the question of labourers, of production chains and the class issues involved in the entire movement. Though it has been widely written that there was a sizeable presence of labourers, unrecorded bargadars and other petty producers who depended on the agricultural production in the acquired land, it remained only as an explicatory information without any major implications in understanding the different modalities of these economic activities, their contestation and the nuanced subsumption into the global circuit of capital. The Singur movement is remembered mainly as a story of how CPI(M) mishandled it, the flaws in the colonial Land Acquisition Act, 1894, and how fast the uprising snowballed into an iconic movement. But the most significant part of this movement has been the participation of a number of labourers, different petty producers who were pulled out, excluded and were then included as the backward 'other' in need of governmental relief, the intervention of the juridico-moral structure of the state. In advocating the necessity for 'developing' this labour force into an advanced proletariat workers, Left ignored the question of class understood as surplus labour, more specifically what Resnik and Wolff (1987) call, the 'class processes'. Following the publication of *Knowledge and Class* in 1987 and *The End of Capitalism* by Gibson-Graham in 1996, the question of class has been rethought as a class process comprising of performance, appropriation, distribution and receipt of surplus. Gibson-Graham on the other hand brings in the concept of 'Other' to capital, the critique of the centric logic that reduces anything outside of capitalocentricity as redundant, the call of the 'primordial', and 'backward' past. In post-development studies, in works of Escobar in particular, this theme of the 'outside', its cultural specificities and the otherness have drawn substantial attention. What all these respective and immensely significant contributions have demonstrated is that there could be a possibility of new Left by adopting a class-focused analysis of capital to resist the development tirade in our contemporary times. The Left has to first abandon its progressivist, dialectical attitude and look for this foreclosed space of the 'outside', its complex manifestation in the disaggregated terrain of capital. What is foreclosed in the Singur movement is the vast world of life, the community lifeworlds and the whole range of experiences which are not incorporated in the singular logic of capital. This forms the space of outside, a space which Chakrabarti et al. (2015) call as *world of the third*, a different language–logic–experience–ethos which the hegemonic corporate capital wants to annihilate to reaffirm its legitimacy. In Chakrabarti et al.'s words:

> If a particular reality as a hegemonic system is produced through foreclosure, would not the perspective or perhaps the standpoint of the foreclosed particular, if made to bear upon the said reality, reality posing as the universal, inaugurate in turn a counter-hegemonic moment? (2012: 34)

Moreover:

> if foreclosure defines and gives life to the hegemonic, then the return of the foreclosed puts to risk the hegemonic; it announces in turn the counter-hegemonic. The return of the foreclosed helps carve out the contours of the *expanded communism*.... This standpoint gives meaning to what is already in the making as part of the production of forms of life. Such forms of life are counter-hegemonic because they are anachronistic to global capitalism. (Chakrabarti et al. 2012: 34)

What is debated so far about Singur is very much invested in a capitalocentric optic. Positions which are termed as anti-capitalist, pre-capitalist and post-capitalist are basically playing with the prefix without questioning the centrality of the capital as the nodal signifier. Hence, to say that a Left politics should constantly strive for transcendence retain its anti-capitalist stand which it lacked in Singur is to basically miss how there could be a whole different engagement with the 'outside' of capital. What is outside in all the discussion on Singur is the absence–presence of the labour issue, of class questions and the disaggregated forms of surplus distribution. Singur had a sprawling chain of production that entailed differing class processes and surplus extraction. As Chakrabarti et al. (2015) have shown, there could be as many as 24 types of class processes, and all the class processes are not exploitative; in fact, there are different communistic class processes to socially distribute the receipt of surplus (p.151). These non-exploitative communistic class processes are not visible from within the delusional cosmology of capitalist class process. In fact, these communistic class processes work as a constitutive outside of this capitalist production chain. These class processes are often interrelated with the social and cultural processes that involve community ties, caste affinities and religious affiliations. We need to see how these processes of surplus distribution were present among the farmers of Singur who for over a decade sustained the dissenting energies and withstood all types of oppression and frustration. What is apparent from their cumulative participation and the determination not to do away with their lands is how they retained some forms of living which were not completely subsumed in the capitalist language–logic–ethos–experiences.

In defining the postcolonial capital, Kalyan Sanyal (2007) talked about how Gibson-Graham's position reeks of a transition hypothesis and why we need to abandon such paradigm to rethink the question of economy as an ensemble of capitalist and non-capitalist forces. He highlighted how the non-capitalist 'need' economy has been sustained by capital through, what he calls, 'reverse accumulation'. We further need to extend this formulation to argue how this 'need economy' entails a whole life-world which cannot be understood in a single economic register. The need economy can be interpreted as a space of 'outside', whose foreclosure, unlike what Sanyal has argued, has made the existence of capital possible in the first place.

The practice of Left politics should begin from this realm of 'outside', this space of 'need economy' which is present and yet foreclosed. Left has to see class as an adjective, a qualifier in the acts of performance, appropriation, distribution and the receipt of surplus. Seeing class through the prism of a process would then help Left to expand its monologism of anti-imperial politics and provide a whole different cartography of radical politics.

CONCLUSION

According to two sources, such as the statistical handbook of the state government and the survey report published by 'Sanhati Udyog', around 83 per cent of the land in Singur was irrigated with a staggering 220 per cent crop density. Singur had perhaps the best kinds of fertile lands in Bengal. The 'Sanhati Report' further stated that 997 acres earmarked for acquisition contained more than 11,000 landholdings of around 2 bighas, where almost 6,000 families depended for their daily livelihood. Four hundred to 450 cart drivers earned their living by daily transporting produces and seeds, whereas 200 families relied on animal husbandry and 150 depended for cultivating vegetables. Five cold storages in neighbouring Ratanpur roughly employed another 500. According to Parthasarathi Banerjee (2006: 4719) in all the villages which were affected, 50 per cent of the population was marginal and small farmers. He also informs that 25–30 per cent were bargadars and landless people who mainly belonged to lower castes. These whopping numbers clearly prove that the Singur question is not only about politics of governmentality, land question, comparative merits of differential development dynamics and the lack of a praxis–oriented politics within a given field, it was also a case of forceful intervention and annihilation of a vibrant life–world comprised of various economic, social and cultural networks. This large number of people who are in some way or the other related to the agricultural produces belongs to different community formations and diverse lineages. The point is that this entire population could not be brought under the capitalist hegemony. It is in their collective practice of reproducing the social, economic and cultural lives, one can glimpse the fleeting moments of alternative language–logic–experience–ethos, the 'world of the third', a whole domain which is excluded and foreclosed in conventional representations of movements and the discussions of political agency. The Left politics should try to retrieve those moments of otherness, these 'alternative narratives of human belonging', so that the world may once again appear as radically heterogeneous. The two quotations mentioned at the very beginning of this chapter indicate a possibility of dialogue between them. If there has to be a paradigm of practice in the Left politics, one should be able to theorize that practice in close connection to possibilities of retrieving the domain of outside, the communistic class processes, and thus dispel the centrality of capital in discussions of resistance. The *world of the third* marks that space of outside, that realm of otherness, 'a different materiality and embodied forms of life *outside* the circuit-camp of global capital with language-knowledge-experience-ethos fundamentally different' (Dhar 2014).

REFERENCES

Baisya, Arup. 2011. '"The Left in Decline": A Historical Perspective'. *Economic & Political Weekly* 46 (47): 77–79.

Banerjee, Parthasarathi. 2006. 'Land Acquisition and Peasant Resistance in Singur, a Brief Account of Peasant Resistance to Land Acquisition for the Tatas Motors Project at Singur in Hoogly District of West Bengal'. *Economic & Political Weekly* 41 (46): 4718–4720.

Banerjee, Sumanta. 2012. 'Revolutionary Movements in a Post-Marxian Era'. *Economic & Political Weekly* 47 (18): 55–61.

Basu, Pranab Kanti. 2013. 'Byarthota Kar, Partyr na Dorshoner?' (Whose Failure it is, the party or the ideology?) In *Bamraj: Totto O Chorchay*, edited by Prabrit Dasmahapatra and Rajesh Bhattacharya. Kolkata: Chorchapad.

———. 2015. 'World of the Third'. *Economic & Political Weekly* 50 (31): 75–80.

Bhattacharya, Dipankar. 2011. 'For a Left Resurgence'. *Economic & Political Weekly* 46 (47): 71–73.

Bhattacharyya, Dwaipayan. 1999. 'Politics of Middleness: The Changing Character of the Communist Party of India (Marxist) in Rural West Bengal (1977–1990)'. In *Sonar Bangla? Agricultural Growth and Agrarian Change in West Bengal and Bangladesh*, edited by Ben Rogaly, B. Harris-White, and Sugata Bose, 59–69. New Delhi: SAGE Publications.

Bhattacharyya, Dwaipayan. 2016. *Government as Practice: Democratic Left in a Transforming India*. Delhi: Cambridge University Press.

Bidwai, Praful. 2015. *The phoenix Moment: Challenges Confronting the Indian Left*. Noida: Harper Collins.

Chakrabarti, Anjan, Anup Kumar Dhar, and Byaadeb Dasgupta. 2015. *The Indian Economy in Transition, Globalization, Capitalism and Development*. Delhi: Cambridge University Press.

Chakrabarti, Anjan, Anup Dhar, and Stephen Cullenberg. 2012. *World of the Third and Global Capitalism*. Delhi: Worldview.

Chakraborty, Dhritiman, Mursed Alam, and Anindya Sekhar Puakayastha. 2016. 'Refolutionary Inflectional Zones of Democracy: Rethinking Post-civil Society Resistance'. *Kairos: A Journal of Critical Symposium* 1, (1): 2016

Chandra, Uday. 2015. 'Rethinking Subaltern Resistance'. *Journal of Contemporary Asia* 45 (4): 563–573.

Chandra, Uday, Grier Heierstad, and Kenneth Bo Nielsen. 2016. *The Politics of Caste in West Bengal.* New York, NY: Routledge.

Chatterjee, Partha. 2011. *Lineages of Political Society, Studies in Postcolonial Democracy.* Ranikhet: Permanent Black.

———. 2012. 'The Debate over Political Society'. In *Reframing Democracy and Agency in India, Interrogating Political Society*, edited by Ajay Gudavarthy, 305–322. New Delhi: Anthem Press.

Comaroff, J., and J. Comaroff. 2006. *Law and Disorder in the Postcolony.* Chicago, IL: University of Chicago Press.

Das, Ritanjan. 2013. 'History, Ideology and Negotiation: The Politics of Policy Transition in West Bengal, India'. Doctoral Thesis. The London School of Economics and Political Science (LSE).

Davis, M. 1983. *Rank and Rivalry: The Politics of Inequality in Rural West Bengal*, Vol. 7. Cambridge: Cambridge University Press.

Day, R. J. 2005. *Gramsci is Dead: Anarchist Currents in the Newest Social Movements.* London: Pluto Press.

Dhar, Anup. 2014. 'Swaraj in Ideas: From "Third World" to "World of the Third"'. Unpublished Working Paper.

Foucault, Michele. 2009. *Security, Territory, Population: Lectures at the College de France, 1977–78.* Translated by Graham Burchell. New York, NY: Picador.

Giddens, Anthony. 1998. *Capitalism and Modern Social Theory: An Analysis of the Writings of Marx, Durkheim and Max Weber.* New Delhi: Cambridge University Press.

Ghosh, Jayati. 2012, 16 June. 'The Emerging Left in the "Emerging" World'. *Economic & Political Weekly* 47 (24): 33–38.

Gibson-Graham, J. K. 1996. *The End of Capitalism (As We Knew It): A Feminist Critique of Political Economy.* Oxford: Blackwell.

Gohain, Hiren. 2011, 17 September. 'Decline of the Left: A Critical Comment'. *Economic & Political Weekly* 46 (38): 79–80.

Gudavarthy, Ajay. 2013. *Politics of Post-Civil Society: Contemporary History of Political Movement in India.* New Delhi: SAGE Publications.

Holloway, John. 2002. *Change the World without Taking Power: The Meaning of Revolution Today.* London: Pluto Press.

Jal, Murzban. 2012, 16 June. 'On Understanding the Decline of the Established Indian Left'. *Economic & Political Weekly.*

Mitra, Ashok. 2011. 'With No Apologies, What the Left Front Did Wrong in West Bengal?' *The Telegraph*, 20 May.

Nielsen, Kenneth Bo. 2010. 'Contesting India's Development? Industrialisation, Land Acquisition and Protest in West Bengal'. *Forum for Development Studies* 37 (2): 145–170.

———. 2015. '"Community" and the Politics of Caste, Class, and Representation in the Singur Movement, West Bengal'. In *New Subaltern Politics, Reconceptualizing*

Hegemony and Resistance in Contemporary India, edited by Alf Gunvald Nilsen and Srila Roy, 202–225. New Delhi: Oxford University Press.

———. 2016. 'The Politics of Caste and Class in Singur's anti-land acquisition struggle'. In *The Politics of Caste in West Bengal*, edited by Uday Chandra, Geir Heierstad and Kenneth Bo Nielsen. New York: Routledge.

O'Brien, K. 1996. 'Rightful Resistance'. *World Politics* 49 (1): 31–35.

Patnaik, Prabhat. 2007. 'In the Aftermath of Nandigram'. *Economic & Political Weekly*, 42 (21): 1893–1895.

———. 2011. 'The Left in Decline'. *Economic & Political Weekly* 49 (29): 12–16.

Resnik, Stephen A., and Richard D. Wolff. 1987. *Knowledge and Class*. Chicago, IL: University of Chicago Press.

Roy, Dayabati. 2014. *Rural Politics in India: Political Stratification and Governance in Bengal*. Delhi: Cambridge University Press.

Ruud, A. E. 2003. *Poetics of village politics*. Delhi: Oxford University Press.

Sanyal, Kalyan. 2007. *Rethinking Capitalist Development: Primitive Accumulation, Governmentality and Postcolonial Capitalism*. New Delhi: Routledge.

Sarkar, Abhirup. 2007. 'Development and Displacement, Land Acquisition in West Bengal'. *Economic & Political Weekly* 42 (16): 1435–1442.

Sau, Ranjit. 2008, 25 October. 'A Ballad of Singur: Progress with Human Dignity'. *Economic & Political Weekly* 42 (22): 2048–2051.

Scott, James. 1985. *Weapons of the Weak: Everyday Forms of Peasant Resistance*. New Haven, CT: Yale University Press.

The Telegraph. 2008. 'Budha Bombshell—CM Vows to Speak Up, CITU, Trinamool Heap Scorn'. *The Telegraph*, 27 August.

Tilly, C., and S. Tarrow. 2007. *Contentious Politics*. Boulder: Paradigm Publishers.

Vanaik, Achin. 2012, 13 October. 'Future Perspective for the Mainstream Indian Left'. *Economic & Political Weekly* 47 (41): 12–14.

Afterword
Politics of Secular Sectarianism*

Ajay Gudavarthy and Nissim Mannathukkaren

The rise of right-wing politics in India is built on the fragmented nature of the struggles waged by the oppressed who constitute the vast majority of the population: 'lower' castes, adivasis, working classes and peasants, women, religious minorities, etc. Countering right-wing political imagination would mean a dismantling of caste-, class-, gender- and religion-based oppressions. This cannot happen without forging a commonality among the oppressed which is at once non-patronizing as well as self-critical.

Political imagination in India has come to a standstill, aiding and abetting the construction of a homogenized cultural and political sphere. The roots of this exist not merely in the right-wing political imagination of a Hindu *rashtra* but also in the secular sectarianism pursued by secular, democratic and progressive political formations. Secular sectarianism of the feminists, Dalits, the Left and religious minorities has, over a period, ghettoised communities and advanced a sectarian political imagination, leading to a political deadend that they now find difficult to negotiate with. Cumulatively, they all seem to have contributed to a shrinking political imagination that has in turn handsomely contributed to the rise of right-wing politics.

---

* This chapter has previously been published in the *Economic & Political Weekly* by Gudavarthy and Mannathukkaren (2014).

Feminist politics in India was silenced after the Shah Bano Case with right-wing forces demanding a uniform civil code. As a result, it was unable to negotiate the competing demands between women's rights and that of religious minorities. It is puzzling why it did not proceed along the lines of equating gendered practices in all religions. For instance, whether the Hadith or the Manusmriti or the Bible, all consider women to be impure during the menstrual cycle, along with many other similar sanctioned practices that place women as less than equal to men. In fact, it was Ambedkar who argued that it is only Dalits and women who face untouchability due to religious sanctions.

Similarly, sections of Dalit politics in India, especially vibrant on social media networks, have adopted a proprietary attitude towards Ambedkar in recent times. This has resulted in an excessive focus on 'trivial and emotive issues' centred around the symbol of Ambedkar rather than on structural issues of Dalit emancipation. Such 'sensational and farcical attempts by Dalit groups' make it also easier for the ruling elites and mainstream caste society to trivialise Ambedkar's ideas and the question of Dalit emancipation (Wankhede 2012). Again, if earlier the idea was that all dispossessed social groups are Dalits, irrespective of their caste, today even individuals seeking to annihilate caste are reduced to the caste into which they are born into; a new kind of *homo sacer*—as bare caste beings. In seeking to construct an authentic standpoint for Dalit oppression, there is also an ignorance of oppressions like gender within certain strands of Dalit activism. There is a lack of internal critique and this is justified, as Gopal Guru and V Geetha argue, 'on the ground that it is not advisable to attack a Dalit self which has not even emerged' (2000: 130).

IDENTITARIAN POLITICS

It is this prison of identitarian politics that becomes the breeding ground for right-wing politics. This shift to a narrower interpretation of anti-caste imagery also led to social justice shrinking to mere political representation, most clearly exemplified by the biggest force in Dalit politics, the Mayawati-led Bahujan Samaj Party (BSP). If Kanshi Ram gave birth to a movement that is an unprecedented and astounding advancement of the politics of the oppressed in India's postcolonial history, its later trajectory has focused on the 'politics of recognition' based on symbolic empowerment alone rather than one which adds to it the 'politics of redistribution' based on material empowerment, a tendency which has reached its apogee under Mayawati.[1]

While the BSP governments have done an excellent job in ensuring communal peace, the original radical agenda of building a *bahujan samaj* uniting Dalits, Other Backward Classes (OBCs), adivasis and religious minorities has been sacrificed at the altar of electoral expediency. The resultant new imaginations of *sarvjan samaj* including the savarna castes have ironically reduced the importance of Dalits themselves (Teltumbde 2014: 29). The argument that the BSP remains the third largest party in the country (in terms of vote share) and thus faces no threat from right-wing forces is an erroneous one, for it does not recognise the party's rapidly eroding support base (losing as much as one-third of it in less than a decade).

The attraction of right-wing forces and their buzzword of development for the marginalized castes arises from the vacuum created by the degeneration of the parties and other secular forces seeking to end caste. To believe at this juncture that the BSP stands for an 'emancipatory politics for dalits' is ignoring reality (Teltumbde 2014: 29). The right-wing forces like the Bharatiya Janata Party (BJP) and the Rashtriya Swayamsevak Sangh (RSS) are also seeking to appropriate caste by advancing a more de-brahmanised mode of Hinduization by including leaders from the Dalit-Bahujan communities. It is not surprising then that sections of the oppressed communities consider the opportunities provided by right-wing political mobilisation as justified mobility towards undoing demeaned social status caused by centuries of abjection.

Dalits being at the margins and the receiving end of the dominant caste society are not the agents on whom the onus is placed to eradicate the horrors of caste, especially when the state and political society create immense divisions among them for their own narrow interests. Dalits do not enjoy political, economic and cultural power to cause paradigm

---

[1] For an argument on how the Dalit mobilisation in Uttar Pradesh has not led to tangible advancement in human development, see Mehrotra (2006).

shifts (Sukumar 2014). But this should not mean that this reality of the force field of caste oppression structured by the dominant castes should exclude a critique of practices of discrimination, including untouchability, within and between various sections of the Dalit community or that of gender as already mentioned.

Sectarianism has been rife also with the secular discourse regarding minority rights in India. It not only assumed that Muslims and other religious minorities are homogeneous but their concerns are disconnected from other political discourses in a democracy, mentally and spatially ghettoising them into a segregated social group. For instance, Muslim political organizations could have talked not only about the witch-hunt against Muslims from Azamgarh and alleged encounter killings in Batla House but also about the same kind of exceptionalism being practised against tribals in Chhattisgarh and racial profiling of citizens from northeast India. In the same breath, it would be incumbent to speak of the plight of Hindus in Baluchistan and Bangladesh, as much as the rights of Kashmiri Pandits who lost their homes. It is important to conjoin the rights of Muslims with questioning the views of Syed Ali Shah Geelani on Hindu religious minorities and women in Kashmir.

EXPECTATIONS FROM MUSLIMS

Muslims, like the Dalits, being a marginalized minority, cannot be expected to be responsible for destroying the logic of communalism and religious majoritarianism. At the same time, the claim to mitigate one's own marginalization and oppression has to be sensitive to the claims of others who are similarly oppressed and marginalized. This has not happened often. For instance, Muslims in Kerala are probably the most empowered in the country because of the strength of the Muslim League as a political party, which is in a position to wield state power. But the liberal Muslim League, while playing an important moderating role in dissipating communal tensions, has been a conservative force allied with the power block rather than addressing marginalisations on the basis of class, gender, and caste within the Muslim community or outside. Citizenship as a political practice is instantiated in the right to speak for others, not in speaking just for one's own self. This becomes important also in a context where neo-liberalism has in a very substantive sense undermined empathy for others, and fraternity and solidarity of all kinds.

Indian democracy, otherwise considered a success story within the postcolonial nations of the world, built its foundations on secular sectarianism of various kinds. This was previously typified as the 'Congress System', where different and conflicting social groups were accommodated within the same political party. This accommodation, however, retained the social status of the groups as they stood into an umbrella formation. It is this politics of forming a coalition of social groups without any sustained attempt to forge intersectional dialogue that is now visibly unworkable and has led to a sharp decline in the electoral prospects of the Congress. It is this very strategy of maintaining a centrist polity that has gradually shifted rightwards through replicating the same strategy of forging a status-quoist coalition but for a different purpose—of realising a Hindu rashtra—by the right-wing political formations.

This decline of the Congress is made even more pronounced by the simultaneous decline of the left parties that have found themselves in a political landscape that can best be typified as a 'no man's land'. Any progressive social project in India cannot proceed without understanding caste, and it is astounding that even after so many decades, the Left is still grappling with the question. Reports about mainstream communist parties point to their own failures in eradicating caste, not in the larger society, but among their own cadres. But this self-critique has not necessarily translated into a structural programme to counter it.

A society suffused with caste hierarchies and culture (or caste privilege itself masquerading as merit) and the lack of secular spaces have prepared the ground for the rapid incursion of Hindutva—modified now to incorporate the oppressed castes without dismantling the hierarchy, and modified also to make it a majoritarian ideology tied now with the economic one of neoliberalism. The failure of the Left in building secular identities, even in their traditional strongholds, is a colossal one. This failure is worsened further by the domination of the upper castes and the exclusion of the marginalised, the Dalits, adivasis and Muslims in the communist movement as in West Bengal (though Kerala does much better, especially with regard to the OBCs). Prabhat Patnaik (2013) calls this exclusion an 'extraordinary phenomenon'.

NEW LOW FOR THE LEFT

Despite the historic lows that the parliamentary Left has touched in the recent Lok Sabha elections, there is a distinct refusal to recognise the severity of the crisis that it is facing. Instead, the same old squabbles among different communist parties are resurfacing centred around theoretical inanities like the inevitability of the 1964 split in the Communist Party of India. In pursuit of a 'correct line', it has neither responded to political exigencies nor overcome the dogmas to which it has often fallen victim. Today, it is faced with a difficult choice; of being either pragmatic or dogmatic, both of which have contributed to its sustained decline. There could not be a starker example of secular sectarianism than the numerous divisions within the communist movement when right-wing forces have achieved a parliamentary majority. The pathologies of secular sectarianism are also evident when there are last-minute attempts by the left parties to cobble up 'secular' electoral coalitions against communal parties before the national elections. These attempts, supposedly meant to counter 'fascist forces', have inevitably been disastrous.

They are the worst examples of the latest avatars of what Marx had called 'parliamentary cretinism', a systematic reduction of the need for multifaceted social transformation across political, economic and cultural spheres to the politics of electoral adjustments. The mainstream communist parties are in the 'conjuncture of late socialism', a contradictory phase in which the ever growing hegemony of capitalism, its practices and values in all spheres is complemented by the upholding of an empty revolutionary rhetoric which masks the real evanescence of socialist dreams (Mannathukkaren 2010).

Parallel to the Left's failures in the attempts to annihilate caste and the construction of class-based selves is the emergence of politics that refuses to engage with class. The glossing over by secular formations of identities like caste and oppressions based on them can be justifiably held partly responsible for this identity-based politics. At the same time, they are not entirely to blame either as we have seen with BSP's trajectory. It is a remarkable paradox that India, which suffers from some of the worst forms of class-based inequities and deprivations, should increasingly generate a politics that glosses over class just as caste was papered over in secular politics. This is especially surprising when there is a significant overlap of caste and class (which nevertheless cannot always be conflated for any resistance struggles). This has serious consequences and is the context in which neo-liberal imaginations of the right become attractive to the exploited classes.

There is a commonly adduced argument from among a Dalit-Bahujan perspective that the differences between the Right, Left and Centre are immaterial with regard to Dalits and the other oppressed castes as the entire political spectrum is equally casteist (Mhaskar 2014). So the binaries of secularism/communalism, Hindu/Hindutva are meaningless as both sides of the binary are equally structured by caste domination. By implication, it does not matter if Dalit-Bahujans become a part of the Hindutva project (Ilaiah 2014). This is a fallacious and vacuous argument. Even assuming that the different political ideologies are equally marked by visible or invisible caste discrimination, it surely cannot be argued that Hindutva and other political projects are the same when it comes to the question of religious minorities in India. The devastating consequences of religious nationalism are starkly evident, especially in terms of the state of the Muslim population in India. The Dalit-Bahujan argument that Hindutva is a bogey imagined by the (casteist) secular intellectual trivialises the significant numbers of lives lost in communal violence (of which a vast majority are lower caste). Further, it is ironical when we consider that the nearly 18 crore Muslim population is overwhelmingly lower caste. For instance, the Pasmanda Muslims on many indicators are worse off than the Dalits. Again, the pitfalls of secular sectarianism that seeks the liberation of one's own without worrying about the consequences for the other are evident.

The Dalit-Bahujan argument that materially too, there are no differences with regard to the Right, the Left and other political formations when it comes to the oppressed castes does not stand up to empirical scrutiny. Despite the ensconcing of the Left movement in caste hierarchies, the successes of class struggles have had a direct material impact on Dalit-Bahujan communities. The best example of this is the agrarian reforms instituted in Kerala, which are considered as the most radical and comprehensive land reforms in India. While even these did not grant land to the actual tiller of the soil—the Dalit agricultural labourer—the securing of tiny plots of homestead land by the agricultural labourer, and a slew of laws protecting manual labour with regard to wages, working hours, pensions and so on (Mannathukkaren 2011) have led to the most empowered working classes in the country. This in turn has significantly contributed to at least some aspects of Dalit well-being like health, education, fertility and nutrition.

The same is the case with Dravidian political mobilisations in Tamil Nadu, which, even when operating in a hierarchical relationship with regard to the Dalits, have had an important impact on human development indicators of Dalits, far superior to those achieved by rightwing governance as in Gujarat. Therefore, the differences between political and ideological regimes, when it comes to caste, are not meaningless. The struggles by the Dalits and adivasis in Kerala to complete the land reforms in Kerala, and the opposition of the dominant communist parties to them demonstrate, on the one hand, the significance of class, and on the other, are a telling commentary on the state of the communist movement in India.

While capital and the market depend on a process of individuation, progressive politics has to move towards affinity and an idea of shared spaces rather than focus on mere claims of essentialised identity, notwithstanding the contribution 'identity politics' has made in highlighting the concerns of some of the most marginalised social groups in India. This, in essence, is also the difference with right-wing political mobilisations. Otherwise, there would be very little distinction between the sectarianism of the 'democratic' kind and the divisive politics of the RSS, the BJP, the Bajrang Dal and the Vishva Hindu Parishad.

OPENING INTERNAL DIALOGUE

The way forward seems to be in opening up internal dialogue within communities as across them. These will have to necessarily go together.

This will include raising difficult questions such as masculinity within anti-caste movements that attract them towards far-right groups like the Shiv Sena, communal sentiments and inward-looking philosophy of the dominant sections of Muslims, the unholy alliance between the politically powerful and their convenient interpretations of the Koran which disallows a more progressive interpretation of justice and equality being the core pillars of Islam.

Questions are also to be asked about the self-righteous tendencies in the Left that refuses to listen and learn that social change cannot be programmed, scientific and sanitised but carries with it a load of uncertainties that need to be incessantly made sense of and within them find the possibilities to break the condensation of the polity into a majoritarian construct. The same goes for the Left's failure in aligning with non-class democratic organizations and its mutual contempt for other left-based political mobilizations. The time has long passed for the parallel running streams of the Left and anti-caste movements to merge. There could not be a more critical juncture than the current one.

Majoritarianism in Indian polity today is growing in the interstices of secular sectarianism that left unanswered various inconvenient questions pertaining to social groups that were considered as the subaltern. It is within this space and growing possibility of conflicts within the subaltern on the one hand, and joining in alliance with the traditional social elite on the other, that right-wing political mobilisation is finding its new space and turning democracy on its head. There cannot be a reversal of this without recognising the intersectionality of oppression and exploitation, and overcoming it. As Bell Hooks argues:

> the struggle to end sexist oppression that focuses on destroying the cultural basis for such domination strengthens other liberation struggles. Individuals who fight for the eradication of sexism without struggles to end racism or classism undermine their own efforts. Individuals who fight for the eradication of racism or classism while supporting sexist oppression are helping to maintain the cultural basis of all forms of group oppression. (2000: 40)

At the same time, this does not mean an anodyne and predetermined recognition that all oppressions are equal and have the same material and symbolic consequences. This is something for actual struggles on the ground to determine.

In terms of dialogue and solidarity within and across communities, a few examples can be cited. The Dalit Intellectuals' Collective is one. It seeks to critique the dominant caste society and its hierarchies, and at the same time wants an 'audit of the Dalit intellectual tradition and culture, which create and sustain internal hierarchies' and thus involve Dalit intellectuals as well as non-Dalit interrogators (Guru and Geetha 2000: 13). The question is how to translate this intellectual initiative into larger political movements. With regard to class, there is a need to go back to examples like the radical potential exhibited by the Dalit Panthers in Maharashtra in the 1970s when it 'understood caste and class as integral themes' in the revolution of the oppressed (Wankhede 2013: 23).

Similarly, within the Muslim community, the Jamaat-e-Islami Hind's (JIH) transformation to engage with secularism is a significant development. This is especially so in the case of Kerala, where the Jamaat movement is at the strongest (Anand 2012). There its movement has made a robust attempt to reach across to other communities, especially Dalits, through social and economic programmes, forums for intercommunity dialogue, publishing a critical and secular newspaper (with an impressive circulation), magazines and so on. It has simultaneously intervened within the community by critiquing the conservative leadership, extremist trends and wrong interpretation of concepts like Jihad, and pushing for a progressive transformation of the religion. The movement is definitely not without blemishes; for example, its complicated relationship to its founding ideology of Islamic revivalism, or the fact that the movement is still upper-caste dominated. Nevertheless, what is significant is a new mode of political and intellectual engagement that has the potential to achieve critical dimensions.

These are some possibilities of the present. Whether they actually fructify to escape the current political and ideological morass remains to be seen.

REFERENCES

Anand, J. 2012. 'Reluctant Democrats—Jamaat-e-Islami Hind (JIH)'. South Asia Citizens Web, 2 August. Available at: http://www.sacw.net/auteur321.html (accessed on 30 September 2014).

Gudavarthy, Ajay, and Nissim Mannathukaren. 2014. 'The Politics of Secular Sectarianism'. *Economic & Political Weekly*, 49 (49): 16–19.

Guru, G., and V. Geetha. 2000, 15 January. 'New Phase of Dalit–Bahujan Intellectual Activity'. *Economic & Political Weekly* 35 (3): 130–134.

Ilaiah, K. 2014. 'A Civil-War Is on the Doorstep of India'. Interview by Mahmood Kooria, 1 September, *Kafila*. Available at: http://kafila.org/2014/09/01/a-civil-war-is-on-the-doorstep-of-india-interview-with-kancha-ilaiah-by-mahmood-kooria/ (accessed on 6 August 2019).

Mannathukkaren, N. 2010. 'The Conjuncture of Late Socialism in Kerala: A Critique of the Narrative of Social Democracy'. In *Development, Democracy and the State: Critiquing Kerala Model of Development*, edited by K. Ravi Raman, 155–171. London and New York, NY: Routledge.

———. 2011. 'Redistribution and Recognition: Land Reforms in Kerala and the Limits of Culturalism'. *Journal of Peasant Studies* 38 (2): 379–411.

Mehrotra, S. 2006, 7 October. 'Well-being and Caste in Uttar Pradesh'. *Economic & Political Weekly* 41 (40): 4261–4271.

Mhaskar, S. 2014. 'No Right Turn'. *Outlook*, 16 October. Available at: http://www.outlookindia.com/article/No-Right-Turn/292290 (accessed on 1 November 2014).

Patnaik, P. 2013. 'In the Long Run: The Social Divide in Bengal'. *The Telegraph*, 16 July. Available at: http://www.telegraphindia.com/1130716/jsp/opinion/story_17110832.jsp#.VG-x4F65fwI (accessed on 6 August 2014).

Sukumar, N. 2014. 'Dalit Revolution and Hindutva Counter Revolution in Indian Politics'. *Round Table India*, 16 September. Available at: http://roundtablein-dia.co.in/index.php?option=com_content&view= article&id=7632:dalit-revolution-and-hindutva-counter-revolution-in-indian-politics&catid= 119&Itemid=132 (accessed on 1 November 2014).

Teltumbde, A. 2014, 4 October. 'Maestro of Identity Politics'. *Economic & Political Weekly* 49 (40): 28–31.

Wankhede, H. 2012. 'In the Name of Amebdkar'. *The Indian Express*, 18 May. Available at: http://archive.indianexpress.com/news/in-ambedkar-s-name/950688/0 (accessed on 1 November 2014).

———. 2013, 29 June. 'Class–Caste Debate Revisited'. *Economic & Political Weekly* 48 (26–27): 23–24.

About the Editor and Contributors

EDITOR

Ajay Gudavarthy is Associate Professor at the Centre for Political Studies of Jawaharlal Nehru University, New Delhi. He has taught earlier as assistant professor at the National Law School of India University, Bengaluru. Dr Gudavarthy became Associate Member, Institute for the Humanities, Simon Fraser University, in 2018. He was visiting professor, Centre for Modern Indian Studies (CeMIS), University of Gottingen, Germany, in 2014, and visiting fellow, Centre for Citizenship, Civil Society and Rule of Law, University of Aberdeen, in 2012. He was visiting faculty at Centre for Human Rights, University of Hyderabad, in 2011, and visiting fellow, Goldsmiths, University of London, in 2010. In 2008, Dr Gudavarthy was Charles Wallace Visiting Fellow, the School of Oriental and African Studies (SOAS), London. His published works include *Re-framing Democracy and Agency in India: Interrogating Political Society* (edited, 2012), *Politics of Post-Civil Society: Contemporary History of Political Movements in India* (SAGE, 2013), *Maoism, Democracy and Globalisation: Cross-currents in Indian Politics* (SAGE, 2014), *Revolutionary Violence versus Democracy: Narratives from India* (SAGE, 2017) and *India after Modi: Populism and the Right* (2018).

CONTRIBUTORS

Seema Ahmed is a PhD Scholar at Jadavpur University, Kolkata. She completed her MPhil from the Institute of Development Studies Kolkata (IDSK) in 2015. Her MPhil thesis was on Girls' Madrasas in West Bengal and their interaction with tradition and modernity.

Her research areas include Muslim women's writings in West Bengal, Islamic feminism, religious studies, etc.

Mursed Alam teaches in the Department of English, Gour Mahavidyalaya, Malda, West Bengal. He is one of the founding members of PSAGS and editorial associate of *Kairos: A Journal of Critical Symposium*. His research areas include subaltern life and politics, Islamic traditions in South Asia, minor discourses, etc. He has published in journals such as *Economic & Political Weekly*, *Rethinking Marxism*, *Journal of Postcolonial Writing*, *Contemporary South Asia* and *South Asia Research*. In 2017, he jointly guest-edited the *Café Dissensus* issue on Muslim life in West Bengal.

Shadab Arab is a doctoral candidate in the Faculty of Sciences of Society at the University of Geneva, Switzerland. His research is an ethnographic study of urban segregation in Mumbai. The research unravels 'a ghetto within a ghetto', where Muslims live cheek by jowl with Dalits. It uses a socio-political lens to explore the new spatially relevant metrics and the socio-spatial interactions between the two minority groups as well as with the urban spaces and civic institutions. His work has contributed to several academic initiatives and publications that explore the intersection of identity, religion and violence.

Dhritiman Chakraborty is currently writing his doctoral thesis, 'Dilemmas of Postcolonial Development in India: An Enquiry into the Politics of two Dissident Movements', from Centre for Studies in Social Sciences, Calcutta (CSSSC), India. His research interests include explorations of postcolonial political, Indian social thinking, political philosophy, postcolonial feminism and literary studies. His recent publications include chapters, 'Who is Afraid of Postcolonial Theory? Development, Accumulation and the Specter of *Outside*' (2019) and 'Governance of Society or Self? Postcolonial Foucault and the Singur Movement in India' (2019). He has jointly written on political movements in contemporary India in *Kairos: A Journal of Critical Symposium* and *Economic & Political Weekly*. He has co-edited a book on American Studies after 9/11 in 2014.

Manas Dutta is Assistant Professor in the Department of History, Kazi Nazrul University, Asansol, West Bengal, India, and his current area of research covers issues related to war and conflict in South Asia, with a special focus on civil–military relations in the Global South. Along with this, he is also investigating, as part of his recent research on war and genocide studies, on the involvement of native Indian soldiers in the First World War, with a special emphasis on their performance in the Western Front.

Samir Gandesha is an Associate Professor in the Department of the Humanities and the Director of the Institute for the Humanities at Simon Fraser University. He specializes in modern European thought and culture, with a particular emphasis on the 19th and 20th centuries. His work has appeared in *Political Theory, New German Critique, Constellations, Logos, Kant-Studien, Philosophy and Social Criticism, Topia, The European Legacy, The European Journal of Social Theory, Art Papers, Radical Philosophy*, the *Cambridge Companion to Adorno* and *Herbert Marcuse: A Critical Reader* as well as in several other edited books. He has co-edited *Arendt and Adorno: Political and Philosophical Investigations* (with Lars Rensmann, 2012), *Spell of Capital: Reification and Spectacle* and *Aesthetic Marx* (with Johan Hartle, 2017). In the Spring of 2017, he was the Liu Boming Visiting Scholar in Philosophy at the University of Nanjing and visiting lecturer at Suzhou University of Science and Technology in China. In February 2019, he was visiting lecturer at Faculdade de Filosofia, Letras e Ciências Humanas Universidade de São Paulo (FFLCH-USP). He is currently editing a book titled *Spectres of Fascism* that, in part, stems from an Institute Free School co-organized with Stephen Collis in 2017, co-editing with Peyman Vahabzadeh, a Festschrift for Ian Angus, and preparing a manuscript on the 'Neoliberal Personality'.

Tirthankar Ghosh teaches at the Department of History, Kazi Nazrul University, Asansol, West Bengal, India, as an Assistant Professor since 2014. His areas of specialization are social history of disaster, ecological and environmental history of India, economic history of India and social and political movements in colonial and postcolonial India. He has contributed in journals, namely *Studies in People's History, Journal of History, Indian Historical Review, Contemporary South Asia, Environment* *and History, South Asia Research, Quarterly Review of Historical Studies* and *Café Dissensus.*

Dickens Leonard presently teaches at the Centre for Comparative Literature, University of Hyderabad. He was awarded PhD from the University of Hyderabad for the thesis titled 'Casteless Community' (2017) on the 19th century Tamil intellectual Iyothee Thass and Tamil Buddhism. He was formerly DAAD-visiting PhD fellow (2016) at the Centre for Modern Indian Studies, Georg-August University, Gottingen, Germany. He has published on anti-caste intellectual thought and also on contemporary Tamil films in internationally renowned journals.

Suratha Kumar Malik (MA, MPhil, PhD) is an Assistant Professor in the Department of Political Science, Vidyasagar University, West Bengal. He was awarded UGC-NET, JRF and Nirman Foundation Fellowship (Lord Bhikhu Parekh endowment). His research interest and specialization includes Dalit and tribal issues and politics, social-political movements, marginalization and identity politics, Indian and Western political thoughts and philosophy. To his credit, he has three books and more than a dozen of articles and chapters in journals and edited books of national and international reputation with renowned publishers. He also presented papers in more than 30 international and national seminars/conferences across the country and abroad. He recently completed the UGC Major Research Project as the Principal Investigator (PI). Ten MPhil students have been awarded degree under his supervision. He is the life member and editorial member of different bodies and organizations.

P. Thirumal is Professor at the Department of Communication, Sarojini Naidu School of Arts and Communication, University of Hyderabad, Telangana, India. His areas of interest and specialization include theory and history of media, histories of technologies and communities, theorizing Dalit emancipatory project, borderland media history and the North East region of India. He has published in *The Indian Economic and Social History Review, Seminar* and the *Economic & Political Weekly* and has written for newspapers, periodicals and websites.

Anindya Sekhar Purakayastha is Associate Professor in the Department of English, Kazi Nazrul University, Asansol, West Bengal, India. He is a Fulbright–Nehru Academic and Professional Excellence Fellow 2018–2019 in the University of Massachusetts Amherst, Amherst. He has contributed in journals such as *International Journal of Zizek Studies, Parallax, Journal of Postcolonial Writing, Contemporary South Asia, Postcolonial Studies, History and Sociology of South Asia* and *Journal of Social Movement Studies*. He co-edits *Kairos: A Journal of Critical Symposium* and is one of the founding members of the Postcolonial Studies Association of the Global South (PSAGS).

Nathalène Reynolds, holder of a doctorate in the history of international relations (Paris I, Panthéon-Sorbonne), is an Associate Researcher at the Pakistan Security Research Unit (PSRU) of Durham University and a Visiting Fellow at the Sustainable Development Policy Institute of Islamabad (SDPI). She has recently published a book titled *Jammu and Kashmir in the Indo-Pakistani Conflict (1947–2004)*.

Tarushikha Sarvesh is working as an Assistant Professor in the Centre for Women's Studies at Aligarh Muslim University. She did her graduation from Lady Shri Ram College, Delhi University, New Delhi, and earned her postgraduate degree in sociology from Jawaharlal Nehru University, New Delhi. Tarushikha was also a part of IIT Kanpur for a short duration. She acquired a PhD degree from G. B. Pant Social Science Institute, Allahabad. Tarushikha has been actively engaged in academic research for the past seven years and has published research papers, articles and interviews in various journals and magazines. Apart from command over various components of sociology and qualitative research methods, her research interests include interdisciplinary areas such as gender and developmental studies, Dalit studies, social inclusion and exclusion, questions of statecraft and state institutions, and issues of indigenous rights and globalization. She is teaching courses related to the said themes. Tarushikha also has training in journalism and has worked as a full-time journalist before joining academia.

Index